ORESTES A. BROWNSON

A BIBLIOGRAPHY, 1826-1876

Compiled and Annotated by

PATRICK W. CAREY

MARQUETTE
UNIVERSITY

PRESS

MARQUETTE STUDIES IN THEOLOGY
No. 10

ANDREW TALLON, SERIES EDITOR

Library of Congress Cataloging-in-Publication Data

Carey, Patrick W., 1940-
    Orestes A. Brownson, a bibliography, 1826-1876 / compiled and
annotated by Patrick W. Carey.
        p.   cm. — (Marquette studies in theology ; #10)
    Includes index.
    ISBN 0-87462-634-X
    1. Brownson, Orestes Augustus, 1803-1876—Bibliography.
2. Universalist churches—United StatesDoctrines—History—19th
century— Bibliography. 3. Transcendentalism (New England)—
Bibliography. 4. Catholic Church—United States—Doctrines—
History—19th century—Bibliography. 5. United States—Church
history—19th century—Bibliography. 6. United States—Intellectual
life—19th century—Bibliography. I. Title. II. Series.
Z8124.6.B76C37 1997
[BX4705.B85]
016.282'092—dc21   96-45810

Printed in the United States of America

MARQUETTE UNIVERSITY PRESS
MILWAUKEE

The Association of Jesuit University Presses

TABLE OF CONTENTS

ACKNOWLEDGEMENTS

I have incurred a number of debts during the last ten years while compiling this bibliography. Former graduate research assistants—Dr. David Schimpf, Dr. Arie Griffioen, James Keane, Anne Slakey, and Ian Levy—have helped to identify sources and have typed this bibliography. Ian Levy and Anne Slakey, moreover, have had a major hand in proofreading and putting the text into final form. The staffs at the Archives of the University of Notre Dame, Harvard University, the Library of Holy Cross College (Worcester, MA), the American Antiquarian Society (Worcester, MA) and especially Ms. Joan Sommers and the Reference and Interlibrary Loan staffs of Memorial Library at Marquette University have located and obtained rare journals, pamphlets and books, and have supplied numerous other resources for this project.

I have also received a number of research grants from the Research division of Marquette's Graduate School to complete this work, and for this I am deeply grateful to Father Thaddeus Burch, S.J., Dean of the Graduate School.

Finally, I am indebted to Dr. Andrew Tallon, director of Marquette University Press, who has encouraged this project throughout and has offered to publish the bibliography and four volumes of a critical edition of Orestes A. Brownson's early (1826-44) writings.

INTRODUCTION

A complete bibliography of Orestes A. Brownson's (1803-76) works is long overdue. Brownson's writings are important and creative contributions to the history of American intellectual life, and are reflective of some major currents in American and European thought during the early and mid-nineteenth century. Yet, there is no comprehensive bibliography of his contributions. This bibliography provides the first useful guide to his numerous writings and to the many central intellectual issues that he addressed.

Brownson was one of the more prolific, hard-hitting, uncompromising, volatile, polemical, creative, mutable, and many-sided American intellectuals. As an author of seven books and twenty-five pamphlets, as a writer of over 1500 essays in more than thirty journals, and as an editor of six popular as well as elite journals of opinion, he commented on various central issues in American religious, philosophical, political, and literary life. His writings, as Arthur Schlesinger Jr. noted some years ago, belong to all Americans,[1] and are especially significant for the history of American intellectual life.

Brownson was a prominent figure in nineteenth-century American life and has been so recognized at least since Schlesinger's 1939 biography and Perry Miller's works on Transcendentalism.[2] Fifteen percent of the entries in Miller's anthology on *The Transcendentalists* (1950) came from Brownson's works—that is, more selections (16) from Brownson than any other person included in the text. Even in Miller's *American Transcendentalists: Their Prose and Poetry* (1957) two of the thirty-six entries are from Brownson. Miller claimed that Brownson was "in many respects the most powerful of the Transcendentalists—at any rate, the hardest hitting." From 1834 to 1844, Brownson was a "major spokesman" for the new school of Coleridge

---

1. Arthur M. Schlesinger Jr., *A Pilgrim's Progress: Orestes A. Brownson* (Boston and Toronto: Little, Brown and Company, 1966), xi-xii.
2. Perry Miller, *The Transcendentalists: An Anthology* (Cambridge: Harvard University Press, 1950) and *American Transcendentalists: Their Prose and Poetry* (Garden City, NY: Doubleday, 1957).

and Carlyle, the German literature, and especially of Victor Cousin's eclecticism; however, his frequent intellectual and religious transformations, and particularly his conversion to Catholicism in 1844, made him, according to Miller, a *persona non grata* among subsequent nineteenth-century intellectuals who "shamefully neglected" his "immense contribution" to American thought.[3]

Although a number of exaggerated claims have been made about Brownson's importance in American history (e.g., *America's Foremost Philosopher*[4]), there is no doubt that he commanded a great deal of public attention in his day and has continued to interest twentieth-century scholars in various fields of American studies (e.g., literature, history, philosophy, religious studies, and political science). Between 1960 and 1995 he was the subject of at least fifteen separate monographs, twenty-five dissertations, and numerous articles. He has also received some attention in the general surveys of American religious, philosophical, and political thought. Labels used to identify Brownson indicate something of his prestige within the United States: e.g., a religious "pilgrim," an American "weathervane," "an American Marxist before Marx," "a Yankee warrior," "a Jacksonian literary critic," "a philosophical expounder on the Constitution," "a reluctant democrat," "a philosophical realist," "a philosopher of freedom."

Although Brownson has been acknowledged as a creative thinker in American political and religious life, his role in American life has not been adequately examined because most scholars have had to rely upon Henry Brownson's twenty-volume collection of his father's works.[5] This collection is inadequate for representing the ferment and development of Brownson's early thought (1826 to 1844) and the scope of intellectual options in early nineteenth century America. Henry Brownson's edition contains what he considered to be the principal writings from his father's Catholic period (i.e., 1844 to 1876). He included only fifty-one of the more than 375 writings from the years 1826 to 1844. Of these fifty-one, nineteen were originally published in 1844 and none of the fifty-one were from the period 1826

---

3. Perry Miller, *The Transcendentalists: An Anthology,* 45.

4. Sidney A. Raemers, *America's Foremost Philosopher* (Washington, DC: St. Anselm's Priory, 1931).

5. Henry F. Brownson, ed., *The Works of Orestes A. Brownson*, 20 vols. (Detroit: Thorndike Nourse, 1882-1887).

to 1835. Henry Brownson selected these writings, too, primarily because of their Catholic leanings. Many scholars who have depended
almost exclusively upon Henry Brownson's collection have been un-
aware of the earliest developments in his thought.

Few scholars have examined the numerous articles Brownson wrote
as a young Universalist in the so-called "Burnt-Over District" of upstate New York from 1826 to 1829, nor his works as a member of the
Workingmen's Party during the years 1829 to 1830.[6] These writings
are particularly significant for the light they shed on the upstate New
York anti-revivalist party and the development of what Nathan Hatch[7]
has called popular theology in the early American republic. A few
scholars like Miller and William Hutchison have examined Brownson's
Unitarian and Transcendentalist works from 1833 to 1844,[8] but no
scholar has systematically examined the numerous articles Brownson
wrote on politics, philosophy, religion and literature in a variety of
Boston Unitarian and Transcendentalist journals during this period.
And, Brownson's voice was a major one, even though his position
became increasingly antithetical to Unitarian and Transcendentalist
positions during those years.

Although Brownson separated himself from American Protestantism after 1844, he continued to express his views on major issues
facing the nation between 1844 and 1876. Historians of American
intellectual life, as Perry Miller claimed, have neglected Brownson's
thought during the period he was a Protestant, but they have almost
totally ignored his contributions during the period he was a Catholic. Such lacuna in the historical record can no longer be justified,
especially now that the American Catholic community represents such
a large segment of the American population. The Catholic voice needs
representation in the histories of intellectual life in this country. This
bibliography will provide scholars with a guide to one major Catholic voice in the nineteenth century, even though that voice was not
always representative not only of the American but also of the Ameri-

6. One exception here is William J. Gilmore's "Orestes A. Brownson and New England
   Religious Culture, 1803-1827," Ph.D. diss., University of Virginia, 1971.
7. Nathan O. Hatch, *The Democratization of American Christianity* (New Haven:
   Yale University Press, 1989).
8. William Hutchison, *The Transcendentalist Ministers: Church Reform in the New
   England Renaissance* (New Haven: Yale University Press, 1959), 154-169, passim.

can Catholic mainstream. But, few intellectuals are ever representative of dominant tendencies in a culture.

Orestes A. Brownson was born to Sylvester and Relief Metcalf Brownson in Stockbridge, Vermont in 1803.[9] His father was a Presbyterian who died when he was three years old. His mother, a Universalist, was unable to support the family after his father's death so when Orestes was six years old she sent him to live with a Calvinist-Congregationalist's relative who raised him until he was fifteen years of age. At one point during his early teenage years he experienced a Methodist-Arminian revival and had what he consider a conversion experience, but he did not join a particular church at the time. In 1818 he rejoined his mother and siblings who all migrated, with many other Vermonters seeking a better living, to Balston Spa, New York, across the Western border of Vermont. In 1822, after hearing a Presbyterian revivalist in upstate New York, he became a Presbyterian; but, after nine months, he withdrew from that association and became a Universalist. These early years reflected the religious flexibility and plasticity of the society in which he lived.

He apparently was educated in the common schools during these early years of his life, but he never received a college education. His unpublished diary for the years 1822 and 1823 (when he was nineteen and twenty years old), though, indicates that he read widely especially in religious literature and polemical tracts. In 1823, he left Balston Spa for Detroit to become a school teacher, but stayed there only for a year. He returned to New York in 1824, decided to become a Universalist minister, and went to Vermont in 1825 where he joined the Universalist Association and was ordained to the Universalist ministry. In 1826, at the age of twenty-three, he published in *The Christian Repository* (Vermont) his first work, a sermon he gave to a Vermont Universalist congregation.

From 1826 to 1829, he served Universalist congregations in Ithaca, Geneva, and Auburn, New York, wrote in some upstate New York

---

9. There are a number of biographies of Brownson worth consulting in addition to Schlesinger's: e.g. Thomas Ryan's *Orestes A. Brownson: a Definitive Biography* (Huntington, Indiana: Our Sunday Visitor, 1976); Theodore Maynard's *Orestes Brownson: Yankee, Radical, Catholic* (New York: MacMillan Co., 1943); Americo D. Lapati's *Orestes A. Brownson* (New York: Twayne, 1965); Henry F. Brownson's *Orestes A. Brownson's Life* 3 vols. (Detroit: H. F. Brownson, 1898-1900).

Universalist papers (i.e., the *Utica Magazine* and the *Cayuga Patriot*), and edited and wrote for the Universalist journal *The Gospel Advocate and Impartial Investigator*. He married Sally Healy on June 19, 1827 at Elbridge, New York, where he had taught her after leaving Detroit. In 1829, he left the Universalist ministry because of conflicts with fellow-Universalists and because of a growing attachment to Frances Wright, the *Free Enquirer*, and the Workingmen's Party of New York—an association some Universalists considered heretical.

From November of 1829 to December of 1830, after leaving the Universalists, he edited the Genesee *Republican and Herald of Reform*,[10] a political voice for the Workingmen's Party in upstate New York, and wrote a few articles for Frances Wright's *Free Enquirer*. During this period he considered himself a social reformer who had lost all hope in the power of contemporary denominational Christianity to provide a religious warrant for needed economic and social reforms. In late 1830, he moved from Auburn to Ithaca where he edited *The Philanthropist*, at the time the only upstate New York Unitarian journal of opinion. By February of 1831, he began to reassert a religious basis for any successful social reforms. The return to religious principles was accompanied by a return to the ministry. This time, he became a non-denominational pastor to a congregation in Ithaca, New York, where he served until mid 1832. In July of 1832, after reading some of William Ellery Channing's essays on the religious sentiment, he became a Unitarian minister and accepted an invitation to Walpole, New Hampshire, where he served until 1834 when he moved to Canton, Massachusetts, to take up a new Unitarian pastorate. During these years at Walpole and Canton (1832 to 1836), he wrote for a number of Unitarian journals (i.e., *The Christian Register*, *The Unitarian*, *The Christian Examiner*, and *The Boston Observer and Religious Intelligencer*).

Essays in these journals helped to develop his reputation as a creative thinker on the social implications and dimensions of Christianity. In July of 1836, George Ripley (1802-80), a fellow Unitarian,

---

10. Extant copies of this journal could not be located, but we know from Brownson's autobiography and from references to the journal in some of his earlier writings that he did edit and write for this journal between 1829 and 1830. See *Works*, 5:63.

invited him to take up a pastorate among the working classes of Boston. Brownson moved his family to Chelsea, outside of Boston, and from there he ministered to the city's working people through the Society for Christian Union and Progress, which he founded. In 1836, moreover, he edited and wrote for the *Boston Reformer*—a journal published to voice the economic and social concerns of workingmen in Boston and to comment on American politics and literature. The same year he also became a charter member of the Transcendentalist Club and wrote his first major book (*New Views of Christianity, Society, and the Church*).

From 1837 to 1841 he held an administrative position in the Hospital of Chelsea, but he also published a few articles in *The Liberator* (1838), an abolitionist journal, and founded, edited, and was the chief contributor to the *Boston Quarterly Review* (1838-42), a first-class journal of systematic commentary on contemporary political, social, and religious ideas and events. Criticisms of some essays in the *Boston Quarterly Review*, particularly his essay on "The Laboring Classes" (July 1840), and his increasing political dissatisfaction with the Democratic Party caused him to sell his journal to John L. O'Sullivan in 1842 and to become a writer for O'Sullivan's *United States Magazine and Democratic Review*. Brownson continued to contribute articles to O'Sullivan's magazine until his views on democracy so clashed with O'Sullivan's that the two parted company at the end of 1842.

From 1842 to 1844, Brownson's religious thought became more and more affiliated with the ecclesial and sacramental positions of the Catholic Church, as was evident particularly in articles he wrote in 1843 for *The Christian World*, a Unitarian journal, and for his own newly established (1844) *Brownson's Quarterly Review*. In October of 1844, after taking instructions in Catholic doctrine from Boston's Catholic bishop John Bernard Fitzpatrick (1812-46), Brownson became a Catholic and thereafter his *Review* became the major forum for expressing a Catholic perspective on American religion, politics, economics, philosophy, and literature. The *Review* was also a platform for intra-Catholic debates on religious and cultural issues.

As a Catholic no less than as a Protestant Brownson changed his viewpoint periodically and developed it in response not only to changing political events and circumstances but also to Catholic as well as Protestant criticisms of his so-called ultraisms. Brownson's ultra-

ultramontanism (especially his views of the pope's temporal authority), his anti-Gallicanism, his rabid anti-Protestantism, and his views
on exclusive salvation, Irish nationalism, American nativism, John
Henry Newman's developmentalism, liberal Catholicism, and
ontologism, to mention a few issues, brought him into conflict with
some fellow Catholics. His former Protestant friends, too, considered his newly developed Catholic positions an extreme reversal of
his former teachings. Some Protestants as well as Catholics, moreover, disagreed with positions he eventually took on emancipation,
reconstruction, strict constitutionalism, and popular or absolute democracy. His *Review* also became the mouthpiece for his own Catholic criticisms of major intellectual and religious movements in the
American Protestant mainstream. Brownson scrutinized, for example,
the theological views of the Transcendentalists Ralph Waldo Emerson
and Theodore Parker, the Mercersburg theology of John Williamson
Nevin, and the Princeton theology of Charles Hodge.

At the end of the Civil War (1864) Brownson suspended his *Review* because of opposition to his religious and political views from
some Catholics and because the number of his subscriptions declined.
He continued, however, to write, publishing his major theological-
political philosophy of American government in *The American Republic* (1865). He also wrote a number of articles for various newspapers and became a regular contributor to *Ave Maria* (1865-72), a
University of Notre Dame journal of religious thought and Catholic
piety; the *Catholic World* (1866-72), a monthly journal of opinion
on contemporary religious and political life edited by the Paulist priest
Isaac Hecker (1819-88); and the *New York Tablet* (1867-72), a Catholic newspaper of political and religious opinion published by James
A. (d. 1869) and Mary Sadlier (1820-1903).

Because of the *Catholic World's* increasing editorial supervision and
censorship of some of his articles and because of his dissatisfaction
with the limited amount of space he had to develop his ideas in the
New York Tablet, Brownson decided in 1872 to recommence his *Review* so that he could develop his ideas fully and without interference. The *Review* resumed in 1873, but Brownson's declining health
and physical exhaustion forced him to cease publication in 1875. In
1876 he moved to Detroit to live with his son Henry. His last article,
"Philosophy of the Supernatural" (January 1876), was published in
the *American Catholic Quarterly Review*, a journal that was explicitly

intended to fill the gap left by the cessation of *Brownson's Quarterly Review*. On 17 April 1876, Brownson died in his son's home.

After publishing *The American Republic*, Brownson had aspirations of writing a major philosophy of religion, summarizing the views and ideas he had been developing throughout his life, but he never had the time, energy, or perhaps temperament to do so. He was also so dependent upon his essays and lectures as a means of financial support that he could not afford to abandon them to write his *magnum opus*. Nonetheless, many of his post-Civil War essays (especially his essays on the "Refutation of Atheism") reveal something of his comprehensive philosophy of religion and provide an outline of what his *magnum opus* might have been.

Throughout his life he was primarily an essayist who responded to the immediate issues of his day. For a variety of reasons, Brownson's essays, particularly those written during his Catholic period, have drawn little attention. Unlike books, which can have a continuing influence upon an intellectual tradition, essays have a tendency to influence their times but are more fleeting than books, remaining buried, as they are, in journals which subsequent generations rarely read. Essays, even when they are significant or contain seminal insights, remain occasional pieces and lose their influence upon subsequent generations unless the writer belongs to the mainstream of a culture's intellectual tradition. And, Brownson belonged to a minority tradition which had not the developed intellectual institutions and financial resources that help to sustain an intellectual tradition. As an essayist, Brownson was prolific. It could be said, as it has been said of some contemporaries, that he never had an unpublished thought. The vast number of his publications make it difficult for scholars to examine the development of his thought without some bibliographic guide that allows the researcher to follow that development in chronological order. His essays, too, are a mixed bag: some are brilliant and seminal, logically developed philosophical discourses; others are period pieces that have little to offer but insights into his own idiosyncratic perspectives or emotional state. Some, too, are repetitious of earlier positions, and others reveal changes in his thought and/or are contradictory to previous positions. Many, moreover, oscillate from topic to topic, following the digressions of his mind as he hurried to prepare his *Review* for publication deadlines.

Because of the above characteristics, Brownson's essays on specific topics must be read chronologically to grasp the changes and developments that occur in his own thought as he responds to changing events, discovers new perspectives in what he is reading, and reacts to critics who have pointed out flaws or inconsistencies in his arguments. Brownson's essays must also be read dialectically. He frequently complained that he was misunderstood because some readers did not grasp the dialectical nature of his positions. That is, he tended to argue one dimension of his view at a time. A single essay did not contain the whole of his thought, but only one side of it at a time. To understand him fully one had to read one essay on a particular topic, where he presented one side of his case, in tandem with another, where he argued the other side. The truth of his position emerged from the dialectical association of the differing essays. During the revolutions of 1848, for example, he argued in favor of political authority and social order because he believed the primary threat to society came from red republicanism in its many forms. After the reactions to the revolutions set in during the 1850s, he argued for political liberty and democracy because, as he read the signs of the times, the primary threat came from political absolutism. Reading these two sets of essays in conjunction, one could discover Brownson's dialectical view of the relation of liberty and authority; reading them separately one could think him either a reactionary political conservative or a liberal democrat, neither of which he was. The developmental and dialectical nature of his thought was evident in his essays on theology, philosophy, and economics as well as in those on political philosophy.

There is no doubt some truth in this explanation of how Brownson should be read, but that way of reading his essays will not always account for some of the extreme positions and exaggerated rhetoric in his decidedly one-dimensional approach to a single essay. He cannot always be freed from the charges of inconsistency, contradiction, exaggeration, and ultraism that characterize some of his essays.

Brownson's essays can be insightful, creative, and astute when he is articulating his own religious and political philosophy and when he is systematically criticizing the philosophical presuppositions of the writers he reviews. Although some of his criticisms of American and European philosophical and religious positions are insightful, even these criticisms are sometimes mixed with an unfair representation of an author's position because of Brownson's tendency to reduce all positions to their presumed ultimate philosophical principles, which some authors never held. Some of his essays can also be pugnacious, polemical, spiteful, and angry diatribes against positions he finds repugnant.

From the mid 1830s to the end of his life, there was a consistent development in his philosophy. Three thinkers had a profound and lasting influence upon that development: Victor Cousin (1792-1867), Pierre Leroux (1797-1871), and Vincenzo Gioberti (1801-52). These philosophers introduced him to the post-Kantian problem of reconciling subject and object, a problem that was central to his philosophical development. Throughout his career as a philosopher he focused upon the conditions and principles of human knowledge and upon ways of synthesizing the objective and subjective dimensions of all thought and life. His philosophy moved from Cousin's eclecticism, to Leroux's objective idealism to Gioberti's ontologism in his attempts to uncover a Christian philosophy that would establish objective grounds for knowledge and a post-Kantian defense for Christian revelation.

Throughout this period he was preoccupied with the questions proposed by Immanuel Kant's search for the conditions for the possibility of knowledge and Christian revelation. For him, the questions of the day could not be satisfactorily answered by simply retrieving the scholastic tradition because the issues were new and the scholastic tradition was incapable of responding to them. He wanted to develop a nineteenth century Christian philosophy that would enable Catholic Christians to meet the challenges raised by Kant, the Transcendentalists, and the other new philosophies that had developed in the Western world since Descartes. After 1850, he saw his own modified traditionalism and ontologism as a legitimate philosophical foundation for addressing the problems of the age.

Whatever the strengths or weaknesses of his positions and his style, Brownson is worth reading as an American intellectual who had an enormous influence on his times. Some of his religious and philosophical positions and criticisms of American society may still appeal to some contemporaries, while some of his attitudes and positions (e.g., his racism, male chauvinism, hyper anti-Protestantism) many will find offensive. For the historian, however, his works provide a gold mine for research into the life of early and mid-nineteenth century America. This bibliography provides a guide to those resources.

The Bibliography

This bibliography is chronologically arranged, partially annotated, cross-referenced, and indexed. Although not fully exhaustive,[11] the bibliography is more comprehensive than any bibliography previously produced. Past bibliographies of Brownson's works (i.e., those in the collected *Works*,[12] and in all the dissertations and biographies) do not contain a complete list of his works. This is the first compilation that contains a complete listing not only Brownson's earliest works (from 1826 to 1836) but also his post Civil War writings (particularly articles he wrote for the *New York Tablet* between 1867 and 1872, articles that have never been identified before and have never been examined by scholars). The current bibliography contains a list of Brownson's seven books, twenty-five pamphlets, and over 1500 articles that he published in over thirty extant journals.[13] The list was established by examining references to Brownson's writings in his autobiography, collected *Works*, unpublished letters and manuscripts,[14]

---

11. In the search for journals, which Brownson edited and/or in which he wrote, I could not locate the Genesee *Republican and Herald of Reform*, nor articles he wrote for the *Utica Magazine*. The only extant copies of the *Boston Reformer*, moreover, are those from July 26 to August 25, 1836 (available from the American Antiquarian Society, Worcester, MA) and others that Brownson pasted in his diary (the diary is most readily available on microfilm roll 10 of the Orestes Brownson Papers in the Archives of the University of Notre Dame; see Thomas T. McAvoy and Lawrence J. Bradley, eds., *A Guide to the Microfilm Edition of the Orestes Augustus Brownson Papers* (Notre Dame, IN: University of Notre Dame Press, 1966). The bibliographical entries for the *Boston Reformer,* which come from Brownson's diary, do not always have exact reference to dates or page numbers. I also could not locate a number of Brownson's numerous letters to editors that were published in newspapers and were vaguely referred to in biographies. The present bibliography, however, is as exhaustive as is possible at the present time.

12. *Works* 20:439-62 contains a useful alphabetized index of titles to writings in Brownson's collected works.

13. See p. 21 for a chronologically arranged list of journals for which Brownson wrote and/or which he edited.

14. These unpublished writings are located at the Archives of the University of Notre Dame and, except for two boxes, are available on nineteen microfilm rolls. *Microfilm Edition of the Orestes Brownson Papers*, Thomas McAvoy, Project Director; Lawrence J. Bradley, Manuscripts Preparator (Notre Dame, IN: University of Notre Dame Press, 1966). A *Supplementary Roll One* was added later.

biographies (especially his son Henry's three-volume work), twenty-five dissertations, and the most important other secondary studies of Brownson's life and thought. An initial reading of Brownson's collected works and his other signed articles also revealed a number of references to his writings that were not either in his collected *Works* or in his own edited journals.

The numerous articles listed in the bibliography came from a variety of religious journals and newspapers, and they vary in length , substance, and worth. The user of this bibliography can generally distinguish the substantial from the insubstantial articles by the following characteristics of the journals to which Brownson contributed. Brownson wrote a number of one-page letters to editors of various newspapers (e.g., *Utica Magazine, Cayuga Patriot, Western Messenger, New York Times, Boston Pilot, Catholic Herald and Visitor, Pittsburgh Catholic,* and *New York Tribune*) and a series of short one-page or even one paragraph columns for newspapers he either edited or to which he contributed (i.e., *Gospel Advocate and Impartial Investigator, Free Enquirer, Philanthropist, Boston Reformer,* and *New York Tablet*). In some of these journals (e.g., *Gospel Advocate and Impartial Investigator, Philanthropist,* and *New York Tablet*), he periodically wrote more substantial articles, most of which were serialized over an extended period of time. Most of his substantial essays, however, are located in other journals listed in this bibliography (i.e., *Christian Repository, Christian Register, Unitarian, Christian Examiner, Boston Observer and Religious Intelligencer, Liberator, Boston Quarterly Review, Christian World, United States Magazine and Democratic Review, Brownson's Quarterly Review, Ave Maria, Catholic World,* and *American Catholic Quarterly Review*).

Providing a list of articles Brownson wrote for journals proved to be a most difficult task. Research assistants identified Brownson's writings in many of the extant journals by paging through them to uncover his signed articles. The method for identifying the writings Brownson published in the *Boston Reformer,* the *Boston Quarterly Review, Brownson's Quarterly Review,*[15] the *Catholic World*

---

15. For this bibliography, I used the AMS reprint edition of the *Boston Quarterly Review* and Johnson reprint of *Brownson's Quarterly Review*. The volumes for the two reprint editions are numbered consecutively. Thus, the first volume of the *Boston Quarterly Review* is numbered volume one, but the first volume of *Brownson's Quarterly Review* in the *Johnson* reprint (called the "whole series") is numbered volume six.

and the *New York Tablet* was more complicated because most of the time Brownson wrote anonymously in these journals. Articles were identified or eliminated as Brownson's by external evidence (i.e., by examining Brownson's unpublished correspondence with editors and others to discover references to his publications; by locating those works that were published in the collected *Works*; and by consulting Henry Brownson's biography, which periodically identified the authors who had written specific articles for the *Boston Quarterly Review, Brownson's Quarterly Review*, and the *Catholic World*) and by internal evidence (i.e., a close investigation of the style, content and internal references that clearly identify Brownson as the author).

I have been studying Brownson's works for well over fifteen years for my teaching and research and have developed the skills necessary to identify Brownson's content and style in anonymous works. Brownson's authorship can frequently be determined by his habits of writing, historical references to himself (which occurred repeatedly in his writings when he was responding to attacks or attacking others), the content of his own distinctive philosophical, theological, and political opinions, and the utter disdain he has for opposing positions. Although content and style are not always conclusive evidence of authorship, they are at times good indicators. Unless the internal evidence is clear that Brownson was the author of a particular article, however, I have chosen not to include that article in the bibliography. Unsigned articles—except those in the *Boston Reformer, Boston Quarterly Review, Brownson's Quarterly Review, Catholic World*, and *New York Tablet*—which are more than likely Brownson's, will be identified as such by an asterisk (*) in front of the bibliographic entry.

The bibliography is arranged chronologically to provide scholars with a guide to Brownson's intellectual developments and to ideological discussions at particular periods in American history. The bibliography is also partially annotated. The titles of a few articles clearly indicate their content and need not be annotated. It was necessary, however, to annotate other articles in order to make this bibliography a useful guide for scholars. Titles of many articles tell the reader nothing about the content and need a brief description to indicate the primary subject matter of the piece. Frequently Brownson used the titles of books or pamphlets he was supposedly reviewing as the title of an article, but the title or the book being reviewed sometimes had nothing to do with the actual content of the article. Brownson periodically used the review format, but it was more often than not a pretext for developing one or another of his own ideas on a subject. At times it was difficult to summarize even partially the main content of a particular article because it contained diverse topics and digressions from what appeared to be the principal thesis of the piece. For the most part I tried to identify the primary subject of a journal article.

For a number of reasons, this bibliography is cross-referenced. Many times Brownson wrote serial articles for journals. Cross-referencing these serial articles makes it easier to follow the development of Brownson's thought on a particular topic. At times, too, Brownson republished some of his earlier articles; the later articles in the series are cross-referenced to the earlier ones. The bibliography, moreover, identifies which articles or selections have been reprinted in the collected *Works* and which ones are republished in various anthologies.[16] The list of abbreviations at the beginning of the bibliography will help to identify these collections.

The bibliography has an index of names, subjects, and some titles of the most important articles and books. Titles to important articles are surrounded by quotation marks; if the title refers to a book the entry is also in italics with the name of the author in parentheses at the end of the entry. The bibliography is intended to help scholars locate writers that Brownson reacted to or whose works he reviewed, and to identify subjects and topics that Brownson addressed. The index, too, is cross-referenced to corresponding topics. Annotating the bibliography made it possible to make the index a useful finding guide for scholars interested in researching particular subject matter and/or Brownson's views of persons and issues.

---

16. Two anthologies of Brownson's works—i.e., Henry F. Brownson's *Literary, Scientific and Political Views of Orestes A. Brownson* (New York: Benziger Brothers, 1893) and D. J. Scannell O'Neill's *Watchwords from Dr. Brownson* (Techny, Ill.: Society of the Divine Word, 1910)—were not cross referenced because the selections in each book were not substantial, many times only a paragraph or a sentence from one of Brownson's writings.

LIST OF JOURNALS
Chronologically Arranged

The Christian Repository (Woodstock, Vermont, 1826). American Antiquarian Society (Worcester, MA).

The Gospel Advocate and Impartial Investigator (Auburn, NY, 1827-1829). Yale University Library (New Haven, CT).

New Harmony Gazette (New Harmony, Indiana, 1828). Library of Congress (Washington, DC).

Cayuga Patriot (Auburn, NY, 1829). Seymour Library and Cayuga County Historical Society (Auburn, NY).

Republican and Herald of Reform (Leroy, NY, 1829-1830). Extant copies not located.

Free Enquirer (New York, NY, 1829-1830). Library of Congress (Washington, DC).

The Philanthropist (Ithaca, NY, 1831-32). Part of vol. 1, Cornell University Library (Ithaca, NY). All of vol. 2, University of Notre Dame Library (Notre Dame, IN).

The Christian Register (Boston, MA, 1831-1834). Henry E. Huntington Library (San Marino, CA).

The Unitarian (Boston, MA, 1834). Boston Public Library (Boston, MA).

The Christian Examiner (Boston, MA, 1834-1836). California State Library (Sacramento, CA).

The Boston Observer and Religious Intelligencer (Boston, MA, 1835). American Antiquarian Society (Worcester, MA).

Boston Reformer (Boston, MA, 1836). American Antiquarian Society (Worcester, MA).

The Western Messenger (Louisville, KY, 1837). American Antiquarian Society (Worcester, MA).

The Liberator (Boston, MA, 1838). Boston Public Library (Boston, MA).

Boston Quarterly Review (Boston, MA, 1838-1842). Reprint. New York: AMS Press, 1965.

Daily National Investigator (Washington, DC, 1842). Georgetown University Library (Washington, DC).

Boston Daily Times (Boston, MA, 1842). American Antiquarian Society (Worcester, MA).

New York Mirror (New York, NY, 1842). Boston Public Library (Boston, MA).

The United States Magazine and Democratic Review (New York, NY, 1842-43). Stanford College Libraries (Stanford, CA).

The Christian World (Boston, MA, 1843). American Antiquarian Society (Worcester, MA).

Brownson's Quarterly Review (Boston, MA, 1844-1855; New York, NY, 1856-1864; 1873-1875). Reprint. New York: Johnson Reprint Co., 1965.

American Review (New York, NY, 1849).

The New York Times (New York, NY, 1852-1875).

The Courier (Boston, 1853). Boston Public Library.

The Catholic Mirror (Baltimore, 1854). University of Notre Dame Library.

Pittsburgh Catholic (Pittsburgh, 1854). University of Notre Dame Library.

Catholic Telegraph and Advocate (Cincinnati, 1854). University of Notre Dame Library.

Catholic Herald and Visitor (Philadelphia, 1862). University of Notre Dame Library.

The New York Tribune (New York, NY, 1865-1875).

Ave Maria (Notre Dame, IN, 1865-1872).

The Catholic World (New York, NY, 1866-1872).

The New York Tablet (New York, NY, 1867-1872). Holy Cross College (Worcester, MA).

Boston Pilot (Boston, 1874). University of Notre Dame Library.

The American Catholic Quarterly Review (Philadelphia, 1876).

ABBREVIATIONS

Abell Aaron I. Abell, ed. *American Catholic Thought on Social Questions.* Indianapolis and New York: Bobbs-Merrill Co., 1968.

BQR *Boston Quarterly Review* (1838-42).

BrQR *Brownson's Quarterly Review* (1844-64; 1873-75).

Carey Patrick W. Carey, ed. *Orestes A. Brownson: Selected Writings.* New York: Paulist Press, 1991.

CW *The Catholic World* (1865-73).

Ellis John Tracy Ellis, ed. *Documents of American Catholic History.* Vol. 1: 1493-1865. Wilmington, Delaware: Michael Glazier, 1987.

Essays Orestes A. Brownson, *Essays and Reviews, Chiefly on Theology, Politics, and Socialism.* New York: D. & J. Sadlier, 1852.

Gaustad Edwin Gaustad, ed. *A Documentary History of Religion in America to the Civil War.* 2nd edition. Grand Rapids: Wm. B. Eerdmans Co., 1993.

GAII *The Gospel Advocate and Impartial Investigator (1827-29)*

Gems David Battle, ed. *Gems of Composition and Criticism Compiled from the Writings of the Late Dr. Orestes A. Brownson.* Huntington, Indiana: Our Sunday Visitor, 1923.

Handy Robert T. Handy, Lefferts A. Loetscher, H. Shelton Smith, eds. *American Christianity.* Vol. 2. New York: Charles Scribner's Sons, 1963.

Kirk Russell Kirk, ed. *Orestes Brownson: Selected Essays* Chicago: Henry Regnery Co., 1955.

Miller Perry Miller, ed. *The Transcendentalists: An Anthology* Cambridge, Mass: Harvard University Press, 1950.

Miller2 Perry Miller, ed. *The American Transcendentalists: Their Prose and Poetry.* Garden City, NY: Doubleday, 1957.

Modern Henry F. Brownson, ed. *Essays on Modern Popular Literature by O. A. Brownson.* Detroit: H. F. Brownson, 1888.

RyanA Alvan S. Ryan, ed. *The Brownson Reader.* New York: P. J. Kenedy & Sons, 1955; reprint New York: Arno Press, 1978.

RyanT   Thomas R. Ryan, ed. *Saint Worship. The Worship of Mary.*
          Paterson, New Jersey: St. Anthony Guild Press, 1963.

Works   Henry F. Brownson, ed. *The Works of Orestes A. Brownson.*
          20 Vols. Detroit: Thorndike Nourse, 1882-87.

BIBLIOGRAPHICAL ENTRIES:
1826-1876

1826

"The Influence of Religion on Prosperity." *Christian Repository* 7 (August, 1826):49-58; *GAII* (September 19, 1829); Carey: 95-101. Religion should influence a person in good times and in bad, bringing hope and softening the heart.

1827

"Circular Letter." *The Gospel Advocate and Impartial Investigator* 5 (October 13, 1827):321-22. Brownson's letter on occasion of annual convention of Universalists; "morality must be the test of a man's character."

"A Fragment." *The Gospel Advocate and Impartial Investigator* 5 (November 10, 1827):355-56. Religion is not blind devotion; what counts in religion is morality.

"An Essay on the Progress of Truth." *The Gospel Advocate and Impartial Investigator* 5-6 (November 17, 1827):361-62; (November 24, 1827):369-71; (December 8, 1827):385-87; (December 15, 1827):393-94; (January 19, 1828):24-26; (February 2, 1828):46-47; (February 17, 1828):55-56; (March 1, 1828):68-69; (March 15, 1828):87-90. On the freedom to pursue the truth; Jesus Christ as the source of the religion of reason; and the march of truth in the evolution of pure religion.

"Reply to L. S. Everett." *The Gospel Advocate and Impartial Investigator* 5 (November 24, 1827):373-74. Brownson's answer to Joseph Rogers Underwood's charges that his position on church organization and discipline was heretical.

"Extract from a Sermon." *The Gospel Advocate and Impartial Investigator* 5 (December 15, 1827):394-95. Acquisition of wisdom.

1828

"A Sermon." *The Gospel Advocate and Impartial Investigator* 6 (January 5, 1828):1-4. On the Book of Revelation (Rev. 5:18), prophecy, and the providence of God.

"Remarks on Universalism." *The Gospel Advocate and Impartial Investigator* 6 (January 5, 1828):6-7; Carey: 102-04. Universal salvation and the character of God.

"Sabbath Schools—No. 1." *The Gospel Advocate and Impartial Investigator* 6 (January 5, 1828):8; (January 19, 1828):27-28. On the evils connected with these schools.

"A Letter to the Rev. William Wisner." *The Gospel Advocate and Impartial Investigator* 6 (March 1, 1828):72-73. Against this Presbyterian's assault upon those who oppose revivalist political ambitions.

"A Sermon. On Zeal in Religion." *The Gospel Advocate and Impartial Investigator* 6 (March 29, 1828):97-101. Sermon on Rom. 10:2; in defense of rational, rather than emotional religion.

"A Sermon. The Faith and Character of the True Christian [Acts 11.26]." *The Gospel Advocate and Impartial Investigator* 6 (April 12, 1828):113-17; Carey: 104-14. Nothing in Christ's preaching is contrary to natural religion.

"The Essayest, No. 1." *The Gospel Advocate and Impartial Investigator* 6 (April 12, 1828):117-18; (May 10, 1828):151-52; (May 24, 1828):167-68; (June 7, 1828):181-82; (June 21, 1828):196-98; (July 5, 1828):213-15; (July 19, 1828):230-31; (August 2, 1828):249-50; (August 9, 1828):262-64; (August 30, 1828):278-79; (September 13, 1828):295-96. The revealed not opposed to the natural; revelation of God as benevolent; faith as intellectual assent; Gospel enjoins charity; religious sentiments; philosophy can elevate human character; utility of religious faith; limits of the Bible.

Untitled. *The Gospel Advocate and Impartial Investigator* 6 (April 26, 1828):133-34. On the dangers of an intolerant religious mind.

"Liberality." *The Gospel Advocate and Impartial Investigator* 6 (May 24, 1828):172. Religious feuds prevented by recognizing that faith depends upon assent to truth based on evidence.

"A Sermon [Ezek. 13:22]." *The Gospel Advocate and Impartial Investigator* 6 (June 7, 1828):177-81. Against religious self-pride and ecclesiolatry; religion is for human happiness.

"The Clergy." *The Gospel Advocate and Impartial Investigator* 6 (June 7, 1828):187-88. Duty to enlighten the mind and improve character; deeds over creeds.

"Answer. To the Request of our Friend in Canada." *The Gospel Advocate and Impartial Investigator* 6 (June 21, 1828):202-04. Devil may exist but its existence is beyond proof or disproof.

"Of the Cause of Evil." *The New Harmony Gazette* 3 (August 13, 1828):330; GAII 6 (July 19, 1828):230-31. Marxist-like view that religion is used for the usurpation and support of the status quo.

"A Sermon. On the New Birth [Jn. 3:3]." *The Gospel Advocate and Impartial Investigator* 6 (August 16, 1828):257-62. Common Christian understanding of spiritual regeneration is opposed; against revivals; regeneration equals moral goodness.

"Free Inquiry." *The Gospel Advocate and Impartial Investigator* 6 (August 16, 1828):257-62. Quasi-Marxist protest against using religion to console the poor; future hope no remedy to present pain.

"A Sermon. On the Salvation of All Men [Titus 2:11]." *The Gospel Advocate and Impartial Investigator* 6 (August 30, 1828):273-78. Originally published in the *Gospel Preacher* (Providence, R. I.). God can and will bestow happiness on all who are capable of receiving it.

"Intolerance." *The Gospel Advocate and Impartial Investigator* 6 (August 30, 1828):279. Against an orthodox Presbyterian who is reprimanded for attacking Universalist Church.

"Universalism no test in a dying hour." *The Gospel Advocate and Impartial Investigator* 6 (August 30, 1828):283-84. On the relation between the experience of dying and the truth of doctrine.

"Sabbath Schools." *The Gospel Advocate and Impartial Investigator* 6 (August 30, 1828):285-86. Against the erroneous instruction and sectarian clerical despotism in such schools. Schools used to favor Christian Party in politics.

"A Sermon. On the Moral Condition of Mankind [Jer. 8:22]." *The Gospel Advocate and Impartial Investigator* 6 (September 13, 1828):289-94. Chief cause of evil is ignorance. Religion's chief aim is to improve human condition here, not hereafter.

"Universalism— An Extract." *The Gospel Advocate and Impartial Investigator* 6 (September 13, 1828):299-300. March of mind theme.

"Missionaries." *The Gospel Advocate and Impartial Investigator* 6 (September 13, 1828):300-01; (November 22, 1828):381-82. Against missionaries; Hindu religion may be as good as Christian.

Untitled. *The Gospel Advocate and Impartial Investigator* 6 (September 13, 1828):301-02. On Matt. 7:31-32. Blasphemy against Holy Spirit.

"Sectarianism." *The Gospel Advocate and Impartial Investigator* 6 (September 13, 1828):302. Against the Presbyterians and the Christian Party in politics.

"Reply to 'L. C.'" *The Gospel Advocate and Impartial Investigator* 6 (October 25,1828):342-43; (November 8, 1828):358-60. Suffering and misery proceed from "imperfect state of society."

Untitled Letter to the Editor. *The Gospel Advocate and Impartial Investigator* 6 (November 8, 1828):360-61. On presenting Christianity in its purity.

"A Sermon. On Endless Punishment [Ps. 9:17]." *The Gospel Advocate and Impartial Investigator* 6 (November 22, 1828):369-74. Doctrine of endless punishment is unmerciful, unjust, useless, contrary to revealed will of God, and not taught in Scripture.

"Questions in Regard to Universalism." *The Gospel Advocate and Impartial Investigator* 6(November 22, 1828):374-76. Response to objections raised against Universalist doctrine.

"The Signs of the Times." *The Gospel Advocate and Impartial Investigator* 6 (December 6, 1828):393-94. Against orthodox clericalism in schools, missions, tracts, and papers.

"Outrage." *The Gospel Advocate and Impartial Investigator* 6 (December 6, 1828):394-95. Against Presbyterians who ousted a member for attending a Universalist meeting.

1829

"A Sermon. On future Judgement and Punishment." *The Gospel Advocate and Impartial Investigator* 7 (January 10, 1829):1-7. God's nature is love; hence, no eternal punishment.

"An Essay On Christianity." *The Gospel Advocate and Impartial Investigator* 7 (January 10, 1829):7 9; (January 24, 1829):20-23; (February 7, 1829):36-38; (February 21, 1829):54-56; (March 7, 1829):68-69; (March 21, 1829):85-87; (April 4, 1829):102-03; (April 18, 1829):117-19; (May 2, 1829):134-35. Christianity is reasonable; man is a progressive being; doctrine of the Trinity is unreasonable; testimony of the Bible is weakest kind of evidence; Bible must be interpreted according to reason; against verbal inspiration because of contradictions in Bible; only the doctrinal part of the Christian scriptures are inspired; miracles are only particular events and cannot prove general truths; the Bible must be studied as any other book; Old Testament does not support Trinity.

"To Our Readers." *The Gospel Advocate and Impartial Investigator* 7 (January 10, 1829):9-10. Brownson assumes editorship of *Gospel Advocate.*

"Sellon's Sermons." *The Gospel Advocate and Impartial Investigator* 7 (January 10, 1829):10-11. On the attempts to reconcile everlasting punishment with God's benevolence.

"A Sermon. Why Men Follow Vice [Prov. 3:17]." *The Gospel Advocate and Impartial Investigator* 7 (January, 24, 1829):17-20. Habit is the demon; solution is education and greater knowledge.

"'A Strange Thing'..." *The Gospel Advocate and Impartial Investigator* 7 (January 24, 1829):23-25; (February 7, 1829):39-41; (March 7, 1829):69-70. Against a tract opposing Universalism; Scripture demonstrates universal salvation.

"A Sermon. On Faith And Its Consequences [Mk. 16:16]." *The Gospel Advocate and Impartial Investigator* 7 (February 7, 1829):33-36. Against idea that one's holiness depends on one's faith and not works.

"An Essay On Divine Goodness No. 1" *The Gospel Advocate and Impartial Investigator* 7 (February 7, 1829):38-39; (March 21, 1829):87-89; (April 18, 1829):119-20; (May 2, 1829):135-36; (September 19, 1829):294-95. On the character of God and the problem of theodicy.

"Albany Christian Register." *The Gospel Advocate and Impartial Investigator* 7 (February 7, 1829):41-42. Response to those who charge that Universalism leads to antinomianism.

"Sunday Affairs." *The Gospel Advocate and Impartial Investigator* 7 (February 7, 1829):42. Against using politics to advance religious views.

"Clerical Influence." *The Gospel Advocate and Impartial Investigator* 7 (February 7, 1829):42. Government declaring fast day in New York State Legislature.

"A Sermon. On the Word of God [Jer. 23:26]." *The Gospel Advocate and Impartial Investigator* 7 (February 21, 1829):49-54. Against false prophets of the day.

"Sunday Memorial." *The Gospel Advocate and Impartial Investigator* 7 (February 21, 1829):56-59. Against using government to enforce religious ideas.

"New-York Gospel Herald." *The Gospel Advocate and Impartial Investigator* 7 (February 21, 1829):59-60. On competition from this new Universalist journal.

"Questions for the Rochester Observer." *The Gospel Advocate and Impartial Investigator* 7 (March 7, 1829):70-71. Against religious bigotry.

"Free Enquirers." *The Gospel Advocate and Impartial Investigator* 7 (March 21, 1829):89-90. Approves of Frances Wright's lectures on knowledge.

"Baptism." *The Gospel Advocate and Impartial Investigator* 7 (March 21, 1829):90-91. Water baptism is not essential to Christian character and development.

"Progress of Truth." *The Gospel Advocate and Impartial Investigator* 7 (March 21, 1829):95. Orthodoxy is dying and converts from orthodoxy to liberalism show the progress of truth.

"A Sermon. On the Refuge of Lies [Is. 28:15]." *The Gospel Advocate and Impartial Investigator* 7 (April 4, 1829):97-102. Knowledge can save us.

"The Times." *The Gospel Advocate and Impartial Investigator* 7 (April 4, 1829):103-05; (May 2, 1829):136-38; (September 5, 1829):280-81. On the nature of American government.

"Rev. Abner Kneeland." *The Gospel Advocate and Impartial Investigator* 7 (April 4, 1829):106-07. Against the Universalist condemnation of Kneeland.

"Infidelity." *The Gospel Advocate and Impartial Investigator* 7 (April 18, 1829):121-23. Brownson defends himself against Universalists who charge that he denies existence of God and the truth of divine revelation.

"Gospel Herald." *The Gospel Advocate and Impartial Investigator* 7 (April 18, 1829):123. Against *Gospel Herald* which charged Brownson with infidelity.

"To James Luckey, Esq." *The Gospel Advocate and Impartial Investigator* 7 (April 18, 1829):127-128; (May 30, 1829):176-78; (June 13, 1829):186-88; (July 25, 1829):234-36. Theodicy; argument for Universalist solution based on the goodness of God; attacks on Calvinists.

"A Question Proposed." *The Gospel Advocate and Impartial Investigator* 7 (May 2, 1829):138-39. Eternal punishment rejected on grounds that it is vindictive and unjust.

"Church and State No.1." *The Gospel Advocate and Impartial Investigator* 7 (May 2, 1829):139-40; (July 25, 1829):240-41; (August 8, 1829):251-53; (August 22, 1829):265-68; (September 5,

1829):284-87; (September 19, 1829):298-99. Against Ezra Stiles Ely and those Presbyterians who are trying to "unite church and state."

"Vindication of Universalism." *The Gospel Advocate and Impartial Investigator* 7 (May 2, 1829):140-41. Believes in revelation: "I hold the bible infallible where light of nature fails."

"A Sermon [Ja. 3:17]." *The Gospel Advocate and Impartial Investigator* 7 (May 16, 1829):147-50. Distinguishes wisdom from above and from below.

"Excommunication." *The Gospel Advocate and Impartial Investigator* 7 (May 16, 1829):151. Against it.

"Service to God—No. 1." *The Gospel Advocate and Impartial Investigator* 7 (May 30, 1829):167-69. On the meaning of true service.

"Review of Amicus." *The Gospel Advocate and Impartial Investigator* 7 (May 30, 1829):169-72; (July 11, 1829):216-18; (August 22, 1829):265. On knowledge of God; against imputed righteousness.

"Forgiveness of Sins." *The Gospel Advocate and Impartial Investigator* 7 (May 30, 1829):172. No use for divine punishment.

"Horrid Impiety." *The Gospel Advocate and Impartial Investigator* 7 (May 30, 1829):172-73. Against Presbyterians.

"Outrage." *The Gospel Advocate and Impartial Investigator* 7 (May 30, 1829):172-73. Presbyterian jailed for speaking out in church.

"My Creed." *The Gospel Advocate and Impartial Investigator* 7 (June 27, 1829):199-201; Carey: 114-17. Assertion of the essential beliefs of true religion.

Untitled. *The Gospel Advocate and Impartial Investigator* 7 (June 27, 1829):201. Brownson charged with being unorthodox.

"Ancient History of Universalism." *The Gospel Advocate and Impartial Investigator* 7 (June 27, 1829):201. On Hosea Ballou's history of Universalism.

"Fourth of July." *The Gospel Advocate and Impartial Investigator* 7 (July 11, 1829):218-19. On the patriotism of the celebration, but criticism of Presbyterians who turn the day into a religious celebration.

"Evangelical Magazine." *The Gospel Advocate and Impartial Investigator* 7 (July 11, 1829):219-20. On the Utica New York Universalist paper and its differences with the *Advocate*.

"A Sermon. On Trusting in Providence [Hab. 3:17-18]." *The Gospel Advocate and Impartial Investigator* 7 (July 25, 1829):227-31. Trusting is not excuse for inactivity and passivity.

"Mr. Reese's Letter." *The Gospel Advocate and Impartial Investigator* 7 (July 25, 1829):236-40. Against the charge that Brownson is an atheist; on primitive revelation.

"Controversy." *The Gospel Advocate and Impartial Investigator* 7 (July 25, 1829):242. On the Reese controversy over atheism.

"Let Us Be Vigilent [*sic*]." *The Gospel Advocate and Impartial Investigator* 7 (August 8, 1829):250-51. Against the political activities of the orthodox and their voluntary societies.

"Miss Frances Wright." *The Gospel Advocate and Impartial Investigator* 7 (August 8, 1829):253-54. Reasons for including Wright's article in paper.

"W. I. Reese." *The Gospel Advocate and Impartial Investigator* 7 (August 22, 1829):264-65. Brownson's belief in the existence of God.

"Existence of God." *The Gospel Advocate and Impartial Investigator* 7 (August 22, 1829):274. God, as represented by revelation, can be known only by revelation.

"Equality, No.1." *The Gospel Advocate and Impartial Investigator* 7 (September 5, 1829):282-83. Critique of privileged classes; against capitalist system.

"Let Us Awake." *The Gospel Advocate and Impartial Investigator* 7 (September 5, 1829):283-84. Introduction to article on church and state; danger from orthodox saints.

"A Sermon. On the Influence of Religion on Prosperity [Ps. 1:3]." *The Gospel Advocate and Impartial Investigator* 7 (September 19, 1829):291-94. Republication of 1826 article.

"The Mission of Christ." *The Gospel Advocate and Impartial Investigator* 7 (September 19, 1829):295-97. Jesus as reformer of humankind.

"Weakness." *The Gospel Advocate and Impartial Investigator* 7 (September 19,1829):299-300. Defense of Frances Wright; Christianity has nothing to fear from free inquiry.

"Early Christians." *The Gospel Advocate and Impartial Investigator* 7 (September 19, 1829):300-01. On the intolerance of primitive Christians.

"Christian Intelligencer." *The Gospel Advocate and Impartial Investigator* 7 (September 19, 1829):301. Hypocrisy of the editor.

"A Sermon. Mankind Authours [*sic*] of Their Own Misery [Prov. 19:3]." *The Gospel Advocate and Impartial Investigator* 7 (October 3, 1829):307-310. Human will is the source of suffering; misuses of the doctrine of divine providence.

"A Gospel Creed." *The Gospel Advocate and Impartial Investigator* 7 (October 3, 1829):310-11; Carey: 117-20. List of Brownson's articles of belief.

"Letter From the Editor." *The Gospel Advocate and Impartial Investigator* 7 (October 17, 1829):329-330. To Brother U. F. Doubleday; on the condition of Universalism in Connecticut.

"Church and State." *The Gospel Advocate and Impartial Investigator* 7 (October 31, 1829):351. Warning against orthodox use of civil institutions.

"Letter From the Editor, No. 2." *The Gospel Advocate and Impartial Investigator* 7 (October 31, 1829):344-45. On Brownson's visit to Charlestown, MA, where orthodoxy is dying out.

"A Sermon [Mt. 17:20]." *The Gospel Advocate and Impartial Investigator* 7 (November 14, 1829):355-58. Faith is interior confidence in one's own powers, a just self-respect.

"Union of Papers." *The Gospel Advocate and Impartial Investigator* 7 (November 14, 1829):362. Union of the *Gospel Advocate* and the *Evangelical Magazine.* Brownson will be leaving editorship.

"Letter to the Editor." *Cayuga Patriot* (November 18, 1829). Reprint "From the *Cayuga Patriot.*" *The Gospel Advocate and Impartial Investigator* 7 (November 28, 1829):378-79. In defense of Frances Wright.

"Universalist Hymn Book." *The Gospel Advocate and Impartial Investigator* 7 (November 28, 1829):377. On church hymns. Brownson no longer a Universalist.

"To the Universalists." *Free Enquirer* 2 (November 28, 1829):38. Brownson ends fellowship as Universalist minister.

"To Robert Dale Owen." *Free Enquirer* 2 (December 12, 1829):55-56. Brownson's discharge from *Gospel Advocate* editorship was not just. Brownson's advocacy of working men's rights.

"Letter to Mr. Doubleday." *Free Enquirer* 2 (December 26, 1829):409. Doubleday criticized Brownson for not separating himself from Wright's religious sentiments.

"Letter to Mr. Doubleday." *Free Enquirer* 2 (December 26, 1829):417. On troubles that caused Brownson to leave *Gospel Advocate.*

1830

"To the Editors of the Free Enquirer." *Free Enquirer* 2 (January 2, 1830):95-96; Carey: 121-3. Brownson's declaration of independence from sectarianism.

Untitled correspondence from Auburn, NY. *Free Enquirer* 2 (January 16, 1830):95-96. Brownson neither religionist nor anti-religionist.

Untitled correspondence from Auburn, NY. *Free Enquirer* 2 (January 23, 1830):103. Brownson tired of religious controversies and "anxious for peace."

1831

"Patrick O'Hara, Chapter VI." *The Philanthropist* 1 (July 23, 1831):141-43; Carey: 59-63. Autobiographical account of the Calvinism Brownson received during his early years.

"On Creeds." *The Christian Register* 10 (July 30, 1831):121. Partial extract from *The Philanthropist*. Right of private judgment; no need for creeds.

An Address on the Fifty-Fifth Anniversary of American Independence. Delivered at Ovid, Seneca County, NY, July 4, 1831. Ithaca: S. S. Chatterton, 1831. Liberty celebrated, yet tyrants of ignorance, superstition and bigotry still to be overcome.

"Strike, but hear." *The Philanthropist* 2 (November 5, 1831):1-3. Bigotry in religious world.

"Unitarianism." *The Philanthropist* 2 (November 5, 1831):3-5. Defense of Unitarian Christianity.

"Church and State." *The Philanthropist* 2 (November 5, 1831):5-8. One need not vent one's spleen against the orthodox.

"To Our Patrons." *The Philanthropist* 2 (November 5, 1831):10-11. Only Unitarian paper in state.

"Letter to Rev. Wm. Wisner." *The Philanthropist* 2 (November 5, 1831):11-14; (November 19, 1831):20-24; (December 3, 1831): 37-42; (December 17, 1831):55-59; (January 31, 1832):109-11; (February 14, 1832):115-19; (February 28, 1832):141-44; (June 12, 1832):228-36. Essence of Christianity is moral freedom and enlargement of soul; only the doctrinal content of Scripture is inspired; God as eternal, intelligent, spiritual, and one; Jesus not consubstantial with Father; necessity of evidence for belief; morality all that is necessary for salvation; Jesus taught righteousness by precepts and example; against Charles Grandison Finney and other evangelists who are not following method of Jesus in teaching that God is father.

"Future State." *The Philanthropist* 2 (November 19, 1831):17-19. Future state can be inferred from capacities of soul itself.

"Religious Discussion." *The Philanthropist* 2 (December 3, 1831):33-35. Unitarianism is little known in this country.

"Justification." *The Philanthropist* 2 (December 3, 1831):35-37. Reprinted in *The Christian Register* 11 (January 7, 1832):2. Christ made no atonement; he was an example.

"Division." *The Philanthropist* 2 (December 3, 1831):44-45. Secession of Restorationists from the General Convention of Universalists.

"Freedom of the Press." *The Philanthropist* 2 (December 3, 1831):45-46. Subscribers should not dictate the direction of a paper.

"Sectarianism." *The Philanthropist* 2 (December 17, 1831):49-51. On the human folly of sectarianism.

"Essay on Reform." *The Philanthropist* 2 (December 17, 1831):51-55; (January 14, 1832):81-85; (February 14, 1832):113-15; (February 28, 1832):129-35; (March 13, 1832):145-50; (June 12, 1832):225-28; (June 26, 1832):241-46. We are responsible for evil and have means to eliminate it; religion is right exercise of our faculties; both piety and social duty produce human happiness; on Brownson's conversion from skepticism to joyful belief in one God; proof of Christianity is the witness within us of the truth; God rules by reason not power; the worship that God requires is "the improvement and exaltation of ourselves."

"Protracted Meetings." *The Philanthropist* 2 (December 17, 1831):62-63; (March 13, 1832):154-55. Revivalists use artificial techniques; their long-term effects must be tested.

"A Sermon on Self-Denial." *The Philanthropist* 2 (December 31, 1831):65-75. On the true doctrine of self-denial that is necessary for social reforms.

"Our Own Concerns." *The Philanthropist* 2 (December 31, 1831):78-79. Ultra-orthodox are increasing their threats against us.

1832

"Justification." *The Christian Register* 11 (January 7, 1832):2. Reprinted from *The Philanthropist,* 2 (December 3, 1831):35-37.

"A Sermon on Righteousness." *The Philanthropist* 2 (January 14, 1832):85-94; Carey: 124-33. Brownson's first sermon as independent minister, defending himself against charges by some that he is a skeptic and by others that he has moved toward "exclusive orthodoxy."

"Dr. Cooper's Case." *The Philanthropist* 2 (January 14, 1832):95. Infidelity is the cause of Thomas Cooper's removal from Presidency of South Carolina College.

An Address, Prepared at the Request of Guy C. Clark, with the Intention of Having it Delivered to the Assembly on the Day of His Execution, February 3, 1832. Ithaca, NY, 1832. Protest against capital punishment and the social havoc it creates.

"Random Thoughts." *The Philanthropist* 2 (February 28, 1832):135-38. Universalist and orthodox parties dangerous; against priestcraft.

"Brief Expositor, No 1." *The Philanthropist* 2 (March 13, 1832):151-53; (June 12, 1832):236-39. On Mt. 25:46. People are justified by conscience.

"The Workingmen." *The Philanthropist* 2 (March 13, 1832):156. On the side of the workingman.

"M. Girard's Will." *The Philanthropist* 2 (March 13, 1832):157. Protest against a society which allows one person to accumulate so much wealth (two million dollars).

"Poverty." *The Philanthropist* 2 (March 27, 1832):161-63. Against *Christian Examiner*'s view that society cannot cure poverty.

"Unitarians not Deists." *The Philanthropist* 2 (May 15, 1832):193-95. Brownson accused of being a Deist; but Unitarians admit both internal and external revelation.

"Orthodox Politeness." *The Philanthropist* 2 (May 15, 1832):202-05. Against the promotion of religious tracts in stagecoaches.

"To our Patrons." *The Philanthropist* 2 (May 15, 1832):206. Money matters.

"Priest and Infidel." *The Philanthropist* 2 (May 29, 1832):209-21. A religion of genuine love opposed to dogmatic Calvinism and skepticism.

"Calvinism and Infidelity." *The Philanthropist* 2 (May 29, 1832):221-22. Calvinism and skepticism lead to infidelity. A religion of genuine love is only cure against dogmatic Calvinism and the skepticism of free inquiry.

"The Moralist, No. 1." *The Philanthropist* 2 (June 26, 1832):246-49. Humans have to cultivate moral nature.

"A Word to Liberal Christians." *The Philanthropist* 2 (June 26, 1832):256. Last issue of *Philanthropist*. We have attempted to defend Christianity against infidels and orthodox, and lived in poverty doing so.

"Treatment of Unbelievers." *The Christian Register* 11-12 (December 8,1832):194; (February 2, 1833):18; (February 23, 1833):30. Charity to unbelievers.

1833

"Channing's Discourses." *The Christian Register* 12 (January 19, 1833):10. Brownson's admiration for Channing's views on the internal evidence of Christianity.

An Address on Intemperance. Delivered in Walpole, NH, February 26, 1833. Keene, NH: J.& J. W. Prentiss, 1833. The causes of intemperance are idleness, debt and melancholy, with the effect being destruction of life. Reform efforts must focus on the force of public opinion and good example. On temperance societies.

"Faith and Works." *The Christian Register* 12 (May 11, 1833):73; (May 25, 1833):82; (June 1, 1833):85-86; (June 15, 1833):93-94; (June 29, 1833):101-02; (August 3, 1833):121-24. On reconciling Paul's view of the necessity of faith and James's view of the necessity of works in the process of salvation.

"Letters to an Unbeliever." *The Christian Register* 12 (October 5, 1833):158; (October 19, 1833):165-66; (October 27, 1833):170; (November 9, 1833):177-78; (November 16, 1833):182; (November 23, 1833):186; (November 30, 1833):190; (December 7, 1833):194; (December 14, 1833):198. Brownson uses his own experience of skepticism to lead an unbeliever to embrace the truth of Christianity by emphasizing that freedom of inquiry and the acceptance of the spirit of Christianity are compatible.

1834

"Christianity and Reform." *The Unitarian* 1 (January, 1834):30- 39; (February, 1834):51-58; Carey: 134-50. Reform party is rising; it embodies the spirit of the gospel.

"The Deist's Immortality, etc." *The Unitarian* 1 (March, 1834):146-47. Review of Lysander Spooner's *The Deist's Immortality* (1834). He got his ideas primarily from Christian writers even though he condemns the orthodox idea of heaven.

"A Letter on the Coldness of New-England Preaching." *The Unitarian* 1 (March, 1834):153-54. On New England way of life.

"The Workingmen's Party." *The Unitarian* 1 (April, 1834):170-77. Review of L. C. Bowles' *Workingman's Library* (1834). Rising position and consciousness of the laboring classes indicates reform and advance.

"Social Evils and Their Remedy." *The Unitarian* 1 (May, 1834):238-44. Review of Charles B. Taylor's *Social Evils and Their Remedy* (1834). The gospel is emphatically the working man's religion and was given "to effect great moral and social reform."

"Motives to Beneficent Action." *The Christian Register* 13 (May 13, 1834):70. Right and duty over vested selfish interests.

"Memoir of Saint-Simon." *The Unitarian* 1 (June, 1834):279-89, 350. On Claude Henri Saint Simon's principle: to each according to his capacities, to each capacity according to its works.

"Rev. Mr. Brownson's Address." *The Christian Register* 13 (June 28, 1834):101; (July 5, 1834):105; (July 19, 1834):114. Delivered to the Boston Young Men's Bible Society, April 20, 1834. Christianity is "the great lever of reform"; take away religion and humans become selfish animals.

"Salvation by Jesus." *The Unitarian* 1 (July, 1834):10. Conversation between Jesus and believer.

An Address, Delivered at Dedham, on the Fifty-Eighth Anniversary of American Independence, July 4, 1834. Dedham: H. Hamm, 1834; see *The Christian Register* 14 (August 23, 1834):6; (September 13, 1834):18 for excerpts. Belief in the power of progress; United States has a providential mission.

"Letter to Rev. Mr. R." *The Christian Register* 14 (August 30, 1834):10. Brownson defends himself against charges of the *Christian Register* that he is radical. He actually wants to elevate the poor, and not bring down the rich.

"Spirituality of Religion "*The Unitarian* 1 (September, 1834):405-13. Review of Ezra Shaw Goodwin's *Sermons* (1834). God meets humans in the inner sanctuary of their hearts, not in outward forms of religion.

"Benjamin Constant *on Religion.*" *The Christian Examiner and General Review* 17 (September, 1834):63-77. Carey: 150-62. Miller: 84-8. Humans are religious by nature; Christianity is religious sentiment itself.

1835

"Principles of Morality." *The Christian Examiner and General Review* 17 (January, 1835):283-301. Review of W. J. Fox's *Sermons on the Principles of Morality* (1833). Brownson against Fox's utilitarianism.

"Essays for Believers and Disbelievers." *The Boston Observer and Religious Intelligencer* 1 (January 1, 1835):2-3; (January 15, 1835):17; (February 5, 1835):42-43; (March 5, 1835):73-74. Difference between believers and unbelievers.

A Sermon, Delivered to the Young People of the First Congregational Society in Canton, on Sunday, May 24th, 1835. Dedham, MA: H. Mann, Printer, 1835. On Mt. 6:33. To desire and love what God desires is to come under the reign of God.

"Accountability for Belief." *The Boston Observer and Religious Intelligencer* 1 (February 26, 1835):66-67. While not accountable for belief, we are responsible for the honesty and diligence with which we seek truth.

"G. E. E.'s Comments on O. A. B." *The Boston Observer and Religious Intelligencer* 1 (April 2, 1835):107. On Brownson's eclecticism: all humans have both truth and error.

"Correspondence," *Boston Investigator* 4 (April 17, 1835):157. Brownson informs the editor, Abner Kneeland, that he is preparing for publication a philosophical history of "modern infidelity."

"Trusting in God." *The Boston Observer and Religious Intelligencer* 1 (April 23, 1835):130; (May 5, 1835):154-55. On the meaning and reasonableness of trust in Divine Providence.

"Remarks on G. E. E." *The Boston Observer and Religious Intelligencer* 1 (May 7,1835):146-47. Brownson, like Victor Cousin, defines religion as the "idea of the holy."

"'He Wants Energy'." *The Boston Observer and Religious Intelligencer* (May 28, 1835):169. On preaching oratory.

"The Infidel." *The Boston Observer and Religious Intelligencer* (June 25, 1835):201-02. Dialogue between father and son on the meaning of infidelity.

"Progress of Society." *The Christian Examiner and General Review* 18 (July, 1835):345-68; Miller: 92-4. Review of William Tait's *An Essay on the Moral Constitution and History of Man* (1834). By Divine Providence individuals and societies progress from strength to perfection.

1836

New Views of Christianity, Society, and the Church. Boston: James
   Munroe & Co., 1836; *Works* 4:1-56; Ryan A: 321-30; Carey: 163-
   92; Miller: 114-23. On the reconciliation of the spiritual and the
   temporal orders of existence in a new church. Religious sentiment
   is permanent; religious institutions are transitory.

"Education of the People." *The Christian Examiner and General Review* 20 (May, 1836):153-69. Education is the only efficient means
   of all social and individual progress.

*A Discourse on the Wants of the Times, Delivered in Lyceum Hall,
   Hanover Street, Boston, Sunday May 29, 1836.* Boston, 1836; see
   also Harriet Martineau, *Society in America* (2 vols., 1837), 2: 402-
   15; *Society in America* (3 vols., 1966), 3: 342-59. The New Church
   of the future should uphold free inquiry and social progress, the
   primary desires of the times.

"Society for Christian Union and Progress." *Boston Reformer* 3 (June
   30, 1836); (July 7, 1836); (July 8, 1836). Goal of Society is to
   form a union for all denominations and encourage moral and religious progress on individual and social level.

Untitled. *Boston Reformer* 3 (July 1, 1836). Religion as a lever of
   reform; advocacy for working man's cause.

"Discourses at the Temple." *Boston Reformer* 3 (July 16, 1836).
   Brownson defends himself against charge of infidelity.

"The Church and Reform." *Boston Reformer* 3 (July 21, 1836). Church
   should unite with Reform Party and take the side of the people.

"Manual Labour Schools." *Boston Reformer* 3 (July 23, 1836):1; (August 11, 1836):1; (August 13, 1836):1; (August 16 1836). These
   schools intend to educate the body and mind, elevating labor to
   ranks of liberal profession.

"Prospects of the Tribune." *Boston Reformer* 3 (July 26, 1836):1.
   Comments on a new monthly periodical published in Washington DC, and Brownson's remarks on literature's function in American society.

"Influence of Slavery on Labor." *Boston Reformer* 3 (July 26, 1836):1-
   2. All slavery is wrong and must cease.

Untitled reply to G. B. M. *Boston Reformer* 3 (July 26, 1836):2. On
   the evidence and nature of biblical revelation.

"The Olive Branch." *Boston Reformer* 3 (July 26, 1836):2. On the
   Protestant and the Episcopal Methodists.

"Responsibility of Society to its Members." *Boston Reformer* 3 (July 28, 1836). In a virtuous society the rich must take responsibility for the poor.

"Sunday Reading." *Boston Reformer* 3 (July 30, 1836):1. Review of Jonathan Farr's *Forms of Meaning and Evening Prayer* (1836) and Brownson's reflections on prayer.

"Signs of the Times." *Boston Reformer* 3 (July 30, 1836):1. Review of John Codman's *Signs of the Times* (1836). The excitement and reforming mood of the times which Codman finds threatening, Brownson finds promising for future progress.

"Reform no. I & II." *Boston Reformer* (July 30, 1836):2. Father and son dialogue on reform; mothers are paid poorly for their hard work.

"The Utica Magazine and Advocate." *Boston Reformer* 3 (July 30, 1836):2. Brownson opposes utilitarian view of religion because it begins with selfishness.

"Inklings of Adventure." *Boston Reformer* 3 (August 2, 1836). Review of N. P. Willis's *Inklings of Adventure* (1836).

"Slavery—Mobs, &c." *Boston Reformer* (?) (August 4, 183?). Southern mobs in Boston protest emancipation of slaves in West Indies.

"Formation of a New Republic in South America." *Boston Reformer* 3 (August 2, 1836):1-2. Comments on the origins of South Peru.

"The Monitor." *Boston Reformer* 3 (August 4, 1836):1. Against the *Monitor* (Concord, NH) which has once again leveled the charge of radicalism.

"The Monitor Again." *Boston Reformer* (date unknown). Response to charges of radicalism.

"Importance of Industry." *Boston Reformer* 3 (August 4, 1836):1. On useful work for the young.

"The Slave Cause." *Boston Reformer* 3 (August 4, 1836):2. On the freedom of two Black women.

"'Stop My Paper.'" *Boston Reformer* 3 (August 4, 1836):2. On freedom of the press.

"We Want Men To Carry Our Principles Into Effect." *Boston Reformer* 3 (August 6, 1836):2. Real changes needed in people before policy changes in government.

Untitled. *Boston Reformer* 3 (August 6, 1836):2. *Boston Reformer* charged with deserting the cause of working men.

"Mr. Arnold's Sixth Semi-Annual Report." *Boston Reformer* 3 (August 9, 1836):1. On emphasizing causes over effects of poverty.

"Holiness, or the Legend of St. George." *Boston Reformer* 3 (August 9, 1836):1. Favorable review of Elizabeth Peabody's *Holiness or the Legend of St. George* (1836).

"Mr. Hallet's Oration." *Boston Reformer* 3 (August 9, 1836):1. Against Benjamin Franklin Hallet's July 4th *Oration* (1836) defining democracy as sovereignty of people and fitness to rule. Sovereignty resides in God.

"Female Education." *Boston Reformer* 3 (August 9, 1836):1-2. Such education should not differ from that of men.

"Radicalism." *Boston Reformer* 3 (August 9, 1836):2. Objects that the term, as a term of reproach, is applied to Brownson and the *Boston Reformer*.

"The Workingmen." *Boston Reformer* 3 (August 9, 1836):2. The *Reformer* does not labor for the Workingmen's Party, but for workingmen.

"Political Parties." *Boston Reformer* 3 (August 11, 1836):2. Principles over parties.

"Letters About the Hudson River." *Boston Reformer* 8 (August 11, 1836):2. Review of Freeman Hunt's *Letters About the Hudson River* (1836). This is not American literature.

"Bancroft's Orations." *Boston Reformer* 3 (August 13, 1836):2. George Bancroft rightly vindicates democracy; democracy part of the outworking of Providence.

"Fresh Water for the City." *Boston Reformer* 3 (August 13, 1836):2. Against inequality of taxation.

Untitled response to 'Young Friend'. *Boston Reformer* 3 (August 23, 1836):2. On Brownson's opposition to monopolies.

"Literary Notices." *Boston Reformer* 3 (August 27, 1836). Favorable review of Edward Everett's *Orations and Speeches* (1836). Everett is a liberal-minded friend of social and moral progress, but not a good politician.

"Nature." *Boston Reformer* 3 (September 6, 1836). Review of Ralph Waldo Emerson's *Nature* (1836). Brownson sees it as harbinger of a new literature, but protests against its pantheism.

"The American Quarterly Review." *Boston Reformer* 3 (September 8, 1836). On the September issue's evaluations of François René Chateaubriand and William Wordsworth.

"Religion." *Boston Reformer* 3 (October 7, 1836). Review of state of religion in various countries.

"Editorial Address." *Boston Reformer* 3 (1836). *Boston Reformer* continues to be political paper, but supports no party; social equality must correspond to political equality.

"Natural and Revealed Religion." *Boston Reformer* 3 (1836). All knowledge of God is revealed.

"Birth Day of America." *Boston Reformer* 3 (1836). Against political factions during celebration of Fourth of July.

"'Our Country Right or Wrong.'" *Boston Reformer* 3 (1836). A principle that can never be defended.

"Hours of Laaour [*sic*]." *Boston Reformer* 3 (1836). Rights of individual workers to determine how many hours they will work.

"The Fourth." *Boston Reformer* 3 (1836). On the Boston celebrations.

"Aristocracy of Our Churches." *Boston Reformer* 3 (1836). Bostonians do not perceive the aristocracy of their own churches.

Untitled response to 'A Subscriber.' *Boston Reformer* 3 (1836). Religion grows out of idea of the infinite, morality out of the idea of duty.

"Dr. Combe on Digestion and Dietetics." *Boston Reformer* 3 (1836). Review of Andrew Combe's *Digestion and Dietetics* (1836). On good health and good morals.

"Literature." *Boston Reformer* 3 (1836). Recommends the *Tribune* which proposes to develop a truly American literature.

Untitled. *Boston Reformer* 3 (1836). On Frances Wright.

"Mr. Abner Kneeland." *Boston Reformer* 3 (1836). On Kneeland's review of Brownson's Discourse on *The Wants of the Times* (1836).

"Catholicism." *Boston Reformer* 3 (1836). Mission of Catholic Church has ended; Christianity has outgrown its childhood.

"Children's Books." *Boston Reformer* 3 (1836). Books for children generally grow out of false notions of education, religion and philosophy.

"Agrarianism." *Boston Reformer* 3 (1836). Equal distribution of wealth would be a curse, not a blessing.

Untitled. *Boston Reformer* 3 (1836). Real obstacle to moral, social and religious regeneration is belief that gospel is impractible.

"Loco Foco-ism in the Pulpit." *Boston Reformer* 3 (1836). *Boston Reformer* does not recommend preaching politics from pulpit.

"The Advertiser." *Boston Reformer* 3 (1836). *Boston Reformer* sides with Martin Van Buren party at times, and at other times with the Whigs.

"Too Much Religion." *Boston Reformer* 3 (1836). Jesus is true reformer and should be imitated.

"A True Sentence." *Boston Reformer* 3 (1836). On putting the Church on the side of liberalism.

"Bulwer's Works." *Boston Reformer* 3 (1836). Freedom in literature.

"The Reformer." *Boston Reformer* 3 (1836). Brownson not a radical.

"The Christian Examiner." *Boston Reformer* 3 (1836). On three articles in the September issue on the institutions of Moses, Victor Cousin's philosophy, and Orville (?) Dewey's unsuccessful Dudleian lecture in favor of Christianity.

"Address to the Democratic Voters of Massachusetts." *Boston Reformer* 3 (1836). Favors Martin Van Buren as president. Against Van Buren Party, but more opposed to William Henry Harrison.

"Bunker Hill Monument." *Boston Reformer* 3 (1836). Monuments are against the republican spirit.

"The Religious Sentiment." *Boston Reformer* 3 (1836). On Benjamin Constant. A translated excerpt on the religious sentiment from his *Religion Considered in its Origin*.

"The Worship of God [written in 1832]." *Boston Reformer* 3 (1836). Reflections on John 4:24. Worship in spirit because God is spirit.

"Sermon at the Temple." *Boston Reformer* 3 (1836). On the necessity of preaching the truth (even those new truths that are not generally received) regardless of the consequences .

"Philothea, a Romance." *Boston Reformer* 3 (1836). Favorable review of Lydia Maria Child's *Philothea, A Romance* (1836).

"Cousin's *Philosophy*." *The Christian Examiner and Gospel Review* 21 (September, 1836):33-64. "Victor Cousin," Miller: 107-14. Brownson's first substantial philosophical article on Victor Cousin. Religion needs a new defense because it has lost its hold on the understanding.

1837

"Letter to James Freeman Clarke." *The Western Messenger* 3 (April, 1837):602-04. People reject religion today because it is almost universally anti-liberal.

"Jouffroy's Contributions to Philosophy." *The Christian Examiner and Gospel Review* 22 (May, 1837):181-217; see also *BrQR* (January, 1845). Review of Théodore Simon Jouffroy's *Cours de Droit Naturel* (1834, 1835). On the psychological method in philosophy, German and American transcendentalism, and on discovering the grounds of moral obligation in consciousness.

Babylon is Falling. A Discourse Preached in the Masonic Temple, to the Society for Christian Union and Progress, on Sunday Morning, May 28, 1837. Boston: I. R. Butts, 1837. Reflections on Rev. 18:11. Babylon is the commercial system which promotes the spirit of gain. Revelation predicts the downfall of the spirit of gain. On the coming struggle or war between the party of privilege and advocates of social equality.

An Address on Popular Education. Delivered in Winnisimmet Village, Sunday Evening, July 23, 1837. Boston: Press of J. Putnam, 1837. On education as the formation of character and the necessity of promoting it not only in schools but in all phases of human development within society, and not only for the elite but for all.

1838

"Rev. Mr. Brownson's Speech." *The Liberator* 8 (January 5, 1838):1-2. A speech commemorating the death of Elijah P. Lovejoy, delivered December 22, 1837 at a meeting of the Massachusetts Anti-Slavery Society. Lovejoy was a martyr of free speech and liberty in opposition to slavery.

"Introductory Remarks." *Boston Quarterly Review* 1 (January, 1838):1-8; Miller: 180-82. There is a power above humans that they cannot alter. Brownson's sympathy with the progress of humanity.

"Christ before Abraham." *Boston Quarterly Review* 1 (January, 1838):8-21. Christianity is not an original revelation with Jesus. Uniqueness of Christianity found not in doctrines, but in the life Jesus and apostles lived.

"Whittier's Poems." *Boston Quarterly Review* 1 (January, 1838):21-33. Review of John G. Whittier's *Poems Written during the Progress of the Abolition Question* (1837). An American poet's mission is to realize the idea of universal freedom.

"Democracy." *Boston Quarterly Review* 1 (January, 1838):33-74; *Works* 15:1-34; RyanA: 36-44. Comments on "Address of the Democratic State Convention of Massachusetts" (1837). Sovereignty belongs not to the people, but to justice.

"Bacon's Poems." *Boston Quarterly Review* 1 (January, 1838):74-83. Review of William Thompson Bacon's *Poems* (1837) as "too uniformly personal."

"Philosophy and Common Sense." *Boston Quarterly Review* 1 (January, 1838):83-106; *Works* 1:1-18; "Francis Bowen," Miller: 83-106. Review of *The Christian Examiner*'s (1837) article "Locke and Transcendentalists." On two kinds of reason: reflective and spontaneous.

"Emerson's Phi Beta Kappa Oration." *Boston Quarterly Review* 1 (January, 1838):106-20. Review of Emerson's *An Oration delivered before the Phi Beta Kappa Society, at Cambridge* (1837). Emerson is an American scholar who embodies in language the spirit of his times.

"The Character of Jesus and the Christian Movement." *Boston Quarterly Review* 1 (April, 1838):129-52. What was original in Jesus was his character of universal love for humanity, not his nature or doctrine.

"Wars must Cease—Cousin's Argument for Wars." *Boston Quarterly Review* 1 (April, 1838):152-61. Review of John Quincy Adams's *An Oration ... on ... the Declaration of Independence* (1837). Because human race is progressive, wars will cease.

"Grund's Americans." *Boston Quarterly Review* 1 (April, 1838):161-92. Review of Francis J. Grund's *The Americans* (1837). Grund supports democracy against aristocracy.

"Tendency of Modern Civilization." *Boston Quarterly Review* 1 (April, 1838):200-38. On the newly established "Boston Association of the Friends of the Rights of Man," a working men's society. Christianity's great contribution to Western civilization is "its great doctrine of the universal brotherhood of humanity," which this association hopes to advance.

"Slavery—Abolitionism." *Boston Quarterly Review* 1 (April, 1838):238-60; *Works* 15:45-63. Review of William E. Channing's *Slavery* (1836). Brownson against slavery, but does not side with abolitionists.

"Letter to William Lloyd Garrison." *The Liberator* 8 (May 11, 1838):73. Brownson's defense of his anti-slavery position in response to Garrison's reaction to Brownson's "Slavery-Abolitionism" article of April, 1838.

"To the Editor of The Liberator." [May, 1838]. Not published in the *Liberator,* but in *The American Catholic Historical Researches,* 11 (April, 1894):50-52. Brownson's defense of his fidelity to Christianity and his anti-slavery position.

"Palfrey on the Pentateuch." *Boston Quarterly Review* 1 (July, 1838):261-310. Review of John Gordon Palfrey's *Academical Lectures on the Jewish Scriptures and Antiquities* (1838). Palfrey fails to articulate principles by which he decides which accounts are inspired and miraculous and which are not, and does not take the German historical criticism of Wilhelm De Welte into consideration.

"Religion and Politics." *Boston Quarterly Review* 1 (July, 1838):310-33. Review of Henry Whiting Warner's *An Inquiry into the Moral and Religious Character of the American Government* (1838). Against the idea that America is a Christian Commonwealth. Freedom, not religion, is the dominant idea of our institutions.

"Sub-Treasury Bill." *Boston Quarterly Review* 1 (July, 1838):333-60; *Works* 15:85-107. Review of various speeches by Daniel Webster and John Calhoun for and against the Sub-Treasury Bill. On the expediency of dispensing with banks in the management of the government's fiscal concerns.

"*The American Democrat.*" *Boston Quarterly Review* 1 (July, 1838):360-77. Review of James F. Cooper's *The American Democrat* (1838). Brownson unable to sympathize with Cooper's fear of the leveling tendency in American society.

"Ultraism." *Boston Quarterly Review* 1 (July, 1838):377-84; *Works* 15:107-12. Review of *The Mother in her Family* (1838). On the vast extent of the reformist mentality in the United States.

"Progress of Civilization." *Boston Quarterly Review* 1 (October, 1838):389-407. Irresistible tendency of the human race toward advancement.

"Carlyle's French Revolution." *Boston Quarterly Review* 1 (October, 1838):407-17; *Works* 19:40-47; RyanA: 152-57; *Modern*: 40-47. Review of Thomas Carlyle's *The French Revolution* (1837). The Revolution manifested an "irrepressible instinct" to assert natural rights.

"Alcott on Human Nature." *Boston Quarterly Review* 1 (October, 1838):417-32; "Alcott's Conversations," Miller: 188-9. Review of Amos Bronson Alcott's *Conversations with Children on the Gospels* (1836). Alcott is a reformer who identifies human instincts too much with the divinity within. His system of education is flawed because of his view of human nature.

"Specimens of Foreign Literature." *Boston Quarterly Review* 1 (October, 1838):433-44; "Ripley's Specimens," Miller: 189-91. Review of George Ripley's translation of *Philosophical Miscellanies* (1838). Study of the works of Cousin, Jouffroy and Constant. Literature of various nations will liberalize our minds.

"Democracy of Christianity." *Boston Quarterly Review* 1 (October, 1838):444-73. Review of Joseph Tuckerman's *Principles and Results of Ministry in Boston* (1838); Félécité de Lamennais's *Affaires de Rome* (1837), and *Paroles d'un Croyant* (1834). On the social dimensions of Christianity.

"Abolition Proceedings." *Boston Quarterly Review* 1 (October, 1838):473-500; *Works* 15:63-85. Review of S. B. Treadwell's *American Liberties and American Slavery* (1838). Brownson separates himself from the abolitionists and their one-dimensional view of justice and reform.

"Mr. Emerson's *Address.*" *Boston Quarterly Review* 1 (October, 1838):500-14; Carey: 193-203; Miller: 198-200. Review of *Divinity School Address* (1838). Against the central doctrine that the soul has its own divine laws, and against Emerson's ahistorical view of Christianity.

1839

"American Literature." *Boston Quarterly Review* 2 (January, 1839):1-26; *Works* 19:1-21. RyanA: 158-66; *Gems*: 5-22; "Emerson," Miller: 431-4; *Modern*: 1-22. Review of Emerson's *Literary Ethics: An Oration delivered before the Literary Societies of Dartmouth College* (1838). Against Emerson's view that liberation is produced from the mere will of man.

"The Eclectic Philosophy." *Boston Quarterly Review* 2 (January, 1839):27-53; see April, 1839; *Works* 2:533-52. Review of Victor Cousin's *Cours de Philosophie* (1836). Cousin's method is the experimental method and is thus distinguished from the transcendentalist method.

"Norton on the Evidences of Christianity." *Boston Quarterly Review* 2 (January, 1839):86-113; "Norton's Evidence," Miller: 205-9. Review of Andrews Norton's *The Evidences of Genuineness of the Four Gospels* (1837). On the miracles question and Brownson's opposition to Norton for placing the truth of Christianity upon mere external historical evidence. Such evidence does not give one sufficient grounds for justifying Christian truths.

"Lieber's Political Ethics." Part I of II. *Boston Quarterly Review* 2 (January, 1839):113-93; see April, 1840. Review of Francis Lieber's *Manual of Political Ethics* (1838). Against politics and morality as Lieber conceives them.

"Prospects of the Democracy." *Boston Quarterly Review* 2 (January, 1839):123-36; *Works* 15:34-44. On the results of the recent elections; Brownson identifies the stationary and the movement parties in the country.

"Wordsworth's Poems." *Boston Quarterly Review* 2 (April, 1839):137-68; "Wordsworth," Miller: 43-6. Review of William Wordsworth's *The Poetical Works* (1832). Poetic sentiment in its essence is not distinguishable from religious sentiment.

"Eclecticism—Ontology." *Boston Quarterly Review* 2 (April, 1839):169-87; see January 1839. Review of Victor Cousin's *Cours de Philosophie* (1836). Cousin recognizes the necessity of ontology and our knowledge of reality outside the self.

"Foreign Standard Literature." *Boston Quarterly Review* 2 (April, 1839):187-205. Review of George Ripley's *Specimens of Foreign Standard Literature* (1839) and Brownson's analysis of Johann Goethe's and Friedrich Schiller's views.

"Pretensions of Phrenology." *Boston Quarterly Review* 2 (April, 1839):205-29; *Works* 9:235-54. Against George Combe's *A System of Phrenology* (1835); accepts facts of phrenology but does not want to make it a "complete system of mental philosophy."

"Our Indian Policy." *Boston Quarterly Review* 2 (April, 1839):229-59. Against war on Indians but in favor of "civilizing" them.

"Bulwer's Novels." *Boston Quarterly Review* 2 (July, 1839):265-97. Brownson has more favorable opinion of Edward Lytton Bulwer's work than Brownson's contemporaries; morality in literature discussed.

"The Currency." Part I of II. *Boston Quarterly Review* 2 (July, 1839):298-326; see January, 1840. The value of the paper currency is subject to constant fluctuations.

"The Kingdom of God." *Boston Quarterly Review* 2 (July, 1839):326-50. Kingdom of God means that Jesus came to establish a dominion of truth and love.

"Unitarianism and Trinitarianism." *Boston Quarterly Review* 2 (July, 1839):378-85. Review of James Walker's *Unitarianism Vindicated* (1839). We should go with the new liberal party emerging out of Unitarianism because Unitarianism as a denomination is dead.

"Ancient Profaneness." *Boston Quarterly Review* 2 (July, 1839):385-87. On Cassius Longinus's *Essay on the Sublime* (English trans., 1834).

"Education of the People." *Boston Quarterly Review* 2 (October, 1839):393-434. Review of *Second Annual Report of the Board of Education* (1839). Humans should be educated for their social, religious and political as well as their individual ends.

"Democracy and Reform." *Boston Quarterly Review* 2 (October, 1839):478-517. Review of Robert Townsend's *An Inquiry into the Cause of Social Evil* (1839); Samuel Osgood's *An Oration delivered on the 4th of July* (1839); Seth J. Thomas's *An Address, delivered before the Democratic Citizens of Plymouth County* (1839); and John T. Tarbell's *An Oration, delivered before the Democratic Citizens of the North part of Middlesex County* (1839). All reformers should sustain the Democratic Party and see democracy as the political application of Christianity. Seek reforms on religious grounds. Whigs are Christian rationalists.

1840

Charles Elwood: or, The Infidel Converted. Boston: Charles C. Little and James Brown, 1840; *Works* 4:173-316. A semi-disguised autobiographical account of the movement from infidelity toward a belief in God and the supernatural origin of Christianity.

"Introductory Statement." *Boston Quarterly Review* 3 (January, 1840):1-20. On the authority of the Bible, the witness within, and the commonly received tradition.

An Oration, delivered before the United Brothers Society of Brown University, at Providence, RI, September 3, 1839. Cambridge: Metcalf, Torry and Ballou, 1839; "American Literature," *Boston Quarterly Review* 3 (January, 1840):57-79; *Works* 19:22-39; *Modern*: 22-39. On the lack of a specific American literature and the cause of it.

"The Currency." Part II of II. *Boston Quarterly Review* 3 (January, 1840):80-116; see July, 1839.

"The People's Own Book." *Boston Quarterly Review* 3 (January, 1840):117-27. Review of Félécité de Lamennais' *The People's Own*

Book (1839). Christianity must be on the side of liberty and social justice, and must help restore people's rights and correct social abuses.

"Education." *Boston Quarterly Review* 3 (April, 1840):137-66. "Observations and Hints on Education," Ryan A: 106-13. On the necessity of educating the people in order to sustain democracy.

"Truth not Dangerous." *Boston Quarterly Review* 3 (April, 1840):167-81. On the necessity of preaching the truth that one knows.

"Lieber's Political Ethics." Part II of II. *Boston Quarterly Review* 3 (April, 1840):181-93. See January, 1839.

"Chevalier's *Letters*." *Boston Quarterly Review* 3 (April, 1840):209-24. Review of Michael Chevalier's *Society, Manners, and Politics in the United States* (1839), which has no clear conception of the nature of our institutions and is too influenced by St. Simonians.

"The School Library." *Boston Quarterly Review* 3 (April, 1840):225-37. Review of Massachusetts Board of Education's *The School Library* (1840). Education depends on good libraries and Brownson opposes the Board's role in the selection of books for libraries.

"The Whig Answer." *Boston Quarterly Review* 3 (April, 1840):238-58. Review of *Answer of the Whig Members of the Legislature of Massachusetts* (1840). Against the newly elected Democratic governor of Massachusetts; Whigs identified with property and Democrats with humanity; the future belongs to the Democrats.

An Oration before the Democracy of Worcester and Vicinity, Delivered at Worcester, Mass., July 4, 1840. Boston: E. Littlefield, 1840. Worcester: M.D. Phillips, 1840. Brownson against banks and American Whigs, and in favor of Democrats who promote the aims of the American Revolution: political and social equality.

"Two Articles from the *Princeton Review,* etc." *Boston Quarterly Review* 3 (July, 1840):265-323. Miller: 240-6. Review of reprints, *Two Articles from the Princeton Review* (1840). Brownson's assessment of the intellectual battles between the Transcendentalists (German, French, as well as American) and the rationalists (like Andrews Norton).

"The Laboring Classes." *Boston Quarterly Review* 3 (July, 1840):358-95. See October, 1840. See also *The Laboring Classes, an Article from the Boston Quarterly Review*. Boston: B. H. Greene, 1840; RyanA: 45-57; Handy: 154-60; Miller: 436-46. Review of Thomas Carlyle's *Chartism* (1840). A Marxist-like critique of American economic system and a call for major systematic changes in the economic, political, and religious orders.

"Progress our Law." *Boston Quarterly Review* 3 (October, 1840):397-409. Sermon preached to Society for Christian Union and Progress in 1838; progress is law of our consciousness.

"A Discourse on Lying." *Boston Quarterly Review* 3 (October, 1840):411-20. A sermon delivered in 1837 and 1838, based on Revelation 21:8, on the lies of the banks who failed to honor their promises.

"The Laboring Classes—Responsibility to Party, etc." *Boston Quarterly Review* 3 (October, 1840):420-512. See July, 1840; *Brownson's Defense. Defense of the article on the laboring classes. From the Boston Quarterly Review.* Boston: B.& H. Greene, 1840. Answering objections to "Laboring Classes" article of July, 1840. On Christianizing democracy and democratizing the church.

1841

"Conversations with a Radical." Part I of II. *Boston Quarterly Review* 4 (January, 1841):1-41. See April, 1841. Conversations between a poor radical prophet and a wealthy conservative on society and reform.

"Our Future Policy." *Boston Quarterly Review* 4 (January, 1841):68-112; see also *Our Future Policy. The Policy to be Pursued Hereafter by the Friends of the Constitution and Equal Rights.* Boston: Greene, 1841; *Works* 15:113-49. Political policy after William Henry Harrison's election; mission of nation to emancipate the proletariat.

"Address to the Workingmen." *Boston Quarterly Review* 4 (January, 1841):112-27. Review of *An Address of the Workingmen of Charlestown, Mass., to their Brethren throughout the Commonwealth and the Union* (1840), an address published on eve of the 1840 election. On the Workingmen's Party, Brownson's sympathy for it, and a reprint of the *Address* (which Brownson wrote).

"Conversations with a Radical." Part II of II. *Boston Quarterly Review* 4 (April, 1841):137-83. See January, 1841.

"Distribution and the Public Lands." *Boston Quarterly Review* 4 (April, 1841):230-56; see also *Public Lands and Distribution Bill.* Boston: B. Greene, 1841; *Works* 15:149-70. Review of series of federal reports and speeches in Congress from 1840-41 concerning the distribution of public land to the states and the disposition of the proceeds from the sale of public lands.

"To the Editors of The Lowell Offering." *Boston Quarterly Review* 4 (April, 1841):261-64. Sympathy with laboring classes, especially the "factory girls" of Lowell, MA.

"Social Evils and their Remedy." *Boston Quarterly Review* 4 (July, 1841):265-91. Government needed to affect social reform; also needed are religion, morality and individual intelligence.

"Emerson's *Essays*." *Boston Quarterly Review* 4 (July, 1841):291-308. Review of Emerson's *Essays* (1841). Emerson has moved away from a cold and dead Unitarianism toward spiritualism, but he ends in pantheism.

"The Secret of the Lord." *Boston Quarterly Review* 4 (July, 1841):308-20. Discourse on Ps. 25:14; fear of God is the beginning of wisdom. On the scriptural meaning of fear.

"Truth is not a Lie." *Boston Quarterly Review* 4 (July, 1841):339-53. Review of William Wollaston's *Religion and Nature Delineated* 5th ed. (1731). On Wollaston's realism and on the symbolic nature of doctrine.

"Executive Patronage." *Boston Quarterly Review* 4 (July, 1841):353-70; *Works* 15:171-85. Review of President John Tyler's *Address to the People of the United States* (1841) in favor of states' rights.

Oration of Orestes A. Brownson Delivered at Washington Hall, July 5th, 1841. [New York, 1841]. July 4th address; Brownson places U. S. Revolution in context of providential history and asserts that its purpose was to alleviate conditions of working classes and give them equality with mercantile and feudal lords.

"The President's Message." *Boston Quarterly Review* 4 (July, 1841):371-90; *Works* 15:186-201. Review of President John Tyler's *Message to the Two Houses of Congress* (June 1, 1841); on fiscal policies and distribution of land.

"Transient and Permanent in Christianity, etc." *Boston Quarterly Review* 4 (October, 1841):436-74. See also *A Review of Mr. Parker's Discourse on the Transient and Permanent in Christianity.* Boston: Greene, 1841. A generally favorable review of Theodore Parker's *Discourse* (1841). The permanent in Christianity resides in the Divine Mind, not in our conceptions or theologies. Brownson's defense of Parker's views of inspiration and authority of Scripture, and of the authority and character of Jesus. Parker criticized, though, for his views of the person of Jesus. The young should not mistake innovation for progress.

"Bancroft's History." *Boston Quarterly Review* 4 (October, 1841):512-18. Review of George Bancroft's *History of the Colonization of the United States* (1841). Against Bancroft's idea of absolute democracy; we need a "limited democracy."

1842

"Church of the Future." *Boston Quarterly Review* 5 (January, 1842):1-27; *Works* 4:57-78. Review of Brownson's New *Views* (1836); the ideal of the new church will be the redemption and sanctification of the race, not just the individual.

"Constitutional Government." *Boston Quarterly Review* 5 (January, 1842):27-59. See also *Constitutional Government*. Boston: Greene, 1842; *Works* 15:231-58. Government has its origins in what is good in human nature; its end is the common good.

"Reform and Conservatism." *Boston Quarterly Review* 5 (January, 1842):60-84; *Works* 4:79-99. Review of James F. Clarke's *The Well-Instructed Scribe* (1841). Clarke espouses reformist doctrine Brownson held for a long time, that the true reformer holds onto the past while exerting himself to conquer the future. Brownson's idea of progress as assimilation (à la Pierre Leroux), not self-development.

"The Distribution Bill." *Boston Quarterly Review* 5 (January, 1842):84-119; *Works* 15:202-31. Favorable review of John Calhoun's *Speech of Mr. Calhoun, of South Carolina, on the Distribution Bill* (1841) and Brownson's understanding of constitutional democracy and the unconstitutionality of distributing the public lands.

"Letter to the Editor." *Boston Daily Times* 12 (March 30, 1842):2. Brownson's reaction to *Boston Daily Times*' views of his "Lecture on the Influence of Property and Civilization."

"Charles Elwood Reviewed." *Boston Quarterly Review* 5 (April, 1842):129-83; *Works* 4:316-61. Review of Brownson's *Charles Elwood* (1840).

"Modern French Literature." *Boston Quarterly Review* 5 (April, 1842):230-51; *Works* 19:48-65; *Modern*: 48-65. Review of George Sand's *Spiridion* (1839); on women's rights issues.

"To Hon. Edmund Burke." *Daily National Investigator* (May 30, 1842). Brownson defends himself against charge of being "agrarian" and "infidel."

"Letter to the Editors." *Daily National Investigator* (June 29, 1842). Brownson defends himself on his "horrible doctrines" concerning property.

*"The Rhode Island Affair." *United States Magazine and Democratic Review* 10 (June, 1842):602-07. Description of the constitutional question regarding universal suffrage in Rhode Island.[17]

*"The Rhode Island Question." *United States Magazine and Democratic Review* 10 (July, 1842):70-83; see also *The Rhode Island Question* (New York: 1842). In favor of changing the Rhode Island Constitution to allow for universal suffrage. See *Brownson's Quarterly Review* (October, 1844) for Brownson's later view of the Rhode Island question.

"Leroux on Humanity." *Boston Quarterly Review* 5 (July, 1842):257-322; *Works* 4:100-39. Review of Pierre Leroux's *De L'Humanité* (1840). Humans defined as progressive animals; hence, Leroux is against the individualism of Augustinian Christianity which does not allow for the improvement of the human race.

"Zanoni." *Boston Quarterly Review* 5 (July, 1842):342-66. Review of Edward Lytton Bulwer's *Zanoni* (1842). Brownson no longer likes Bulwer's works; he criticizes Bulwer as excessively sentimental.

"Introductory Address." *Boston Quarterly Review* 5 (July, 1842):366-71. On Brownson's return to preaching in April of 1842 (he ceased preaching in 1839 to assume a position in the government) and the new course his preaching will take.

"Parker's Discourse." *Boston Quarterly Review* 5 (October, 1842):385-512. Review of Theodore Parker's *A Discourse on Matters Pertaining to Religion* (1842). Brownson's criticisms of Parker's subjectivist views of religion are based upon Pierre Leroux's philosophy of the synthesis of the subjective and the objective, the natural and the supernatural.

"End of the Volume." *Boston Quarterly Review* 5 (October, 1842):513-16. On the reasons for cessation of *Boston Quarterly Review* and on Brownson's arrangements with *Democratic Review*.

---

17. This article as well as the one immediately following may be from the pen of John O'Sullivan, editor of the *Review*. This was at least the view of George Dennison, *The Dorr War. Republicanism on Trial, 1831-1861* (Lexington, KY: University of Kentucky Press, 1976), 113-14. The *National Union Catalogue*, however, attributes "The Rhode Island Question" to Brownson. Both articles were written by the same author.

"Schmucker's Psychology." *United States Magazine and Democratic Review* 11 (October, 1842):352-73; *Works* 1:19-57. Review of Samuel Schmucker's *Psychology* (1842). Importance of tradition in one's understanding of the grounds of knowledge.

"Young America." *New York Mirror* 20 (October 22, 1842):338. We are the people of the future; we must write our own literature.

"Brook Farm." *United States Magazine and Democratic Review* 11 (November, 1842):481-96; *Brook Farm* [New York, 1842]. Brownson's enthusiastic support for Brook Farm. On the age's burning question of social equality and the various solutions to the problem.

"Synthetic Philosophy." Part I of III. *United States Magazine and Democratic Review* 11 (December, 1842):567-78; *Works* 1:58-129. See January and March, 1843. Under the influence of Pierre Leroux, Brownson describes his newly emerging view of philosophy as the science of life. All thought, as all life, is the result of the interaction or synthesis of the subject and object.

The Mediatorial Life of Jesus. A Letter to Rev. William Ellery Channing, D. D. Boston: Charles C. Little and James Brown, 1842; *Works* 4:140-72; RyanA: 260-72; Carey: 205-31. On Brownson's application of Pierre Leroux's philosophical principles to Christianity and theology, and his rejection of Channing's views on the divinity of humanity. All life comes through communion, and divine life through communion with Christ.

1843

"Synthetic Philosophy." Part II of III. *United States Magazine and Democratic Review* 12 (January, 1843):38-55. See December, 1842 and March, 1843.

"The Mission of Jesus." Part I of VII. *The Christian World* 1 (January 7, 1843):2. See January 14, January 21; "The Church and Its Mission," February 4, February 11, February 25; "Discipline of the Church," April 15, 1843. Brownson outlines his view of life by communion. The salvific life of Christ raised human life to communion with God, and this divine life is passed on to Christians through the church and its sacraments.

"The Mission of Jesus." Part II of VII. *The Christian World* 1 (January 14, 1843):1. See January 7, 1843.

"The Mission of Jesus." Part III of VII. *The Christian World* 1 (January 21, 1843):2. See January 7, 1843.

"What Shall I Do to Be Saved?" *The Christian World* 1 (January 28, 1843):2. Christians have access to salvific life through the medium of Christ's body, the church.

"The Church and Its Mission." Part IV of VII. *The Christian World* 1 (February 4, 1843):1-2. See January 7, 1843. Carey: 99-107.

"The Church and Its Mission." Part V of VII. *The Christian World* 1 (February 11, 1843):2. See January 7, 1843. Carey: 107-13.

"The Church and Its Mission." Part VI of VII. *The Christian World* 1 (February 18, 1843):1-2. See January 7, 1843. Carey: 113-21.

"Mediation of the Church." *The Christian World* 1 (February 25, 1843):1-2. Gospel announces mediatorial grace; Jesus is the mediator and he must have a continuing means of mediation.

"The Community System." *United States Magazine and Democratic Review* 12 (February, 1843):129-44. On the battles between individualism and community and Brownson's philosophy of communion.

"Democracy and Liberty." *United States Magazine and Democratic Review* 12 (April, 1843):374-87; *Works* 15:258-81; RyanA: 58-67; Miller2: 340-47. Against notion that *vox populi est vox Dei*; Brownson's changing religious views correspond to his changing perspectives on democracy and liberty.

"Entering into Life." *The Christian World* 1 (April 1, 1843):1. Brownson no longer holds transcendentalist and spiritualistic view of church; spirit of Christ found embodied only in the church.

"The Sacrifice of Our Lord Mediatorial." *The Christian World* 1 (April 8, 1843):1-2. Comments on the New York *Churchman* (March 11, 1843); sin deprives sinner of ability to repent; sacrifice of Christ is mediatorial.

"Discipline of the Church." Part VII of VII. *The Christian World* 1 (April 15, 1843):1-2. See January 7, 1843. Brownson's views of the sacraments as means of salvation. Brownson struck by the similarity of his ideas and language to that of the Catholic Church.

"Remarks on Universal History." Part I of II. *United States Magazine and Democratic Review* 12 (May, 1843):457-74. See June, 1843; *Remarks on Universal History* [n. p., 1843]; "The Philosophy of History," *Works* 4:361-92; "Philosophy of History," RyanA: 188-

205. Humans made for progress; growth and development are from without rather than from within the self.

"Popular Government." *United States Magazine and Democratic Review* 12 (May, 1843):529-37; *Works* 15:281-96. Article on the *United States Magazine*'s opposition to Brownson's views of democracy.

"Remarks on Universal History." Part II of II. *United States Magazine and Democratic Review* 12 (June, 1843):569-86; see May, 1843; "The Philosophy of History," *Works* 4:392-423.

"The Present State of Society." *United States Magazine and Democratic Review* 13 (July, 1843):17-38. See also *The Present State of Society*. New York, 1843; *Works* 4:423-60; Kirk: 11-69. On social justice and the injustices in United States. Against the divorce between politics, religion and morality.

An Oration on the Scholar's Mission. Boston: B. H. Greene, 1843; Burlington, Vt.: V. Harrington, 1843. "The Scholar's Mission." *Works* 19:65-87; RyanA: 114-25; *Modern*; 65-87. An address given to the Gamma Society of Dartmouth College, Hanover, N. H., on July 26, 1843, and to the alumni and friends of the University of Vermont on August 1, 1843. A scholar as a providential person, must be religious, instructing and inspiring people to fulfill human progress and destiny.

"Origin and Source of Government." Part I of III. *United States Magazine and Democratic Review* 13 (August, 1843):129-47; see September and October, 1843; "Origin and Ground of Government," *Works* 15:296-327. On Brownson's philosophy of the constitution of the state.

"Origin and Source of Government." Part II of III. *United States Magazine and Democratic Review* 13 (September, 1843):241-62; see August and October, 1843; "Origin and Ground of Government," *Works* 15:327-361. All power is of God; no government is legitimate if it does not subsist by divine right.

"Origin and Source of Government." Part III of III. *United States Magazine and Democratic Review* 13 (October, 1843):353-77; see August and September, 1843; "Origin and Ground of Government," *Works* 15:361-404. Fulfilling human destiny demands freedom; government's role is to guarantee freedom. United States government is a constitutional republic.

1844

Social Reform. An Address before Society of the Mystical Seven in the Wesleyan University, Middletown, Conn. August 7, 1844. Boston: Waite, Pierce & Co., 1844. On poverty in society, the tendency to separate labor and capital, criticisms of various proposed solutions to complicated social problems, and the necessity of reviving faith in God and in the realities of the spiritual world as a remedy for social evils.

"Introduction." *Brownson's Quarterly Review* 6 (January, 1844):1-28. Catholic Church is favorable to freedom and progress, but needs more reforming.

"Berkeley and Idealism." *Brownson's Quarterly Review* 6 (January, 1844):29-56. Review of *Encyclopédie Nouvelle* (1836), edited by P. Leroux and J. Reynaud. Brownson reviews Leroux's article on Berkeley and idealism.

"The Church Question." *Brownson's Quarterly Review* 6 (January, 1844):57-84; *Works* 4:461-83. Review of *Tracts for the Times* (1839). True church exists now only in fragments.

"Demagoguism." *Brownson's Quarterly Review* 6 (January, 1844):84-104; *Works* 15:434-51. Necessary virtues absent from popular government; there must be loyalty to eternal justice.

"Life and Speeches of John C. Calhoun." *Brownson's Quarterly Review* 6 (January, 1844):105-31; *Works* 15:451-72. Review of *Life of John C. Calhoun* (1843) and *Speeches of John C. Calhoun, delivered in the Congress of the United States, from 1811 to the Present Time* (1843). Calhoun is a true political leader; Van Buren only follows political tide.

"History of Philosophy." Part I of III. *Brownson's Quarterly Review* 6 (April, 1844):137-74; see April and July, 1844; "Kant's Critic of Pure Reason," *Works* 1:130-62; "Kant's Critique of Pure Reason," RyanA: 206-18. Review of Immanuel Kant's *Critik der Reinen Vernunft* (1828). Brownson's classification of four root systems of philosophy and his criticisms of Kant's transcendentalist philosophy as the science of knowing, not a science of life or being.

"No Church, No Reform." *Brownson's Quarterly Review* 6 (April, 1844):175-94; *Works* 4:496-512. Church must return to its unity and catholicity before authentic social reforms are possible; reform only possible with superhuman aid.

"Necessity of Liberal Education." *Brownson's Quarterly Review* 6 (April, 1844):194-208; *Works* 19:88-99; *Modern*: 88-99. Review of George Junkin's *The Bearings of College Education on the Welfare of the whole Community* (1843). On educating the elite for the benefit of the entire community.

"Origin and Constitution of Government." *Brownson's Quarterly Review* 6 (April, 1844):208-42; *Works* 15:405-33. Review of *The Democratic Review* (December, 1843). Response to attack upon Brownson's view of government; Brownson not opposed to democracy, only certain theories of it.

"Nature and Office of the Church." *Brownson's Quarterly Review* 6 (April, 1844):243-56; *Works* 4:484-95. Most important question of the age is the necessity of the church.

"Mr. Calhoun and the Baltimore Convention." *Brownson's Quarterly Review* 6 (April, 1844):257-69; *Works* 15:473-83. On party politics relative to Calhoun and Van Buren.

"Kant's Critic of Pure Reason." Part II of III. Brownson's Quarterly Review 6 (July, 1844):281-309; see April and October, 1844; *Works* 1:162-86. Philosophy defined; necessity of revelation for Christian Idealism.

"Church Unity and Social Amelioration." *Brownson's Quarterly Review* 6 (July, 1844):310-327; *Works* 4:512-26. Associations of reform should be under Church's guidance.

"Hildreth's Theory of Morals." *Brownson's Quarterly Review* 6 (July, 1844):328-49; *Works* 14:236-54. Review of Richard Hildreth's *Theory of Morals* (1844). Brownson disgusted with Hildreth's claim that morals have no foundation outside the human constitution; divine will is law and foundation of obligation.

"Bishop Hopkins on Novelties." *Brownson's Quarterly Review* 6 (July, 1844):349-67; *Works* 4:527-42. Review of John Henry Hopkin's *The Novelties Which Disturb our Peace* (1844). Brownson disappointed with Hopkins for asserting the Protestant rather than the Catholic side of Episcopalianism.

"Come-outerism: or the Radical Tendency of the Day." *Brownson's Quarterly Review* 6 (July, 1844):367-85; *Works* 4:542-58. On social justice; Brownson's change from a revolutionary to a conservative reformer.

"Sparks on Episcopacy." *Brownson's Quarterly Review* 6 (July, 1844):386-96; *Works* 4:558-67. Review of Jared Sparks's *Letters*

on the Ministry, Ritual, and Doctrines of the Protestant Episcopal
Church (1844). On Brownson's difficulties in perceiving the unity
and catholicity of the Protestant Episcopal Church.

"The Presidential Nominations.—Texas.—Mr. Calhoun." Brownson's
Quarterly Review 6 (July, 1844):396-407; Works 15:484-93. Comments on Baltimore Democratic Convention's nomination of James
K. Polk; Henry Clay and Theodore Frelinghuysen represent very
worst of Whiggism.

"Kant's Critic of Pure Reason." Part III of III. Brownson's Quarterly
Review 6 (October, 1844):417-49; see April and October, 1844;
Works 1:186-213.

"Fourierism Repugnant to Christianity." Brownson's Quarterly Review
6 (October, 1844):450-87. Review of Charles Pellarin's Charles
Fourier, sa Vie et sa Theorie (1843); and the journal The Phalanx:
Organ of the Doctrine of Association vol. 1, nos. 14 and 15. Fourierism denies necessity of Church and is, therefore, impotent to affect social reform.

"The Anglican Church Schismatic." Brownson's Quarterly Review 6
(October, 1844):487-514; Works 4:567-89. Response to article in
the New York Churchman against Brownson's article "Bishop
Hopkins on Novelties," July, 1844.

"The Protective Policy." Brownson's Quarterly Review 6 (October,
1844):514-32; Works 15:493-507. Against James K. Polk who favors "a tariff which discriminates in favor of home industry."

"The Suffrage Party in Rhode Island." Brownson's Quarterly Review 6
(October, 1844):532-44; see "The Rhode Island Affair" and "The
Rhode Island Question," June and July, 1842; Works 15:508-18.
Review of Might and Right (1844) by a Rhode Islander in favor of
the extension of suffrage.

1845

"Literary Policy of the Church of Rome." Brownson's Quarterly Review 7 (January, 1845):1-29; Works 6:520-49. Review of Methodist Quarterly Review (July, 1844). Response to charges raised against
Catholic hostility to the press, literature, science as well as revelation and religion.

"The British Reformation." Brownson's Quarterly Review 7 (January,
1845):29-53; Works 6:568-92. Review of John H. Hopkins's Six-
teen Lectures on the Causes, Principles, and Results of the British Ref-

ormation (1844). Brownson's view that the Reformers cannot be freed from the charge of schism.

"Jouffroy's Ethical System." *Brownson's Quarterly Review* 7 (January, 1845):53-76; see *The Christian Examiner and Gospel Review* (May, 1837); *Works* 14:266-89. Review of Théodore Simon Jouffroy's *Cours de Droit Naturel* (1835). Brownson has changed his mind and now rejects Jouffrey's principle doctrines and the eclectic school of thought.

"Native Americanism." *Brownson's Quarterly Review* 7 (January, 1845):76-98; *Works* 10:17-37; *Essays*: 420-44. Review of Fenelon's (pseudonym) *Catholicism compatible with Republican Government, and in full Accordance with Popular Institutions* (1844). True Americanism means that "merit makes the man," not native birth.

"The Recent Election." *Brownson's Quarterly Review* 7 (January, 1845):130-34; *Works* 15:519-23. On Brownson's support for James Polk, his hopes for the new administration, and his analysis of the Texas question.

"The Church against No-Church." *Brownson's Quarterly Review* 7 (April, 1845):137-94; *Works* 5:337-89. *Essays*: 1-68. Review of "The Church," *The Christian Examiner and Religious Miscellany,* January, 1845. Must distinguish between objective revealed truths and subjective apprehension; need infallible authority independent of Bible to determine its genuine sense.

"Salve for the Bite of the Black Serpent." *Brownson's Quarterly Review* 7 (April, 1845):194-222. Review of Dr. Evariste Gyphendole's (pseudonym of Abbé Antoine Martinet) *Onguent contre la Morsure de la Vipère Noire* (1843) as an allegory on the Protestant disease and its cure.

"Parkerism, or Infidelity." *Brownson's Quarterly Review* 7 (April, 1845):222-49. Review of Theodore Parker's *The Relation of Jesus to his Age and the Ages* (1845) and *The Excellence of Goodness* (1845). Parker is not a Christian teacher, but an infidel.

"Miss Fuller and the Reformers." *Brownson's Quarterly Review* 7 (April, 1845):249-57. Review of Margaret Fuller's *Women in the Nineteenth Century* (1845). Book lacks thesis and suffers from the transcendentalist-reformist mentality relative to women's rights.

"Catholic Magazine and Ourselves." *Brownson's Quarterly Review* 7 (April, 1845):258-62. Review of article on Brownson's *Review* in *The United States Catholic Magazine and Monthly Review* (March,

1845). Brownson's denial that he is an eclectic and his autobiographical reflection on his conversion as a revolution in his mind.

"Transcendentalism, or the latest Form of Infidelity." Part I of III. *Brownson's Quarterly Review* 7 (July, 1845):273-32; see October, 1845, October, 1846; *Works* 6:1-50. "Transcendentalism," RyanA: 219-31. Review of Theodore Parker's *A Discourse of Matters pertaining to Religion* (1842). Parker's system is pantheistic and subjectivist; Brownson denies Parker's distinction between reason and understanding.

"Protestant Love of Liberty." *Brownson's Quarterly Review* 7 (July, 1845):323-41. Review of Nathaniel Ward's *The Simple Cobbler of Aggawam in America* (1645; reprint 1843) and Brownson's denial that Protestantism supports civil and religious liberty (as Ward's book demonstrates).

"Hildreth's Joint Letter." *Brownson's Quarterly Review* 7 (July, 1845):341-52; *Works* 14:255-66. Review of Richard Hildreth's *A Joint Letter to O. A. Brownson and the Editor of the North American Review* (1845), and Brownson's reactions to Hildreth's criticisms and theory of morals.

"The Episcopal Observer versus The Church." *Brownson's Quarterly Review* (April, 1845):352-79; *Works* 5:389-416; *Essays*: 69-100. Review of *The Episcopal Observer*, 1 (May, 1845). Brownson's response to criticisms of his article "The Church against no Church" (April, 1845).

"Modern Idolatry." *Brownson's Quarterly Review* 7 (July, 1845):380-97; *Works* 19:100-18; *Modern*; 100-18. Review of Friedrich Schiller's *The Aesthetic Letters, Essays, and the Philosophical Letters of Schiller* (1845). Brownson's critique of the leading doctrine as "unwholesome," putting humanity in place of God.

"Ireland, O'Connell, &c." *Brownson's Quarterly Review* 7 (July, 1845):398-408; *Works* 15:573-84. On the repeal movement in Ireland and Brownson's criticisms of Daniel O'Connell's unprovoked attacks upon American slavery and his interference in American domestic policies.

"Transcendentalism, or latest form of Infidelity." Part II of III. *Brownson's Quarterly Review* 7 (October, 1845):409-42; see July, 1845 and October, 1846; *Works* 6:50-83.

"Professor Park against Catholicity." *Brownson's Quarterly Review* 7 (October, 1845):442-514; *Works* 6:353-426. Review of and reply to Edwards A. Park's charges against Catholicism, which were delivered at Harvard's Dudleian lecture and published in the *Bibliotheca Sacra and Theological Review* (August, 1845). On the standard and authority for judging the infallible Catholic Church.

"Catholicity Necessary to Sustain Popular Liberty." *Brownson's Quarterly Review* 7 (October, 1845):514-30; *Works* 10:1-16; *Essays:* 369-86; Gaustad: 442-45. Without Roman Catholic Church it is impossible to preserve democratic government.

"Native American Civility, Religious Liberty, etc." *Brownson's Quarterly Review* 7 (October, 1845):530-40. On the compatibility of Catholicism with American institutions and freedoms, and the native American's practical violation of religious liberty.

1846

"Faith not possible without the Church." *Brownson's Quarterly Review* 8 (January, 1846):1-40; *Works* 5:417-56. Review of *The Episcopal Observer* (August, 1845). Impossible to elicit act of faith and to be saved without the Roman Catholic Church. Continuation of arguments contained in "The Church against No-Church" (April, 1845).

"National Greatness." *Brownson's Quarterly Review* 8 (January, 1845):40-61; *Works* 15:523-45. On the standard by which national greatness must be measured, the standard of a nation fulfilling "the true and proper end of man."

"Dangers of Jesuit Instruction." *Brownson's Quarterly Review* 8 (January, 1846):62-89; see also *A Review of the Sermon by Dr. Potts, on the Dangers of Jesuit Instruction.* St. Louis: Keith and Woods, 1846; review of William. S. Pott's, *Dangers of Jesuit Instruction* (1845). On the necessity of parental religious education of children, Catholic rights and duties in this regard, and on the benefits of Jesuit education.

"Methodist Quarterly Review." *Brownson's Quarterly Review* 8 (January, 1846):89-107; *Works* 6:550-67. Review of "Brownson's Quarterly Review," *Methodist Quarterly Review* (July, 1845); see "Literary Policy of the Church of Rome," *Brownson's Quarterly Review* (January, 1845). Brownson's continuing comments on the charges against the Catholic Church.

"The Roman Church and Modern Society." *Brownson's Quarterly Review* 8 (January, 1846):107-27. Review of Edgar Quinet's *The*

Roman Church and Modern Society (1845). Brownson's view of the continuity between Luther, Voltaire, modern reformers, and infidelity; and Catholicism's opposition to modern infidel tendencies.

"The Church a Historical Fact." *Brownson's Quarterly Review* 8 (April, 1846):153-71; *Works* 5:457-75. Review of Robert Manning's *The Shortest Way to end Disputes about Religion* (1846). Brownson's assertions that the simple historical existence of the Catholic Church is presumption in its favor.

"Presbyterian Confession of Faith." Part I of IV. *Brownson's Quarterly Review* 8 (April, 1846):203-53; see October, 1846, April, October, 1846. *Works* 6:160-211. Review of *The Constitution of the Presbyterian Church* (1838); Brownson challenges 1832 and 1833 Presbyterian confession of faith on its understanding of the authority, rule and interpretation of Scripture.

"Schiller's Aesthetic Theory." *Brownson's Quarterly Review* 8 (April, 1846):253-72; *Works* 19:118-29; *Modern*; 118-29. Response to John Weiss's view that Schiller's theory is not repugnant to Christianity; Brownson admits no Christianity independent of the church and criticizes Schiller's view that human self-development proceeds from a primitive to an aesthetic state.

"Liberalism and Catholicity." *Brownson's Quarterly Review* 8 (July, 1846):273-327; *Works* 5:476-527. Liberalism is no-churchism and between it and Catholicism there is no middle ground—in response to a liberal Protestant's arguments against Brownson's claim that the church has a role in eliciting an act of faith.

"Newman's Development of Christian Doctrine." *Brownson's Quarterly Review* 8 (July, 1846):342-68; *Works* 14:1-28; RyanA: 260-72. Review of John Henry Newman's *An Essay on the Development of Christian Doctrine* (1845). Although Newman comes to Catholic conclusions in this work, his theory of development of Christian doctrine (not discipline or theology) is "essentially anti-Catholic and Protestant." Newman does not distinguish clearly enough Christian doctrine (which for Brownson is the same as revelation) from Christian theology and discipline.

"Protestantism ends in Transcendentalism." *Brownson's Quarterly Review* 8 (July, 1846):369-99; *Works* 6:113-34; *Essays*: 209-33; Gaustad: 440-42. Review of *Margaret, A Tale of the Real and Ideal, Blight and Bloom* (1846). The fundamental principle of Protestantism is private judgment. When logically followed out to its ultimate conclusion, this principle ends in Transcendentalism, which is the only logically consistent form of Protestantism.

"Transcendentalism. Concluded." Part III of III. *Brownson's Quarterly Review* 8 (October, 1846):409-39; see July and October, 1845; *Works* 6:83-113.

"Presbyterian Confession of Faith." Part II of IV. *Brownson's Quarterly Review 8* (October, 1846):439-72; see April, 1846, and April and October, 1847; *Works* 6:211-43.

"War and Loyalty." *Brownson's Quarterly Review* 8 (October, 1846):493-518; *Works* 16:1-25; *Essays*: 321-49. Review of Fletcher Webster's *An Oration delivered before the Authorities of the City of Boston* (1846). Brownson asserts resistance to laws of state must be founded upon infallible law above individual and state.

"Bishop Fenwick." *Brownson's Quarterly Review* 8 (October, 1846):518-34; *Works* 14:470-85; *Gems*: 222-33. A character sketch of Boston's Bishop Benedict Joseph Fenwick; Brownson's autobiographical account of his contacts with him.

"Thornberry Abbey." *Brownson's Quarterly Review* 8 (October, 1846):534-44; *Works* 19:130; *Modern*; 130-142. A favorable review of *Thornberry Abbey* (1846); Brownson's reflections on the creation of a national literature, and especially of a national Catholic literature.

1847

"The Two Brothers; or, Why are you a Protestant?" Part I of IV. *Brownson's Quarterly Review* 9 (January, 1847):1-39; see April, July, 1847; January, 1848; *The Two Brothers; or, Why are you a Protestant?* Detroit: H. F. Brownson, 1888; *Works* 6:244-82. A fictitious dialogue between a convert to Catholicism and his Presbyterian brother on the grounds of Protestantism and responses to typical Protestant charges against Catholicism.

"Newman's Theory of Christian Doctrine." *Brownson's Quarterly Review 9* (January, 1847):39-86; *Works 14*:28-74. Review of J. Spencer Northcote's *The Fourfold Difficulty of Anglicanism* (1846). Against theories of development by assimilation or accretion because they are fatal to sufficiency of original revelation.

"Madness of Antichristians." *Brownson's Quarterly Review 9* (January, 1847):86-99; *Works 14*:414-28; *Gems*: 250-62. Review of Jules

Michelet's *The People* (1846). Brownson's assertion that the principal spirit of the day is the "supremacy of man"; the relation of love of God to love of neighbor.

"Natural and Supernatural." *Brownson's Quarterly Review 9* (January, 1847):100-16; *Works 3*:1-17. Conversation on the end and means of salvation, whether natural or supernatural.

"Religious Novels." *Brownson's Quarterly Review 9* (January, 1847):116-28; *Works 19*:143-54; *Modern*; 143-54. Review of *Dunigan's Home Library* (1846). See *"Thornberry Abbey"* (October, 1846). Brownson's criticism of Catholic literature as sentimental and/or didactic.

"The Two Brothers; or, Why are you a Protestant?" Part II of IV. *Brownson's Quarterly Review 9* (April, 1847):137-63; see January, July, 1847; January, 1848; *Works 6*:282-308.

"Protestant Dissensions." *Brownson's Quarterly Review 9* (April, 1847):163-90. Review of Pharacellus Church's *Religious Dissensions: their Cause and Cure* (1838); and Zebulon Crocker's *The Catastrophe of the Presbyterian Church in 1837* (1838). On Presbyterian lamentations over divisions in the church and on using the Bible alone as the means of procuring Christian unity. Brownson asserts that the Protestant principle of private interpretation vitiates any prospects for unity.

"Presbyterian Confession of Faith." Part III of IV. *Brownson's Quarterly Review 9* (April, 1847):190-215; see April, October, 1846; October, 1847.

"Recent Publications." *Brownson's Quarterly Review 9* (April, 1847):216-49; *Works 19*:155-89; *Modern*; 155-89. Review of *The Chapel of the Forest, and Christmas Eve* (n.d.); *Lorenzo* (1844); *The Elder's House, or the Three Converts* (n.d.); and John D. Bryant's *Pauline Seward* (1847). Brownson's criticism of Catholic novels and his insistence upon exclusive salvation.

"R. W. Emerson's Poems." *Brownson's Quarterly Review 9* (April, 1847):262-76; *Works 19*:189-202; *Gems*: 165-81; *Modern*; 189-202. Review of Emerson's *Poems* (1847). An excellent manifestation as poetry, but devoid of the truth, goodness, and beauty of revelation.

"The Two Brothers; or, Why are you a Protestant?" Part III of IV. *Brownson's Quarterly Review* (July, 1847):277-305; see January, April, 1847; January, 1848; *Works 6*:308-37.

"The Jesuits." *Brownson's Quarterly Review* 9 (July, 1847):305-34. Review of Michelet's and Quinet's *The Jesuits* (1845); Arsene Cahour's *Des Jesuites par un Jesuite* (1844). Brownson's defense of the Jesuits in opposition to Michelet's and Quinet's charges that they are anti-progressive in their views of human nature and religion.

"Slavery and the Mexican War." *Brownson's Quarterly Review* (July, 1847):334-67; *Works 16*:25-59. Review of *Speech of the Hon. R. B. Rhett, of South Carolina, on the Oregon Territory Bill, excluding Slavery from that Territory,—the Missouri Compromise being proposed and rejected* (1847). Agrees with Robert Barnwell Rhett that sovereignty rests with states not Union. Brownson against further expansion of slavery, yet against immediate emancipation. Mexican war unjust.

"American Literature." *Brownson's Quarterly Review* 9 (July, 1847):384-403; *Works* 19:203-20; *Modern*; 203-20. Review of editor Charles Hoffman's *The Literary World* (1847). Brownson's comments on the growth and goal of national literature, a literature that is above national interests as its end.

"The Great Question." *Brownson's Quarterly Review* 9 (October, 1847):413-58; *Works* 5:527-72. Review of W. G . Penny's *The Exercise of Faith impossible except in the Catholic Church* (1847). On conversion to Catholicism and the importance of stressing the absolute necessity of the church as the means of salvation.

"Political Constitutions." *Brownson's Quarterly Review* 9 (October, 1847):458-85; *Works* 15:546-73; *Essays*: 293-321. Review of Joseph De Maistre's *Essay on the Generative Principle of Political Constitutions* (1847). Brownson's arguments on the limits and value of speculative and practical reason, his traditionalism, and the role of divine providence in the generation of unwritten constitutions (even republican constitutions).

"The Dublin Review on Developments." *Brownson's Quarterly Review* 9 (October, 1847):485-526; *Works* 14:75-116. Review of "Doctrinal Developments," *The Dublin Review* (July, 1847). Church does not develop doctrine, rather it renders infallible judgement on the deposit.

"St. Stanislaus Kotska." *Brownson's Quarterly Review* 9 (October, 1847):526-38. Review of *The Life of St. Stanislaus Kotska* (1847) and Brownson's evaluation of Alban Butler's *Lives of the Saints* (1756-59).

"Presbyterian Confession of Faith." Part IV of IV. *Brownson's Quarterly Review* 9 (October, 1847):539-54; see April, October, 1846; April, 1847.

1848

"Admonitions to Protestants." Part I of III. *Brownson's Quarterly Review* 10 (January, 1848):1-20; see April, July, 1848; "A Letter to Protestants," *Works* 5:241-270. On the failures of Protestantism, the obligation to worship God; the insufficiency of reason, nature, and revelation to reach human destiny.

"Dr. Jarvis's Reply to Milner." *Brownson's Quarterly Review* 10 (January, 1848):20-48; *Works* 7:117-44. Review of S. F. Jarvis's *A Reply to Dr. Milner's "End of Religious Controversy"* (1847). Brownson's view of the necessity of an infallible church as the rule of faith.

"Novel-Writing and Novel-Reading." *Brownson's Quarterly Review* 10 (January, 1848):48-71; *Works* 19:221-44; *Modern*; 221-44. Review of John D. Bryant's *Pauline Seward* (1847). Brownson's comments that Catholic novels should reflect the spirit of the church, not of the age.

"Labor and Association." *Brownson's Quarterly Review* 10 (January, 1848):71-101; *Works* 10:38-68; *Essays*: 444-79. Review of Matthew Briancourt's *Organization of Labor and Association* (1847). A critical examination of the principles, ends, and means that the associationists advocate to improve society.

"The Two Brothers; or, Why are you a Protestant? Concluded." Part IV of IV. *Brownson's Quarterly Review* 10 (January, 1848):101-16; see January, April, and July, 1847; *Works* 6:337-52.

"Pius the Ninth, and the Political Regeneration of Italy." *Brownson's Quarterly Review* 10 (January, 1848):117-34. On political conditions in Italy prior to Pius' inauguration and on his subsequent liberal political reform measures in the papal states.

"Admonitions to Protestants." Part II of III. *Brownson's Quarterly Review* 10 (April, 1848):137-63; see January, July, 1848; *Works* 5:270-302.

"Catholicity and Political Liberty." *Brownson's Quarterly Review* 10 (April, 1848):163-83. By its principles and institutions Catholicism has executed a powerful influence in favor of civil liberty.

"Thornwell's Answer to Dr. Lynch." Part I of III. *Brownson's Quarterly Review* 10 (April, 1848):198-222; see July, October, 1848; *Works* 6:427-52; *Essays*: 100-68. Review of James H. Thornwell's *The Apocryphal Books of the Old Testament* (1845). Brownson's reaffirmation of Patrick Lynch's argument that the church's infallibility is the guarantee that these books are inspired.

"Ventura's Funeral Oration." *Brownson's Quarterly Review* 10 (April, 1848):255-65; *Works* 10:69-79. Review of Gioacchino Ventura's *Oraison Funèbre d'O'Connell* (1847). Criticism of Ventura's argument in favor of an alliance of religion and liberty in European politics.

"The Dublin Review and Ourselves." *Brownson's Quarterly Review* 10 (April, 1848):265-72; *Works* 14:116-26. Review of *The Dublin Review* (January, 1848). Brownson believes that revelation was given in its entirety to apostles and delivered completely to their successors.

"Thornwell's Answer to Dr. Lynch." Part II of III. *Brownson's Quarterly Review* 10 (July, 1848):273-305; see April, October, 1848; *Works* 6:452-85.

"Admonitions to Protestants." Part III of III. *Brownson's Quarterly Review* 10 (July, 1848):305-27; see January, April, 1848; *Works* 5:302-30.

"The Church, as it was, is, and ought to be." *Brownson's Quarterly Review* 10 (July, 1848):327-45; *Works* 7:179-96. Review of James F. Clarke's *The Church, as it was, as it is, as it ought to be* (1848). Brownson's reflections on the importance of the church as the indispensable means of Christianity.

"Recent European Events." *Brownson's Quarterly Review* 10 (July, 1848):380-410; *Works* 16:102-32. On mob revolutions and the form of government best suited to France.

"The Expulsion of the Jesuits." *Brownson's Quarterly Review* 10 (July, 1848):415-16. Report of liberals' expulsion of Jesuits from Rome and the imprisonment of the Pope.

"Thornwell against Infallibility." Part III of III. *Brownson's Quarterly Review* 10 (October, 1848):417-52; see April, July, 1848; *Works* 6:485-519; *Essays*: 168-209.

"Legitimacy and Revolutionism, Conservatism and Reform." *Brownson's Quarterly Review* 10 (October, 1848):453-82; *Works* 16:60-81; *Essays*: 386-420. Brownson defends himself against charge that he is hostile to liberty; against current political atheism.

"Grantley Manor, or Popular Literature." *Brownson's Quarterly Review* 10 (October, 1848):482-506; *Works* 19:244-68; *Modern*: 244-68. Review of Georgiana Fullerton's *Grantley Manor* (1848). Brownson's emphasis on exclusive salvation and on the radical differences between Protestantism and Catholicism.

"Doctrinal Developments." *Brownson's Quarterly Review* 10 (October, 1848):525-39; *Works* 14:126-41. Review of *The Dublin Review* (1848). John H. Newman capitulates to spirit of the times; Brownson asserts we cannot know what apostolic tradition is unless church informs us.

"St. Dominic and the Albigenses." *Brownson's Quarterly Review* 10 (October, 1848):539-62. Review of Henri-Dominique Lacordaire's *Vie de Saint Dominique* (1841) and Brownson's denial that St. Dominic participated in the Albigensian wars.

1849

"The Catholic Press." *Brownson's Quarterly Review* 11 (January, 1849):1-24; *Works* 19:269-93; *Modern*; 269-93. Review of *United States Catholic Magazine and Monthly Review* 7 (1848); and *The Freeman's Journal and Catholic Register* 9 (1848). Tendency of the newspapers to pander to the popular interests, the necessity of using the press to communicate Catholic truths, and the weaknesses and new opportunities of Catholic journals.

"Hawkstone, or Oxfordism." *Brownson's Quarterly Review* 11 (January, 1849):24-58; *Works* 7:145-78. Review of William Sewell's *Hawkstone* (1848). Catholic church and history.

"*Shandy M'Guire:* or Irish Liberty." *Brownson's Quarterly Review* 11 (January, 1849):58-90; *Works* 16:144-77. Review of Paul Peppergrass's *Shandy M'Guire* (1848). Brownson's comments on Irish politics; he does not sympathize with desire for independent Ireland.

"Authority and Liberty." *Brownson's Quarterly Review* 11 (April, 1849):137-62; *Works* 10:111-37; *Essays*: 262-92. Review of J. D. Nourse's *Remarks on the Past, and its Legacies to American Society* (1847). On contemporary forms of Neo-platonism, the attempts to create a new rational and universal religion, and the denial of authority in the process; Brownson's view of the dialectical union of authority and liberty.

"The Republic of the United States." *Brownson's Quarterly Review* 11 (April, 1849):176-95; *Works 16:*82-102. Review of Nahum Capen's *The Republic of the United States of America* (1848). Against demagogue courtiers of democracy; reason and effort necessary to produce virtue in people.

"Channing on the Church and Social Reform." Part I of II. *Brownson's Quarterly Review* 11 (April, 1849):209-39; see October, 1849; *Works* 10:137-68. Review of William Henry Channing's *The Christian Church and Social Reform* (1848). On the real, the ideal, and the actual, and the issue of reform and development. God alone can actualize the ideal.

"The Saints and Servants of God." *Brownson's Quarterly Review* 11 (April, 1849):239-53. Review of F. W. Faber's series *The Saints and Servants of God* (1848-49), including the lives of Ss. Philip Neri, Peter Claver, and Cardinal Odeschalchi. On the English Oratorians, study of the lives of the saints, and promotion of Catholic asceticism and holiness.

"Waterworth's Council of Trent." *Brownson's Quarterly Review* 11 (April, 1849):253-65. Review of James Waterworth's *The Canons and Decrees of the Sacred and Ecumenical Council of Trent* (1848). On English Catholics and the necessity of promoting an uncompromising doctrine of the papacy.

"The Vision of Sir Launfal." *Brownson's Quarterly Review* 11 (April, 1849):265-74; *Works* 19:308-17; *Gems:* 133-43; *Modern:* 309-17. Review of J. R. Lowell's *The Vision of Sir Launfal* (1848). Brownson's views on the nature and function of poetry.

"Civil and Religious Toleration." *Brownson's Quarterly Review* 11 (July, 1849):277-309; *Works 10:*207-38. Review of Pierce C. Grace's *Outlines of History* (1848). On the meaning and extent of religious liberty, religious toleration, and exclusive salvation.

"The College of the Holy Cross." *Brownson's Quarterly Review* 11 (July, 1849):372-97. See also *Remarks on the Petition for an Act Incorporating the College of the Holy Cross.* Boston: B.H. Greene, 1849; Review of *House Document, No. 130. Commonwealth of Massachusetts. Report of the Joint Standing Committee on Education* (April 13, 1849). Reasons for incorporating the College of the Holy Cross, even though it is exclusively Catholic.

"H. M. S. Field's *Letter from Rome.*" *Brownson's Quarterly Review* 11 (July, 1849):309-30. Review of Henry M. Field's *The Good and the Bad in the Roman Catholic Church* (1849). On the Protestant Field's respect for Catholic spirituality, but his unjustified calls for reforms in the Catholic Church.

"The Church in the Dark Ages." *Brownson's Quarterly Review* 11 (July, 1849):330-57; *Works* 10:239-66. Review of Kenhelm Digby's *Mores Catholici* (1841); S. R. Maitland's *The Dark Ages* (1844); and *The Christian Examiner and Religious Miscellany* (May, 1849). No need to rehabilitate the middle ages; that is a romantic Protestant notion born out of German Romanticism and the Oxford movement.

"Catholic Secular Literature." *Brownson's Quarterly Review* 11 (July, 1849):358-72; *Works* 19:293-308; RyanA: 167-73; *Modern:* 293-308. Review of Enna Duval's *Spirit Sculpture* (1849). Brownson's views that Catholic novels make a schism between the spiritual and the secular orders of life.

"Presidential Veto." *American Review* 20 (August, 1849):111-23; see *Brownson's Quarterly Review* (April, 1850):243-65.

"Protestantism in a Nutshell." *Brownson's Quarterly Review* 11 (October, 1849):413-38; *Works* 6:135-60; *Essays:* 234-62. Review of James Balmes's *El Protestantismo comparado con el Catolicismo* (1849). On the variability and mutabality of error within Protestantism, and the moral disease of pride at the heart of the movement.

"Channing on Christendom and Socialism." Part II of II. *Brownson's Quarterly Review* 11 (October, 1849):438-74; see April, 1849; *Works* 10:169-206.

"Socialism and the Church." *Brownson's Quarterly Review* 11 (October, 1849):91-127; *Works* 10:79-110; *Essays:* 479-521; Kirk: 71-122. On Charles Fourier's brand of socialism. A diatribe against socialism. Emphasis on the supernatural and surrender to God as conditions for the true good.

"Naomi: or Boston Two Hundred Years ago." *Brownson's Quarterly Review* 11 (October, 1849):476-95. Review of Eliza Buckminster Lee's *Naomi* (1848). Brownson's sympathy for the old Puritans, and his criticisms of the unjustified attacks upon Puritans by the new liberal Christians.

"Bushnellism: or Orthodoxy and Heresy Identical." Part I of IV. *Brownson's Quarterly Review* 11 (October, 1849):495-517; see January, April, and July, 1851; *Works* 7:1-22. Review of Horace

Bushnell's *God in Christ* (1849); and Joseph H. Allen's *Ten Discourses on Orthodoxy* (1849). The Fall and its effect; union of Christian with Christ is mystical not hypostatic.

"The Licentiousness of the Press." *Brownson's Quarterly Review* 11 (October, 1849):517-43; *Works* 16:133-44. The radical European press in times of revolutionary agitation needs to be restrained; against Catholic liberals.

1850

"An a priori Autobiography." *Brownson's Quarterly Review* 12 (January, 1850):1-38; Works 1:214-52. Review of W. B. Breene's *Remarks on the Science of History; followed by an a priori Autobiography* (1849). Book dedicated to Pierre Leroux; Leroux's influence on Brownson (learned ontologism from Leroux); on Leroux's strengths and weaknesses.

"Conversations of an Old Man and his Young Friends." Part I of IV. *Brownson's Quarterly Review* 12 (January, 1850):87-104; see April, July, and October, 1850; *Works* 10:267-84. Dialogue between authority and liberty.

"Morell's *Philosophy of Religion.*" *Brownson's Quarterly Review* 12 (April, 1850):159-90; *Works* 3:18-50. Review of John Daniel Morell's *The Philosophy of Religion* (1849). Morell asserts that since religion originates in and is determined by nature, it is subject to rational investigation; his thinking excludes the supernatural from his definition of religion.

"Reply to the Mercersburg Review." Part I of II. *Brownson's Quarterly Review* 12 (April, 1850):191-228; see July, 1850; *Works* 3:51-90. Review of *The Mercersburg Review* (January, 1849-50). John Williamson Nevin and his school are Eutychian and monothelite; Brownson rejects Nevin's rule of faith.

"Conversations of an Old Man and his Young Friends." Part II of IV. *Brownson's Quarterly Review* 12 (April, 1850):228-43; see January, July, and October, 1850; *Works* 10:285-300.

"The Presidential Veto." *Brownson's Quarterly Review* 12 (April, 1850):243-65. Review of James A. Williams' *The Plan of the American Union, and the Structure of its Government* (1848). The editor of the *American Review* article of the same title (see August, 1849) changed Brownson's original article. He reprinted it here without deletions or changes. Historical and philosophical reflections on presidential powers in a democratic constitutional government.

"The Christian Examiner's Defence." *Brownson's Quarterly Review* 12 (July, 1850):298-330; *Works* 7:197-229. Review of *The Christian Examiner and Religious Miscellany* (March, 1850). On James Freeman Clarke's reply to Brownson's article "The Church against No-Church" (April, 1845); defends himself against charge of frequent intellectual changes.

"Capes's *Four Years' Experience.*" *Brownson's Quarterly Review* 12 (July, 1850):330-53; *Works* 20:1-23. Review of J. M. Capes's *Four Years' Experience of the Catholic Religion* (1849). Brownson's discussion of the motives of credibility for Catholicism and of the influence of religion upon civilization.

"The Mercersburg Theology." Part II of II. *Brownson's Quarterly Review* 12 (July, 1850):353-78; see April, 1850; *Works* 3:90-116. Review of *The Mercersburg Review* (May, 1850).

"Conversations of an Old Man and his Young Friends." Part III of IV. *Brownson's Quarterly Review* 12 (July, 1850):379-93; see January, April, and October, 1850; Works 10:300-14.

"Vincenzo Gioberti." *Brownson's Quarterly Review* 12 (October, 1850):409-48; Works 2:101-40. Submissiveness of laity; laity rather than clergy need reforming.

"Dana's *Poems and Prose Writings.*" *Brownson's Quarterly Review* 12 (October, 1850):466-*90; Works* 19:317-342; *Modern*: 317-42. Review of Richard H. Dana's *Poems and Prose Writings* (1850). Brownson's understanding of the relation of art to truth, goodness, and beauty in the canons of literary and aesthetic criticism.

"The Cuban Expedition." *Brownson's Quarterly Review* 12 (October, 1850):490-516; *Opiniones de un Anglo-Americano acerca de la expedicion cubana, y les anexienistas. Traducido del Brownson's Quarterly Review correspondiente al mes de Octubre del 1850,* par E. J. G. Nueva Orleans: Impr. de la Patria, 1850; *Works 16*:272-98. Review of Richard B. Kimball's *Cuba and the Cubans* (1850). On Narciso Lopez's military attempt to create and support a revolution in Cuba; republicanism against barbarism.

"Conversations of an Old Man and his Young Friends." Part IV of IV. *Brownson's Quarterly Review* 12 (October, 1850):516-28; see January, April, and July, 1850; *Works* 10:315-27.

1851

"Bushnell on the Trinity." Part II of IV. *Brownson's Quarterly Review* 13 (January, 1851):1-29; see October, 1849; April, July, 1851; *Works* 7:22-49.

"The Higher Law." *Brownson's Quarterly Review* 13 (January, 1851):80-97; *Works* 17:1-17; *Essays:* 349-67. Review of Moses Stuart's *Conscience and the Constitution* (1850). Brownson accepts the higher law, but it must be sought in God through the Church; Church essential for constitution of society.

"The Decline of Protestantism." *Brownson's Quarterly Review* 13 (January, 1851):97-120; *Works* 7:567-79. Review of John Hughes's *The Decline of Protestantism and its Cause* (1850); and *Developments of Protestantism, and other Fragments,* reprinted from the *Dublin Review* and the *London Tablet* (1849). Brownson's assertion that Catholic attacks upon Protestantism in England and the United States signal a new and more aggressive Catholic posture.

"Bushnell on the Incarnation." Part III of IV. *Brownson's Quarterly Review* 13 (April, 1851):137-64; see October, 1849; January, July, 1851; *Works* 7:49-75.

"Webster's Answer to Hulsemann." *Brownson's Quarterly Review* 13 (April, 1851):198-230; *Works* 16:178-209. Review of *Correspondence of the Austrian Charge d'Affaires and Mr. Webster* (1851). Brownson's views on the "unjustified" Hungarian rebellion; United States had right to rebellion against a tyrant, not against monarchy *per se.*

"Savonarola." *Brownson's Quarterly Review* 13 (April, 1851):230-66. Article contains a translation of a chapter of Alexis-François Rio's *De la Poésie Chrétienne,* which is a Catholic defense of Savonarola as a faithful son of the Church and a promoter of Christian art against paganism; Brownson's brief comments on Rio's work and Christian art.

"Cooper's *Ways of the Hour.*" *Brownson's Quarterly Review* 13 (July, 1851):273-97; *Works* 16:326-49. On the mixed and complex character of American government and institutions in reaction to James Fenimore Cooper's *Ways of the Hour* (1850).

"Nature and Faith." *Brownson's Quarterly Review* 13 (July, 1851):297-318. Review of Richard Whately's *Essays (Third Series) on the Errors of Romanism having their Origin in Human Nature* (1845). Criticisms of Whately's theory that Roman errors and superstitions originated in the corrupt tendencies of human nature. Nature is the foundation upon which revelation rests.

"Bushnell on the Mystery of Redemption." Part IV of IV. *Brownson's Quarterly Review* 13 (July, 1851):318-61; see October, 1849; January, April, 1851; *Works* 7:75-116.

"The French Republic." *Brownson's Quarterly Review* 13 (July, 1851):362-82; *Works* 16:252-72. Review of *Discours pronounce par M. de Montalembert* (1851). On Charles R. F. de Montalembert's advocacy of order and defense of religious liberty; relative merits of republicanism and monarchy.

"The Fugitive Slave Law." *Brownson's Quarterly Review* 13 (July, 1851):383-411; *Works* 17:17-39. Review of Theodore Parker's *The Chief Sins of the People* (1851). Slavery is an evil but abolition may be even greater evil if it threatens union; abolitionist principles opposed to freedom.

"Newman on the True Basis of Theology." *Brownson's Quarterly Review* 13 (October, 1851):417-52; *Works* 3:117-50. Review of Francis William Newman's *The Soul, her Sorrows and her Aspirations* (1850). Existence of God known through reason; nature and grace distinguishable but not separable.

"Saint-Bonnet on Social Restoration." *Brownson's Quarterly Review* 13 (October, 1851):452-92; *Works* 14:197-235. Against self-development of any kind; there is development of Christian doctrine which occurs outside the self. Progress is in doing, not being.

"The Edinburgh Review on Ultramontane Doubts." *Brownson's Quarterly Review* 13 (October, 1851):527-556. Review of "Ultramontane Doubts," *The Edinburgh Review* (April, 1851). *Works* 10:329-56. Brownson is "ultra-ultramontanist."

1852

Essays and Reviews, Chiefly on Theology, Politics, and Socialism. New York: D. & J. Sadlier, 1852. Writings Brownson collected and edited to provide readers with an overview of his philosophy of Christianity since becoming a Catholic.

"Preface," to *Essays and Reviews, Chiefly on Theology, Politics, and Socialism.* April 7, 1852. A defense of five lectures Brownson gave in St. Louis on Catholicity and Civilization.

"Christianity and Heathenism." *Brownson's Quarterly Review* 14 (January, 1852):1-37; *Works* 10:357-94. On the separation of Christianity and religion from literature; the relation of the secular to the spiritual orders of human existence.

"Willitoft, or Protestant Persecution." *Brownson's Quarterly Review* 14 (January, 1852):37-66; *Works* 10:395-411. Review of James McSherry's *Willitoft, or the Days of James the First* (1851); novel of a conversion to Catholicism, and reflections on Anglicanism and the independence of the spiritual order.

"Piratical Expeditions against Cuba." *Brownson's Quarterly Review* 14 (January, 1852):66-96; *Works* 16:298-326. Objections to privately organized military attempts to invade Cuba and incite rebellion.

"*Sick Calls.*" *Brownson's Quarterly Review* 14 (January, 1852):115-31; *Works* 10:585-95. Review of Edward Price's *Sick Calls* (1851). Brownson's comments on exclusive salvation and spiritual solace for the poor.

"Anti-Kossuth Lecture by Orestes A. Brownson, of Boston, at Cincinnati." *New York Times* (February 19, 1852): 2. Summary of Brownson's lecture .

"The Existence of God." *Brownson's Quarterly Review* 14 (April, 1852):141-64; *Works* 1:253-75. Review of Francis William Newman's *The Soul, her Sorrows and her Aspirations* (1850). Traditionalism against ontologism; mind cannot originate the idea of God; it must be revealed to humans.

"The Two Worlds, Catholic and Gentile." *Brownson's Quarterly Review* 14 (April, 1852):165-94. Review of Pope Pius IX's *Encyclical Letter* (1850), *Letters of the Count de Montalembert* (1851), *Acts of the Synod of Thurles* (1851), *Speech of ... Paul Cullam* (1851), *Speech of John Hughes* (1851), *Letters of ... Michael O'Connor* (1852), and other works. Brownson defends himself against the charge that he is too harsh in treating Protestants as gentiles; on the fundamental distinctions between gentiles (naturalists) and Catholics (supernaturalists).

"Austria and Hungary." *Brownson's Quarterly Review* 14 (April, 1852):195-227; *Works* 16:209-26. Review of Jacques Mislin's *Les Saints Lieux* (1851). Opposition to Kossuth's Hungarian revolution.

"Paganism in Education." *Brownson's Quarterly Review* 14 (April, 1852):227-47; *Works* 10:551-63. Review of Jean Gaume's *Le Ver Rongeur des Societes Modernes* (1851). Brownson's criticisms of

Gaume's thesis that eliminating Greek and Roman classic texts from education would free it from paganism.

"Protestantism and Government." *Brownson's Quarterly Review* 14 (April, 1852):263-78; *Works* 10:411-26. Review and criticism of Hugh A. Garland's *A Course of Five Lectures . . . On Protestantism and Government* (1852). Garland reacted to a series of talks Brownson gave in St. Louis on the Catholic and supernatural origin of all true civilization. Brownson maintains his argument here while he refutes Garland's views on Catholic despotism.

"Morris on the Incarnation." *Brownson's Quarterly Review* 14 (July, 1852):285-328; *Works* 14:141-82. Review of John Brande Morris's *Jesus the Son of Mary* (1851). Brownson detests Puseyites; Morris wishes to bring Protestants into church by removing obstacles; Brownson wants to attack, putting Protestants on the defensive.

"The Works of Daniel Webster." *Brownson's Quarterly Review* 14 (July, 1852):341-82; *Works* 19:343-81; *Gems*: 61-97; *Modern*: 343-81. Review of *The Works of Daniel Webster* (1851). Common law is anterior to Constitution and the ground of all our liberties.

"Bancroft's *History of the United States.*" *Brownson's Quarterly Review* 14 (October, 1852):421-59; *Works* 19:382-418; *Modern*: 382-418. Review of George Bancroft's *History of the United States* Vol. 4 (1852). Brownson's understanding of history as an inductive, not a speculative, science; Bancroft is a democratic philosophical historian.

"The Christian Register's Objections." *Brownson's Quarterly Review* 14 (October, 1852):459-92; *Works* 7:230-58. Reactions to a *Christian Register's* review of Brownson's *Essays and Reviews* (1852) and comments on the limits and benefits of logic and reason in leading one to faith.

"Politics and Political Parties." *Brownson's Quarterly Review* 14 (October, 1852):493-523; *Works* 16:350-79. On relation of states to federal government and the emergence of political parties in the United States.

"Rights and Duties." *Brownson's Quarterly Review* 14 (October, 1852):523-50; *Works* 14:290-316. Review of Juan Donoso-Cortes's letter in *La Civilita Cattolica* (May 3, 1852). Humans are bound to obey God because rights belong only to God and duties only to humans.

1853

"The Worship of Mary." *Brownson's Quarterly Review* 15 (January, 1853):1-25; Works 8:59-85; RyanT: 93-122. Review of Alphonsus Liguori's *The Glories of Mary* (1852); and J. B. Morris's *Jesus the Son of Mary* (1851). Venerating Mary is worshipping God in his works.

"The Two Orders, Spiritual and Temporal." *Brownson's Quarterly Review* 15 (January, 1853):26-62; *Works* 11:1-36. Review of Artaud de Montor's *Histoire des Souverains Pontifes Romains* (1847). On political atheism, i.e., the separation of religion from politics.

"Protestantism not a Religion." *Brownson's Quarterly Review* 15 (January, 1853):87-111; *Works* 10:426-49. Review of Jean Marie Vincent Audin's *The Life of Henry the Eighth* (1852). Protestantism presented as the substitution of the temporal for the spiritual.

"Catholics of England and Ireland." *Brownson's Quarterly Review* 15 (January, 1853):111-29; *Works* 16:390-408. Review of "Parliamentary Prospects," *The London Quarterly Review* (October, 1852). On changes in British government since Protestant Reformation and the effects of these changes upon Catholics.

"The Spiritual not for the Temporal." *Brownson's Quarterly Review* 15 (April, 1853):137-65; *Works* 11:36-62. Review of Alphonse Muzzarelli's *De Auctoritate Romani Pontificis in Conciliis Generalibus* (1810); F. P. Kenrick's *The Primacy* (3rd ed. 1848); Charles R. Montalembert's *Des Intérêts Catholiques an XIXe Siècle* (1852); on the supremacy of the spiritual order over the temporal.

"A Consistent Protestant." *Brownson's Quarterly Review* 15 (April, 1853):185-218; *Works* 7:259-84. Review of Theodore Parker's *Two Sermons preached before the Twenty-eighth Congregational Society in Boston* (1853). Brownson's argument that Parker is the consistent Protestant who supports a free religion, subject to no authority.

"Ethics of Controversy." *Brownson's Quarterly Review* 15 (April, 1853):262-78. Review of *L'Ami de la Religion* (February, 1853). Brownson favors *L'Ami* over *Univers* in controversy on the use of classics in Catholic schools, and is against the traditionalists (Bonnetty) in the controversy with Abbé Cognot of *L'Ami* because the traditionalists deny natural reason its rightful powers. On the ethics of internal Catholic debates.

An Oration on Liberal Studies, delivered before the Philomathian Society, of Mount Saint Mary's College, Md., June, 29, 1853. Baltimore:

Hedian & O'Brien, 1853; "Liberal Studies," *Works* 19:431-46;
Modern; 431-46. On the relationship of the liberal education of
the elite for the "wants of a free state."

"The Spiritual Order Supreme." *Brownson's Quarterly Review* 15 (July,
1853):281-315; *Works* 11:62-94. Review of l'Abbé Jager's *Histoire
de l'Eglise de France pendant la Revoltion* (1852). On the French
Revolution, Gallicanism, and the temporal order as oriented to
the spiritual.

"Philosophical Studies on Christianity." *Brownson's Quarterly Review*
15 (July, 1853):332-65; *Works* 3:151-79. Review of Aguste
Nicholas's *Etudes philosophique sur Christianisme* (1852), D. Juan
Donoso Cortes's *Ensayo sobre el Catolicismo, el Liberalismo, y el
Socialismo* (1851), Louis Veuillot's *Les Libres Penseurs* (1850).
Brownson's criticisms and comments on laymen applying religious
principles to the social and political issues of the day, and his explanation of his own modified form of ontologism and traditionalism.

"The Fathers of the Desert." *Brownson's Quarterly Review* 15 (July,
1853):379-97; Carey: 233-41. Review of Richard Challoner's *The
Lives of the Fathers of the Eastern Deserts* (1852). On monasticism
and its value; superiority of supernatural.

"J.P. Healy, Esquire." *The Courier*, (Boston) October 17, 1853. Obituary.

"The Eclipse of Faith." *Brownson's Quarterly Review* 15 (October,
1853):417-44; *Works* 7:284-303. Review of Henry Rogers's *The
Eclipse of Faith* (1853). An argument chiefly against modern spiritualism (such as transcendentalism) that denies all forms of external authority or mediation; Brownson's reflections upon the Catholic and infidel tendencies within Protestantism.

"Garneau's History of Canada." *Brownson's Quarterly Review* 15 (October, 1853):444-65. Review of F. X. Garneau's *Histoire du Canada*
(1852) and Brownson's summary of main historical events in that
history.

"'Errors of the Church of Rome.'" *Brownson's Quarterly Review* 15
(October, 1853):465-97; *Works* 7:304-34. Review of George W.
Burnap's "The Errors and Superstitions of the Church of Rome,"
published in the *Christian Examiner* (July, 1853). Brownson's remarks on the charges of Catholicism's ultra-conservativism, corporate spirit, and unfriendliness to the diffusion of the Bible.

"J. V. H. on Brownson's Review." *Brownson's Quarterly Review* 15 (October, 1853):497-529; *Works* 14:317-47. Review of Jedediah V. Huntington's "Brownson's Review and the Idea of Right," *Truth-Teller* (July 16, 1853). Brownson's denial that he is a psychologist or a pantheist; asserts that all rights belong to God and that obligations are grounded in the will of God.

"Cardinal Wiseman's *Essays.*" *Brownson's Quarterly Review* 15 (October, 1853):529-42; *Works* 10:450-62. Review of Nicholas Wiseman's *Essays on Various Subjects* (1853). Favorable review; great task of the day is to show that temporal is dependent on the spiritual; the two are not united in form, but at their source.

1854

"Uncle Jack and his Nephew." Part I of *IV. Brownson's Quarterly Review* 16 (January, 1854):1-29; see January, April, and October, 1854; *Uncle Jack and his nephew; or Conversations of an Old Fogy with a Young American.* Detroit: H. F. Brownson, 1888; *Works* 11:165-92. An autobiographical dialogue between an ultramontane Catholic and a young Protestant sympathetic to Gallicanism on the issue of church-state relations; natural against vested rights.

"Schools of Philosophy." *Brownson's Quarterly Review* 16 (January, 1854):30-60; *Works* 1:276-305. The psychological school against the ontological (Brownson in favor of latter); doctrine of creation not integrated into Aristotle or his scholastic followers.

"The Case of Martin Koszta." *Brownson's Quarterly Review* 16 (January, 1854):60-86; *Works* 16:226-51. Brownson's defense of Austria's imprisonment of Koszta; United States government's case in support of Koszta "untenable."

"You go too Far.'" *Brownson's Quarterly Review* 16 (January, 1854):87-106; *Works* 11:95-114. Review of Jean Gosselin's *The Power of the Pope during the Middle Ages* (1853). Brownson defends his views on the temporal authority of the pope against those Catholics who claim his perspective is immoderate.

"Uncle Jack and his Nephew." Part II of IV. *Brownson's Quarterly Review* 16 (April, 1854):137-66; see January, July, and August, 1854; *Works* 11:192-221.

"Protestantism Developed." *Brownson's Quarterly Review* 16 (April, 1854):166-86. Review of J. H. McColloh's *Analytical Investigations concerning the Credibility of the Scriptures* (1852). On whether or not there was a divine foundation of the ministry for the word and for an authoritative church. McColloh denies such a foundation and thereby threatens the developments of churchly Protestantism.

"Temporal Power of the Popes." *Brownson's Quarterly Review* 16 (April, 1854):187-218; *Works* 11:114-36. Review of *The Metropolitan Magazine* (February and March, 1854). Temporal authority of the pope defended as at least a logical deduction from Catholic dogma.

"The Mercersburg Hypothesis." *Brownson's Quarterly Review* 16 (April, 1854):253-65; *Works* 14:183-97. Response to *Mercersburg Review* (January, 1854). On the principle of development; difficult to see how John W. Nevin and Philip Schaff can avoid becoming Catholics.

"The Black Warrior Case." *Brownson's Quarterly Review* 16 (April, 1854):271-72. On the Spanish seizure of the American steamer Black Warrior at Havana.

"Uncle Jack and his Nephew." Part III of IV. *Brownson's Quarterly Review* 16 (July, 1854):273-305; see January, July, and August, 1854; *Works* 11:221-51.

"To The Editors of the *Catholic Mirror*." *Catholic Mirror* (Baltimore) 5 (July 22, 1854):5.

"Native Americanism." *Brownson's Quarterly Review* 16 (July, 1854):328-54; "Native Americans," *Works* 18:281-300. Review of Charles François Delery's *A Few Words on Native Americanism* (1854). On the historical and cultural priority of native-born Americans and necessity of foreigners respecting and assimilating Anglo-American culture.

"Schools and Education." *Brownson's Quarterly Review* 16 (July, 1854):354-76; *Works* 10:564-84. Review of Arsene Cahours's *Des Etudes Classiques et des Etudes Professionnelles* (1852). Cahours opposes Gaume's view on the use of classics in education; Brownson comments on the American Common School system.

"The Turkish War." *Brownson's Quarterly Review* 16 (July, 1854):376-95; *Works* 16:408-27. Brownson prefers Russia to the allied western powers (France and England) in the conflict.

"To the Editor of the *Pittsburgh Catholic*." *Pittsburgh Catholic* 11 (August 12, 1854):182.

"To the Editors of the *Catholic Telegraph*." *Catholic Telegraph and Advocate* (Cincinnati), August 22, 1854.

The Spirit-Rapper, an Autobiography. Boston: Little, Brown, & Co.,
   1854; *Works* 9:1-234. Brownson connects spirit-manifestation with
   modern philanthropy, visionary reforms, socialism, and
   revolutionism. All spirit manifestations are induced by Satan, but
   not without cooperation of free will.

"Uncle Jack and his Nephew." Part IV of *IV. Brownson's Quarterly
   Review* 16 (October, 1854):408-47; see January, April, and July,
   1854; *Works* 11:251-87.

"Know-Nothingism; or Satan warring against Christ." Part I of II.
   Brownson's Quarterly Review 16 (October, 1854):447-87; see January, 1855; *Works* 18:300-38. On the necessity of separating the
   legitimate sentiment of American nationality and the anti-Catholic sentiment; defense of his article on "Native Americanism" (July,
   1854), and insistence on the supra-nationalism of Catholicism.

"Sumner on Fugitive Slaves." *Brownson's Quarterly Review* 16 (October, 1854):487-502; *Works* 17:39-53. Review of the *Speeches of the
   Hon. Charles Sumner* (1854). Brownson asserts equality of all races
   and unnaturalness of slavery but opposes abolitionist party.

"Works of Fisher Ames." *Brownson's Quarterly Review* 16 (October,
   1854):502-514; *Works* 16:379-90. Review of *Works of Fisher Ames*
   (1854), reflections on the "Old Federalists" (i.e., Ames) during
   George Washington's administration, and the need for a contemporary Federalist corrective.

"Church and State." *Brownson's Quarterly Review* 16 (October,
   1854):514-24. Review of Joseph von Radowitz's *Neue Gespräche
   aus der Gegenwart uber Staat und Kirche* (1851). On a Catholic
   statesman's views of government and the relations of church and
   state in Germany that are similar to Brownson's.

"End of the Eleventh Volume." *Brownson's Quarterly Review* 16 (October, 1854):536-40. On the history of the *Review* and the recent
   hostility towards it.

1855

"Gratry on the Knowledge of God." Part I of *II. Brownson's Quarterly
   Review* 17 (January, 1855):1-21; see July, 1855; *Works* 1:324-43.
   On the means and conditions of the knowledge and love of God,
   and on the synthetic relation of love, knowing, revelation and reason, intuition and reflection, in coming to a knowledge of and
   union with God.

"Ritter's History of Philosophy." *Brownson's Quarterly Review* 17 (January, 1855):22-42. Review of Heinrich Ritter's *The History of Ancient Philosophy* (1838). Brownson's views of reason's role in the discovery of truth and his evaluations of selected Ionian and Pythagorian philosophers.

"Radowitz's Fragments." *Brownson's Quarterly Review* 17 (January, 1855):43-61. Review of Joseph von Radowitz's *Gasammelte Schriften* (1853). Brownson's comments on and translations of a few excerpts of Radowitz's political doctrines.

"Luther and the Reformation." *Brownson's Quarterly Review* 17 (January, 1855):61-91; *Works* 10:463-91. Review of Jean Marie Vincent Audin's *History of the Life, the Writings, and the Doctrines of Luther* (1854). Brownson's views of the motives of the Reformation, and his assault on nationalism as a denial of the supremacy of the spiritual.

"Russia and the Western Powers." *Brownson's Quarterly Review* 17 (January, 1855):91-114; *Works* 16:427-49. In defense of Brownson's modified support for Russia against France and England.

"The Know-Nothings." Part II of II. *Brownson's Quarterly Review* 17 (January, 1855):114-35; see October, 1854; *Works* 18:338-80. Review of Franklin Pierce's *Message of the President of the United States* (1854).

"Romanism in America." *Brownson's Quarterly Review* 17 (April, 1855):145-82; *Works* 7:508-43. Review of Rufus W. Clark's *Romanism in America* (1855). Comments on common Protestant objections to Catholicism.

"Liberalism and Socialism." *Brownson's Quarterly Review* 17 (April, 1855):183-209; *Works* 10:526-50; Kirk: 123-60. Review of Don Juan Donoso Cortes's *Ensayo sobre el Catolicismo, el Liberalismo, y el Socialismo* (1851), and Pierre Leroux's *De l'Humanité* (1840). On true liberalism; nativism is a kind of civil despotism; the Maine liquor law is part of this despotism.

"*Questions of the Soul.*" *Brownson's Quarterly Review 17* (April, 1855):209-27; *Works 14*:538-47. Review of Isaac T. Hecker's *Questions of the Soul* (1855). A real American book that is designed to meet the ontological needs of the age.

"What Human Reason can do." *Brownson's Quarterly Review* 17 (April, 1855):227-46; *Works* 1:306-23. Review of Etienne Chastel's *De la Valeur de la Raison Humaine* (1854). On the necessity of supernatural revelation and therefore of traditionalism. Brownson grew up among naturalists and needed to put reason within the context of supernatural revelation.

"The Papal Conspiracy Exposed." Brownson's Quarterly Review 17 (April, 1855):246-70; *Works* 7:543-66. Review of Edward Beecher's *The Papal Conspiracy Exposed* (1855). Brownson's assertion of the mutual antagonism between Catholicism and Protestantism, denial of any Catholic conspiracy, and outline of nativist violence against Catholics.

"Relations of the Pope to the Civil Power: Letter from O. A. Brownson." *New York Times* (July 27,1855):5.

"Gratry on the Knowledge of God." Part II of II. *Brownson's Quarterly Review* 17 (July, 1855):281-300; see January, 1855; *Works* 1:343-61.

"Italy and the Christian Alliance." *Brownson's Quarterly Review* 17 (July, 1855):355-93. Review of Giovanni Perrone's *Il Protestantesimo e la Regola di Fede* (1853) and Gabrielle Bibbia's *Dissertazione Storico—Teologica contro le Bibbliche Società de' Protestanti* (1852). Importance of the rule of faith; on decline of controversy among Catholics.

"Rome after the Peace." *Brownson's Quarterly Review* 17 (July, 1855):300-22. A translation of a fragment of Charles R. F. de Montalembert's "History of the Western Monks" from *Revue des Deux Mondes* (January 1, 1855) on corruptions after the peace of Constantine. Comments on Montalembert's political principles of liberty in the midst of the current rush toward absolutism among some French Catholics.

"Ferrier's *Institutes of Metaphysic." Brownson's Quarterly Review* 17 (July, 1855):32238. Review of James F. Ferrier's *Institutes of Metaphysics* (1854). Analysis and criticism of Ferrier's view of the conditions of all knowledge.

"Wilberforce on Church Authority." *Brownson's Quarterly Review* 17 (July, 1855):33954. Review of Robert I. Wilberforce's *An Inquiry into the Principles of Church Authority* (1855). Analysis of the organic nature of the church and its priority to the individual. Individuals live the divine life by communion with the body of Christ.

"A Know-Nothing Legislature." *Brownson's Quarterly Review* 17 (July, 1855):393-411. Review of Charles Hale's *Our Houses are our Castles* (1855) and Massachusetts Legislature reports on the Nunnery Inspection Committee. Analysis of the anti-Catholic proceedings of the Legislature as illustrative of the anti-American nativist tendencies, not illustrative of the popular sentiment or the republican values of the states or the country.

"The Temporal Power of the Pope." *Brownson's Quarterly Review* 17 (October, 1855):417-45; *Works* 11:137-64. Review of *The Temporal Power of the Pope; containing the Speech of the Hon. Joseph R. Chandler* (1855). On the independence, rights and prerogatives of the spiritual order in the face of the temporal; and the rights and prerogatives of the pope, as representative of the church and the spiritual order, over the temporal order.

"Hume's Philosophical Works." *Brownson's Quarterly Review* 17 (October, 1855):445-73; see "The Problem of Causality," October, 1874; "The Problem of Causality," *Works* 1:381-407. Review of David Hume's *The Philosophical Works* (1854). On the value of Hume's criticism of the limits of empiricism in understanding causality, and the post-Humean attempts to avoid skepticism, including Brownson's attempt to show how intuition and reflection combine in arriving at the notion of causality.

"The Know-Nothing Platform." *Brownson's Quarterly Review* 17 (October, 1855):473-98. On the split over slavery in the Know-Nothing Party's national convention in Philadelphia.

"Ventura on Philosophy and Catholicity." *Brownson's Quarterly Review* 17 (October, 1855):499-524; "Philosophy and Catholicity," *Works* 3:180-204. Review of Gioacchino Ventura's *La Raison Philosophique et la Raison Catholique* (1851-53). Against the divorce of reason and faith.

"Wordsworth's *Poetical Works.*" *Brownson's Quarterly Review* 17 (October, 1855):525-38; *Works* 19:418-30; *Modern*: 418-30. Review of William Wordsworth's *The Poetical Works* (1854). Brownson's views on the Giobertian philosophy of art as a standard for judging the beautiful in poetry.

"The Irish in America." *Brownson's Quarterly Review* 17 (October, 1855):538-47. Review of William Carleton's *The Poor Scholar* (1854) and Mary Sadlier's *New Lights, or Life in Galway* (1853). On Evangelical hatred of Catholicism and the necessity of defending the Irish because they are Catholic, not just because they are Irish. Against political demagoguery among the Irish. Respect for the virtues of the Irish people.

1856

"The Constitution of the Church." *Brownson's Quarterly Review* 18 (January, 1856):1-25; see July, 1875; *Works* 8:527-51. Review of Robert I. Wilberforce's *An Inquiry into the Principles of Church Authority* (1855). On the organic nature of the church, and on the papacy as essential to the very conception of the church in the visible order.

"The 'End of Controversy Controverted.'" *Brownson's Quarterly Review* 18 (January, 1856):26-62. Review of John H. Hopkins's *The "End of Controversy" Controverted* (1855) and Francis Patrick Kenrick's *A Vindication of the Catholic Church* (1855). Brownson's refutation of Hopkins on the role of faith, translations of the Bible, and use of catechisms.

"Catholicity and Literature." *Brownson's Quarterly Review* 18 (January, 1856):62-81; *Works* 19:447-64; *Modern*; 447-64. Review of William B. MacCabe's *Bertha* (1856) and *Florine, Princess of Burgundy* (1855), as well as William Carleton's *Willy Reilly* (1856). Brownson's application of 'gratia supponit naturam' to analysis of literature.

"Transcendental Road to Rome." *Brownson's Quarterly Review* 18 (January, 1856):81-102. Review of "Transcendental Road to Rome," *Christian Review* (October, 1855) which was itself a review of Isaac Hecker's *Questions of the Soul.* On the relation between reason and revelation, nature and grace, in Hecker's works—against the criticism that Hecker is traditionalist and/or transcendentalist.

"Great Britain and the United States." *Brownson's Quarterly Review* 18 (January, 1856):102-20; *Works* 16:471-88. England's peace with United States is in her best interests.

"*Le Correspondant.*" *Brownson's Quarterly Review* 18 (January, 1856):121-34. Review of *Le Correspondant* (October, 1855), which is reorganized and promises to be a Catholic paper that avoids both a dangerous absolutism and a false liberalism.

"'The Church and the Republic.'" A Lecture delivered February 13, 1856 in New York Tabernacle. *New York Times* (February 15, 1856): 3. Church must be one of the constitutive elements of the Republic in order for it to preserve both freedom and authority.

"Protestantism in the Sixteenth Century." *Brownson's Quarterly Review* 18 (April, 1856):137-73; *Works* 10:491-525. Review of l'Abbé Jean Charles Benjamin Poisson's *Essai sur les Causes du Succes du*

Protestantisme au Seizieme Siecle (1839). On Poisson's Gallican view of the success of the Reformation and Brownson's defense of his ultramontane interpretation of history.

"The Blakes and the Flanagans." *Brownson's Quarterly Review* 18 (April, 1856):195-212; *Works* 20:23-39. Review of Mary Sadlier's *The Blakes and the Flanagans* (1855). Brownson's reflection on the regrettable nationalism among the Irish, on Catholic schools, and on nurturing and preserving the faith of the young.

"Montalembert on England." *Brownson's Quarterly Review* 18 (April, 1856):225-52; *Works* 16:489-513. Brownson's agreements and disagreements with Montalembert on English constitutional government.

"The Day-Star of Freedom." *Brownson's Quarterly Review* 18 (April, 1856):252-67; Works 12:103-16. Review of G. L. Davis's *The Day-Star of Freedom, or the Early Growth of Toleration in the Province of Maryland* (1855). Brownson's view of the historical insignificance of colonial Maryland, and the difference between Maryland toleration and American religious liberty; Puritans, not Catholics, are the source of religious liberty in America.

"The Church and the Republic." *Brownson's Quarterly Review* 18 (July, 1856):273-307; *Works* 12:1-32. Church must be one of the constitutive elements of a republic; government's duty to protect freedom of religion.

"The Unholy Alliance." *Brownson's Quarterly Review* 18 (July, 1856):325-48; *Works* 16:450-71. Review of W. G. Dix's *The Unholy Alliance; an American View of the War in the East* (1856). On peace treaty between Russia and allies; what is really needed for regeneration of East is reunion of Orthodox and Roman Catholic churches.

"Collard on Reason and Faith." *Brownson's Quarterly Review* 18 (July, 1856):348-74; *Works* 3:205-29. Review of Maurice Collard's *Raison et foi* (1855). Brownson's call for a new apologetic that pays attention to Protestant subjective feelings as well as to their logical objections against Catholicism. Catholics must address the unscholastic culture of modern non-Catholics.

"Gratry's Logic." *Brownson's Quarterly Review* 18 (July, 1856):375-94; *Works* 1:362-80. Review of Auguste Gratry's *Philosophie. Logique* (1855). Brownson's criticisms of Gratry's attempts to make logic "a mere development of psychology." Brownson bases his logic on ontology, reason, and the nature of things.

"Introduction." James Balmes, *Fundamental Philosophy.* Trans. Henry F. Brownson. 2 vols. New York: D. & J. Sadlier & Co., 1856: vii-xvi; "Balmes' Philosophy," *Works* 2:462-67. Brownson's introduction to his son Henry's translation. Brownson recommended its translation primarily because of Balmes's refutation of Bacon, Locke, Hume, Condillac, Kant, Fichte, Schelling, and Spinoza.

"Mission of America." *Brownson's Quarterly Review* 18 (October, 1856):409-44; *Works* 11:551-84; Abell: 19-37. Review of Martin J. Spalding's *Miscellanea* (1855). America is future of the world. Divine providence has given her a mission and task of working out in the world a higher order of civilization by means of Christianity.

"The Church and Modern Civilization." *Brownson's Quarterly Review* 18 (October, 1856):462-85; *Works* 12:117-36. Review of *Oeuvres completes de A. F. Ozanam* (1855). Reflection on the church's historical relations with Western culture; the Protestant-Catholic controversy now turns on church's contributions to civilization, not on dogma and ritual.

"E. H. Derby to his Son." Part I of V. *Brownson's Quarterly Review* 18 (October, 1856):485-504; see January, April, July, and October, 1857; *Works* 7:335-52. Review of E. H. Derby, *The Catholic. Letters addressed by a Jurist to a Young Kinsman proposing to join the Church of Rome* (1856). Brownson's use of patristic sources to argue against Derby's detailed reasons for his son not joining the Catholic church.

"The Presidential Election." *Brownson's Quarterly Review* 18 (October, 1856):504-13. Against Millard Fillmore and John C. Fremont because they are supported by the Know-Nothings. Favors James Buchanan the Democrat. On inappropriateness of slavery, Maine liquor law, and Catholicism as political issues.

"The Church in the United States." *Brownson's Quarterly Review* 18 (October, 1856):514-24; *Works* 20:40-50. Review of Henry De Courcy's *The Catholic Church in the United States* (1856). De Courcy's judgement on anything American is not to be trusted and his book on American Catholicism is little more than a series of newspaper articles without systematic organization, but intended to glorify France's contribution to Catholicism in this country.

1857

"Brownson on the Church and the Republic." *Brownson's Quarterly Review 19* (January, 1857):1-29; *Works* 12:33-58. Review of "Brownson on the Church and the Republic," *Universalist Quarterly and General Review* (October, 1856). Popular governments are impracticable without the church; church has moral authority and works upon the wills of the governed as well as those who govern.

"E. H. Derby to his Son." Part II of V. *Brownson's Quarterly Review 19* (January, 1857):29-57; see October, 1856; April, July, and October, 1857; *Works* 7:352-78.

"Maret on Reason and Revelation." Part I of II. *Brownson's Quarterly Review 19* (January, 1857):58-89; see "Necessity of Divine Revelation," July, 1858; *Works* 1:438-67. "Dignity of Human Reason," RyanA: 232-42. Tradition necessary to bring to reflective awareness what is ontologically present in intuition; history and tradition are proper media for detecting and establishing fact of supernatural providence.

"Slavery and the Incoming Administration." *Brownson's Quarterly Review 19* (January, 1857):89-114; *Works* 17:54-77. Slavery issue must be left to the states; Brownson supports "Union Principles" against Know-Nothingism and abolitionists.

"Archbishop Hughes on the Catholic Press." *Brownson's Quarterly Review 19* (January, 1857):114-41; *Works* 20:50-73; *Gems*: 234-49. Review of John Hughes's *Reflections and Suggestions in Regard to what is called the Catholic Press in the United States* (1856). On Hughes's criticisms of national divisions in the Catholic press. Brownson's denial that he supports an American Catholic party against a party of Catholic foreigners, and his defense of his own publications on Americanization and other American Catholic issues.

"E. H. Derby to his Son." Part III of V. *Brownson's Quarterly Review 19* (April, 1857):145-84; see October, 1856; January, July, and October, 1857; *Works* 7:378-414.

"Spiritual Despotism." *Brownson's Quarterly Review 19* (April, 1857):191-224; *Works* 7:479-507. Review of "Spiritual Despotism," *Methodist Quarterly Review* (January, 1850). On Catholic violations of religious liberty and progress.

"Ailey Moore." Brownson's *Quarterly Review 19* (April, 1857):224-48; *Works* 20:73-83. Review of Richard Baptist O'Brien's novel *Ailey Moore* (1856). Comments on Irish relations with Anglo-Saxons.

"The Slavery Question Once More." Brownson's *Quarterly Review 19* (April, 1857):248-77; *Works* 17:77-94. On the Dred Scott case; Brownson regrets that the Catholic Chief Justice Roger Taney did not follow his religion in the decision.

"E. H. Derby to his Son." Part IV of V. Brownson's *Quarterly Review 19* (July, 1857):281-327; see October, 1856; January, April, and October, 1857; *Works* 7:414-57.

"Christianity and the Church Identical." Brownson's *Quarterly Review 19* (July, 1857):327-48; *Works* 12:59-79. Review of "A Response to O. A. Brownson," *Universalist Quarterly and General Review* (April, 1857). Brownson's reactions to a Universalist criticism of his article "The Church and the Republic," (July, 1856) and his re-assertion that the Catholic Church is identical with Christianity and necessary in society to prevent anarchy and/or tyranny.

"Present Catholic Dangers." Brownson's *Quarterly Review 19* (July, 1857):349-74; *Works* 12:136-60. Review of "Present Catholic Dangers," *Dublin Review* (January, 1857). Reflections on the *Dublin Review*'s conflict with *The Rambler*, a conflict between the "convert party" and the native Catholic party; all the traditions of Catholics are not Catholic Tradition.

"Religious Liberty in France." Brownson's *Quarterly Review 19* (July, 1857):389-413; *Works* 16:514-35. Review of Charles de Montalembert's "Des Appels comme d'Abus et des Articles Organiques du Concordat," *Le Correspondant* (April, 1857). Catholic Church being allied with imperial governments; freedom of the church is condition of political freedom.

The Convert; or, Leaves from my Experience. New York: Dunigan & Brother, 1857; *Works* 5:1-200; "The Convert," RyanA: 286-303; Carey: 242-49; Miller: 45-47; Miller2: 40-47. Brownson's public account of his intellectual journey to Catholicism.

"E. H. Derby to his Son." Part V of V. Brownson's *Quarterly Review 19* (October, 1857):417-43; see October, 1856; January, April, and July, 1857; *Works* 7:457-79.

"Aspirations of Nature." Brownson's *Quarterly Review 19* (October, 1857):459-503; *Works* 14:548-77. Review of Isaac T. Hecker's

Aspirations of Nature (1857). Hecker does not understand the Fall to be as devastating as it was; has too much confidence in reason at expense of revelation.

"C. J. Cannon's Works." *Brownson's Quarterly Review 19* (October, 1857):503-27. Review of Charles James Cannon's *Dramas* (1857), *Poems Dramatic and Miscellaneous* (1851), and *Ravellings from the Web of Life* (1855). Excerpts from these works and a brief delicate review of literature Brownson considered popular and lacking literary merit.

"Le Vert's *Souvenirs of Travel.*" *Brownson's Quarterly Review 19* (October, 1857):528-42. Review of Octavia Walton le Vert's *Souvenirs of Travel* (1857) and comments on the "genuine outpourings" of an unsophisticated Southern lady.

"British Preponderance." *Brownson's Quarterly Review 19* (October, 1857):542-55; *Works* 16:536-47. On Adam Smith and against British industrial and mercantile system.

1858

"Popular Objections to Catholicity—Lecture by Dr. Orestes A. Brownson." *New York Times* (January 18, 1858): 5. Summary of a lecture given January 12 at the Academy of Music, New York City.

"Conversations of Our Club." Part I of VII. *Brownson's Quarterly Review* 20 (January, 1858):1-31; see April, July, and October, 1858; January, April, and July, 1859; *Works* 11:289-317. Dialogue on relation of religion to Catholicity, nationalism, liberty, politics and economics.

"The Church an Organism." *Brownson's Quarterly Review* 20 (January, 1858):103-27; *Works* 12:79-102. Review of "Christianity as an Organization," *Universalist Quarterly and General Review* (October, 1857). Continuation of Brownson's discussion with a Universalist on the church's role in the Republic (see "Christianity and the Church Identical" July, 1857). Church's claims rest not only on historical evidence, but on interior revelation.

"Conversations of Our Club." Part II of VII. *Brownson's Quarterly Review* 20 (April, 1858):171-209; see January, July, and October, 1858; January, April, and July, 1859; *Works* 11:317-53.

"The Princeton Review and *The Convert.*" *Brownson's Quarterly Review* 20 (April, 1858):244-87; *Works* 5:196-240. Review of "Brownson's Exposition of Himself," *The Biblical Repertory and*

Princeton Review (January, 1858). Brownson's response to stricture upon his view of Presbyterianism in *The Convert* and his reason's for abandoning Presbyterianism.

"Revivals and Retreats." *Brownson's Quarterly Review* 20 (July, 1858):289-322; Carey: 249-67. Sensible devotions, through retreats and parish missions, help prepare people for a lively consciousness and experience of God and moral duty.

"Conversations of Our Club." Part III of VII. *Brownson's Quarterly Review* 20 (July, 1858):347-89; see January, April, and October, 1858; January, April, and July, 1859; *Works* 11:353-92.

"Necessity of Divine Revelation." Part II of II. *Brownson's Quarterly Review* 20 (July, 1858):389-413; see January, 1857. "Maret on Reason and Revelation," *Works* 1:467-89.

"Clapp's *Autobiographical Sketches.*" *Brownson's Quarterly Review* 20 (July, 1858):413-24. Review of Theodore Clapp's *Autobiographical Sketches* (1857). Reflections on Clapp's liberal Christianity (Unitarianism and Universalism).

"Conversations of Our Club." Part IV of VII. *Brownson's Quarterly Review* 20 (October, 1858):425-66; see January, April, and July, 1858; January, April, and July, 1859; *Works* 11:393-431.

"The English Schism." *Brownson's Quarterly Review* 20 (October, 1858):491-513; Works, 12: 161-82. Review of C. J. M.'s *Alice Sherwin* (1858). An historical novel of the times of Sir Thomas More and the English Schism; reflections on the cause of the English Reformation.

"An Exposition of the Apocalypse." Brownson's Quarterly Review 20 (October, 1858):514-23. Review of *An Exposition of the Apocalypse of St. John the Apostle* (1858) by a Catholic priest who shares Brownson's view of the age's need.

1859

"Primitive Elements of Thought." *Brownson's Quarterly Review* 21 (January, 1859):58-90; *Works* 1:408-37. Review of Flavien Hugonin's *Etudes Philosophiques* (1856-57). Main objective is to reassert the divine creative act, which is the basis upon which philosophy can be in accord with Christianity. That divine act exists among our primitive notions.

"Conversation of Our Club." Part V of VII. *Brownson's Quarterly Review* 21 (January, 1859):90-129; see January, April, July, and

October, 1858; April and July, 1859; *Works* 11:431-68. On theocracy.

"The Trial and Conviction of Count de Montalembert." *Brownson's Quarterly Review* 21 (January, 1859):141-43. Protest against the French government's imprisonment of Charles R. F. de Montalembert.

"Conversations of Our Club." Part VI of VII. *Brownson's Quarterly Review* 21 (April, 1859),145-90; see January, April, July, and October, 1858; January and July, 1859; *Works* 11:468-510. On the church and the revolution.

"Politics at Home and Abroad." *Brownson's Quarterly Review* 21 (April, 1859):191-225; *Works* 16:548-80. Struggle for national identities in Europe; significance of Andrew Jackson and the American movement toward a popular democracy.

"The Mortara Case; or, the Right of Parents to the Custody and Education of their Children." *Brownson's Quarterly Review* 21 (April, 1859):226-46. On religious liberty and parental rights. Support for the Roman government's taking of a baptized child from its Jewish parents and providing for the child's Christian education.

"Pere Felix on Progress." *Brownson's Quarterly Review* 21 (April, 1859):262-80; *Works* 12:182-200. Review of Celestin Joseph Felix's *Le Progres par le Christianisme* (1858). On the qualities of a good preacher and Felix's inability to counter, at the affective level, those who hold the doctrine of progress.

"Conversations of Our Club." Part VII of VII. *Brownson's Quarterly Review* 21 (July, 1859):281-324; see January, April, July, and October, 1858; January and April, 1859; *Works* 11:510-51. On the church and revolution.

"Public and Parochial Schools." *Brownson's Quarterly Review* 21 (July, 1859):324-42; *Works* 12:200-16; RyanA: 126-32. Review of John B. Purcell's *Pastoral Letter on the Decrees of the Second Provincial Council of Cincinnati* (1859). Brownson's support for good public schools as well as good Catholic schools that Americanize students.

"Lamennais and Gregory XVI." *Brownson's Quarterly Review* 21 (July, 1859):372-95; *Works* 12:216-38. Review of *Censure de Cinquante-six Propositions Extraites de divers Ecrits de M. de la Mennais, et de ses Disciples* (1835). Brownson holds *Mirari vos* infallible in condemning errors; Catholics may fail but church never does for it is more than simply an aggregate of believers.

"Napoleonic Ideas." *Brownson's Quarterly Review* 21 (July, 1859):396-410; *Works* 16:581-94. Review of Napoleon-Louis Bonaparte's *Des Idées Napoléaniennes* (1839). Napoleon is a despot under guise of liberty; England only bulwark of liberty in Europe.

"Romanic and Germanic Orders." *Brownson's Quarterly Review* 21 (October,1859):493-526; *Works* 12:238-69. Review of John M'Elheran's *The Condition of Women and Children among the Celtic, Gothic, and other Nations* (1858). Brownson's opposition to this book which argued that Catholicism was Celtic and Protestantism was Germanic.

"The Roman Question." *Brownson's Quarterly Review* 21 (October,1859):526-40; *Works* 18:418-30. Review of Edmond About's *The Roman Question* (1859). On papal temporal authority over the papal states.

1860

"Christianity or Gentilism?" *Brownson's Quarterly Review* 22 (January, 1860):1-42; *Works* 12:270-305. Review of *Pope or President?* (1859). Brownson's reaction to this nativist publication, his doctrine of the Incarnation, and his views on the mediation of grace through humanity.

"Manahan's *Triumph of the Church.*" *Brownson's Quarterly Review* 22 (January, 1860):51-74; *Works* 12:305-25. Review of Ambrose Manahan's *Triumph of the Church in the Early Ages* (1859). Brownson's comments on the relation between Catholicism and the moral development of civilization.

"The Bible against Protestants." *Brownson's Quarterly Review* 22 (January, 1860):75-95; *Works* 7:580-97. Review of Bishop Lawrence Shiel's *The Bible against Protestantism and for Catholicity* (1859). Catholic Church does not reveal new truths; Bible is word of God interpreted in light of Catholic tradition.

"*The True Cross.*" *Brownson's Quarterly Review* 22 (January, 1860):96-118; *Works* 8:280-99. Review of C. Malan's *The True Cross* (1858). On the supernatural; Catholic understanding of merit.

"The Yankee in Ireland." *Brownson's Quarterly Review* 22 (January, 1860):118-30; *Works* 20:83-93. Review of Paul Peppergrass's *Mary*

Lee (1860). Brownson's view of the weakness of Irish writers and his controversy with Peppergrass on literary criticism.

"Limits of Religious Thought." *Brownson's Quarterly Review* 22 (April, 1860),137-74; Works 3:230-56. Review of Henry L. Mansel's *The Limits of Religious Thought Examined* (1859). Brownson's criticisms of Mansel's epistemology and his fideism (demolishing reason in order to prove the necessity of revelation).

"*Études de Théologie.*" *Brownson's Quarterly Review* 22 (April, 1860):174-207; *Works* 19:465-93; *Modern*; 465-93. Review of Charles Daniel's and Jean Gagarin's *Études de Théologie, de Philosophie, et d'Histoire* (1859-60). On the error of Ontologists— faith not dependent on philosophy; rather, philosophy useful in constructing science of theology and defending faith.

"Ventura on Christian Politics." *Brownson's Quarterly Review* 22 (April, 1860):207-36; "Christian Politics," *Works* 12:325-50. Review of Gioacchino Ventura de Raulica's *Le Pouvoir Politique Chrétien* (1858). Brownson's views of the separation of religion from politics and the revolutionary spirit of the day.

"Burnett's *Path to the Church.*" *Brownson's Quarterly Review* 22 (April, 1860):237-53; *Works* 20:93-107. Review of Peter H. Burnett's *The Path which led a Protestant Lawler to the Catholic Church* (1860). On California governor's reasons for becoming Catholic and effective means to overcome Protestant doubts and indifference.

"American College at Rome." *Brownson's Quarterly Review* 22 (April, 1860):253-61. Review of *Alla Santità di N. S. Pio IX, in Occasione della Visita da Lui fatta al Nuovo Collegio Americano* (1860). On necessity of Roman education of American clergy to avoid excessive nationalism.

"The Papal Power." *Brownson's Quarterly Review* 22 (July, 1860):273-302; *Works* 12:351-75. Review of Jean Gosselin's *The Power of the Pope during the Middle Ages* (1853). Brownson's view that the pope held temporal powers *jure divino* as well as *jure humano*, and his assertion that politics cannot be wholly separated from religion.

"Politics at Home." *Brownson's Quarterly Review* 22 (July, 1860):360-91; *Works* 17:94-120. Brownson supports republican theory of government; he opposes slavery, but distinguishes between the political and the moral question.

"Rationalism and Traditionalism." *Brownson's Quarterly Review* 22 (October, 1860):409-45; *Works* 1:490-520. Review of *Annales de*

Philosophie Chrétienne (March, 1860). Against Augustin Bonnetty and traditionalists who reduce all science to faith; peripathetics and traditionalists share same mistake—no distinction between intuitive and reflective order.

"Rights of the Temporal." *Brownson's Quarterly Review* 22 (October, 1860):462-96; *Works* 12:376-405. Review of Thomas Hughes's *School Days at Rugby* (1859). On the laity's rights and role in the church, and the rights of lay society. Spiritual supremacy does not imply the absorption of the temporal.

1861

"Ward's *Philosophical Introduction.*" *Brownson's Quarterly Review* 23 (January, 1861):1-32; *Works* 14:348-79. Review of William G. Ward's *On Nature and Grace* (1860). Brownson opposed to Aquinas's systematic order; Ward's problems stem from fact that he starts with Aquinas's *pars secunda*; Ward does not consider the creative act and the Incarnation as the basis of all moral life.

"Separation of Church and State." *Brownson's Quarterly Review* 23 (January, 1861):65-97; *Works* 12:406-38. Review of Celestin Joseph Felix's *Le Progres par le Christianisme* (1858-60). Supremacy of the spiritual, yet the temporal has its freedom; the state is not absolutely autonomous, but it does have a relative autonomy in temporal order.

"Harmony of Faith and Reason." *Brownson's Quarterly Review* 23 (January, 1861):117-31; *Works* 3:257-71. Review of A. C. Baine's *An Essay on the Harmonious Relations between Divine Faith and Natural Reason* (1861). Method for demonstrating that natural reason is below faith but not contrary to it.

"*Christ the Spirit.*" *Brownson's Quarterly Review* 23 (April, 1861):137-63; *Works* 3:272-97. Review of Etha Hitchcock's *Christ the Spirit* (1861). Book attempts to get rid of historical Christ; Brownson believes uncultured Catholics should rely on faith not their simple reasoning.

"Pope and Emperor." *Brownson's Quarterly Review* 23 (April, 1861):163-88; *Works* 12:439-63. Review of Jean-Mamert Cayla's *Pape et Empereur* (1860). Brownson opposes the recommendation of this book which calls for separation of church in France from communion with Rome; Brownson argues that such a "political blunder" would unite church and state.

"The Monks of the West." *Brownson's Quarterly Review* 23 (April, 1861):238-64. Review of Charles R. F. de Montalembert's *Les Moines d'Occident* (1860). On the influence of the monks in founding modern civilization through the agency of monastic life and discipline, and on the American conditions that have led to Civil War, and the need for new monks in the West.

"Gioberti's Philosophy of Revelation." *Brownson's Quarterly Review* 23 (July, 1861):281-324; "Vincenzo Gioberti," *Works* 2:140-82. Review of Gioberti's *Della Filosofia della Rivelazione* (1856). Neither in philosophy nor in theology is Gioberti Brownson's guide or master; against Gioberti's works and political spirit.

"Catholic Polemics." *Brownson's Quarterly Review* 23 (July, 1861):355-78; *Works* 20:107-30; RyanA: 331-40. Review of Charles Frederic Hudson's *Christ our Life* (1861). Brownson describes the new apologetic that is needed to meet the needs of intelligent Protestants.

"The Great Rebellion." *Brownson's Quarterly Review* 23 (July, 1861):378-402; *Works* 17:121-43. Support for Union and Constitution; Southern Confederate States have no legitimate authority.

"Sardinia and Rome." *Brownson's Quarterly Review* 23 (July, 1861):403-16; *Works* 18:431-44. Review of Charles R. F. de Montalembert's *Deuxieme Lettre a M. le Comte de Cavour* (1861). Montalembert's and Brownson's views on temporal power of pope and necessity of making some adjustments to modern developments in Italy.

"Various Objections and Criticisms Considered and Answered." *Brownson's Quarterly Review* 23 (October, 1861):417-62; *Works* 20:130-70. Brownson responds to criticisms of his article "Catholic Polemics" (July, 1861); he defends his Giobertian philosophy, his criticisms of scholasticism, and especially his views on hell and the meaning of the future condition of the reprobate.

"The Philosophy of Religion." *Brownson's Quarterly Review* 23 (October, 1861):462-91; *Works* 2:182-210. On Vincenzo Gioberti's philosophy of religion; five of Gioberti's errors summarized.

"Reading and Study of the Scriptures." *Brownson's Quarterly Review* 23 (October, 1861):492-509; *Works* 20:171-87. RyanA: 304-18. Review of *Introduction Historique Critique aux Livres de Nouveau Testament (1861)*. Church has received the sense of Sacred Scriptures from Holy Spirit but church's guidance does not destroy reason.

"Slavery and the War." *Brownson's Quarterly Review* 23 (October, 1861):510-46; *Works* 17:144-78; *Brownson on the Rebellion*. St. Louis: Gray, 1861. Review of Augustin Cochin's *L'Abolition de l'Esclavage* (1861). Slavery is great moral and political wrong; providence may have brought on war as means of emancipation and the reinforcing of the Union.

"The End of the Eighteenth Volume." *Brownson's Quarterly Review* 23 (October, 1861):547-48. Brownson denies that he has become a Protestant, defends himself against Catholics who question his orthodoxy.

1862

The War For The Union. Speech by Dr. O. A. Brownson. How the War should be Prosecuted. The Duty of the Government, and the Duty of the Citizen. New York: George F. Nesbitt & Co., 1862. A speech on August 28, 1862 at Willard's Hotel in Washington, DC. Advocates the elimination of slavery as a war measure to preserve the Union.

"The Reunion of all Christians." *Brownson's Quarterly Review* 24 (January, 1862):1-34; *Works* 12:464-96. Review of Adrien Nampon's *Étude de la Doctrine Catholique* (1852). Need for a new apologetic: life by communion, and the creative act as the dialectic principle of grace and nature.

"Archbishop Hughes on Slavery." *Brownson's Quarterly Review* 24 (January, 1862):34-66; *Works* 17:179-210. Review of "Brownson's Review," *Metropolitan Record* (October 12, 1861). On Hughes's protest against Brownson's view that slavery was cause of Civil War; Hughes contends northern abolitionists brought on the war.

"Catholic Schools and Education." *Brownson's Quarterly Review* 24 (January, 1862):66-85; *Works* 12:496-514; RyanA: 133-48. Reasons why many Catholics do not support Catholic schools.

"The Punishment of the Reprobate." *Brownson's Quarterly Review* 24 (January, 1862):85-113; *Works* 20:187-215. Brownson's response to criticism that his view on the future condition of the reprobate did not coincide with "the common and universalistic belief of the Catholic people."

"The Struggle of the Nation for Life." *Brownson's Quarterly Review* 24 (January, 1862):113-32; *Works* 17:211-27. Review of *The First Annual Message of the President of the United States* (December 3, 1861). Panegyric on behalf of heroic sacrifice and courage in the

Civil War; war between two ideas of government—states rights and federal union.

"Our Nineteenth Volume." *Brownson's Quarterly Review* 24 (January, 1862):132-34. Brownson reports that the *Review* will become more general and "catholic," appealing not only to Roman Catholics.

"The Church not a Despotism." *Brownson's Quarterly Review* 24 (April, 1862):137-72; *Works* 20:215-48. Church is governed by law; laity have the right to voice theological opinions without prior permission.

"Essays on the Reformation." Part I of III. *Brownson's Quarterly Review* 24 (April, 1862):172-94; see July and October, 1862; *Works* 12:514-36. The Trinitarian structure of Brownson's thought and philosophy of history; on the social and political sources of the Reformation, and the fact that in its united forms the Reformation was Catholic in its motivation.

"State Rebellion, State Suicide." *Brownson's Quarterly Review* 24 (April, 1862):194-220; *Works* 17:228-53. Sovereignty belongs to territory not people, hence injustice of Southern succession; no ground now for slavery to exist.

"Emancipation and Colonization." *Brownson's Quarterly Review* 24 (April, 1862):220-40; *Works* 17:253-72. Review of Agénor de Gasparin's *The Uprising of a Great People* (1862). On the meaning of Lincoln's election; call for immediate emancipation of slaves.

"Weninger's *Protestantism and Infidelity.*" *Brownson's Quarterly Review* 24 (April, 1862):240-63. Review of Francis X. Weninger's *Protestantism and Infidelity* (1862). On Weninger's desire to conduct missions among Protestants and Brownson's emphasis upon the Catholic more than the Protestant causes of infidelity and divisions of Christianity.

"Letter from Dr. Brownson." *Catholic Herald and Visitor* (Philadelphia) (April 22, 1862):6. Defends his orthodoxy *vis-à-vis* his ideas on the temporal power of the pope. Rome has not condemned his position.

"Essays on the Reformation." Part II of III. *Brownson's Quarterly Review* 24 (July, 1862):273-303; see April and October, 1862; *Works* 12:536-66. Protestant movement was honest movement of reform.

"Lacordaire and Catholic Progress." *Brownson's Quarterly Review* 24 (July, 1862):303-33; *Works* 20:249-78; RyanA: 341-48. Review of Charles R. F. de Montalembert's *Le Pere Lacordaire* (1862).

Necessity of liberty outside and inside church; on the mission of intelligent laymen.

"What the Rebellion Teaches." *Brownson's Quarterly Review* 24 (July, 1862):333-60; *Works* 17:273-92. Review of James Keogh's *Catholic Principles of Civil Government* (1862). Governing power a trust; *non est potestas nisi a Deo.*

"Meditations of St. Ignatius." *Brownson's Quarterly Review* 24 (July, 1862):360-73; *Works* 14:577-89. Review of Liborio Siniscalchi's *The Meditations of St. Ignatius, or the "Spiritual Exercises" expounded* (1862). Brownson's difficulties with methods of prayer and meditation, and his own views of the subjective assimilation of grace through meditation.

"Confiscation and Emancipation." *Brownson's Quarterly Review* 24 (July, 1862):373-96; *Works* 17:293-316. On Charles Sumner's views of the war powers of the federal government published in his *Indemnity for the Past and Security for the Future* (1862); Brownson favors voluntary emancipation of Negroes to territory where they will not have to face racial prejudice.

"Literary Notices and Criticisms—What and Where is the Church?" *Brownson's Quarterly Review* 24 (July, 1862):397-400. Brownson defends his view of the infallibility of the church in explaining why he rejected for publication an article submitted to him by a "Brownsonian."

"Essays on the Reformation." Part III of III. *Brownson's Quarterly Review* 24 (October, 1862):409-50; see April and July, 1862; *Works* 12:566-607. Reformation was "the continuance of the evolution of the idea;" Protestant doctrines and sects were only the temporary accidents of the Reform movement.

"Slavery and the Church." *Brownson's Quarterly Review* 24 (October, 1862):451-87; *Works* 17:317-52. Brownson accepts abolition because it is necessary to preserve union; he does not accept negroes as equal to whites.

"The Seward Policy." *Brownson's Quarterly Review* 24 (October, 1862):487-521; *Works* 17:353-85. On the Lincoln administration's "faults and shortcomings," particularly the compromising policy toward the Southern rebellion.

"Froschammer on the Freedom of Science." *Brownson's Quarterly Review* 24 (October, 1862):521-33; *Works* 20:289-92. Review of Jakob Froschammer's journal *Athenäum* (1862). On the German

Catholic philosopher's views on intellectual freedom in the Catholic Church; science and philosophy must have freedom.

"Catholicity, Liberalism, and Socialism." *Brownson's Quarterly Review* 24 (October, 1862):533-44; *Works* 20:279-89. Review of Donoso Cortes's *Essay on Catholicism, Liberalism and Socialism* (1862). On the shallow theology of the schools; Brownson not in Jesuit school of theology. He defines his own theology.

"End of the Nineteenth Volume." *Brownson's Quarterly Review* 24 (October, 1862):544-46. Brownson again defends himself against his Catholic critics. He also states that while the War continues, the *Review* will not continue anti-Protestant articles because both Catholics and Protestants must work together to reunite the nation.

1863

"Faith and Theology." *Brownson's Quarterly Review* 25 (January, 1863):1-29; *Works* 8:1-28. History, facts, and revelation; relation between authoritative faith and authoritative science.

"Conscripts and Volunteers." *Brownson's Quarterly Review* 25 (January, 1863):55-77. On the expensive, inefficient, unequal and unjust system of volunteerism as a method of recruiting for national armies, and on the necessity of conscription.

"Mrs. Sadlier's *Old and New.*" *Brownson's Quarterly Review* 25 (January, 1863):77-88. Review of Mary Sadlier's *Old and New* (1862). Sadlier writes for moral and religious purposes and her works should be judged by moral and religious rather than artistic standards. On the American propensity to gain wealth and its evil consequences upon character.

"The President's Message." *Brownson's Quarterly Review* 25 (January, 1863):88-116; "The President's Policy," *Works* 17:386-412. Review of *Annual Message of the President to both Houses of Congress* (December 1, 1862). On Lincoln's message to Congress, the locus of national sovereignty, and Brownson's developing theory of government.

"Faith and Reason—Revelation and Science." *Brownson's Quarterly Review* 25 (April, 1863):129-60; *Works* 3:565-95. Review of Richard Simpson's *Bishop Ullathorne and the Rambler* (1862) and his *Forms of Intuition. Papers from the Rambler* (n.d.). Brownson and the synthetic method; chief problem is with the scientific rationalists.

"Sermons by the Paulists." *Brownson's Quarterly Review* 25 (April, 1863):160-75. Review of *Sermons preached at the Church of St. Paul the Apostle* (1862). On difference between Paulists and Brownson on origin of sin and pure nature.

"Mr. Conway and the Union." *Brownson's Quarterly Review* 25 (April, 1863):175-204. Review of M. F. Conway's *The War a Reactionary Agent* (1863). Brownson's criticisms of Conway's call for cessation of war and division of country into two nations, one slave and one free. On the administration's war measures.

"Reform and Reformers." *Brownson's Quarterly Review* 25 (April, 1863):227-43; *Works* 20:292-308. Review of Jakob Froschammer's *Einleitung in die Philosophie und Grundriss der Metaphysik; Zur Reform der Philosophie* (1858) and his *Menschenseele und Physiologie* (1855). Need for freedom in Catholic science and reform in philosophy and theology.

"Orthodoxy and Unitarianism." *Brownson's Quarterly Review* 25 (July, 1863):256-89; "The Mysteries of Faith," *Works* 8:28-58. Review of Rev. Anthony Kohlmann's *Unitarianism* (1821); intelligible and supra-intelligible form one dialectical whole.

"Walworth's *Gentle Skeptic.*" *Brownson's Quarterly Review* 25 (July, 1863):312-41; "Science and the Sciences," *Works* 9:254-68; "Science and the Sciences," RyanA: 243-56. Review of Clarence Walworth's *The Gentile Skeptic* (1863). Role of science in teleological order; possession of revelation does not preclude scientific investigation.

"Stand by the Government " *Brownson's Quarterly Review* 25 (July, 1863):342-67. Review of John Baker's *The Rebellion* (1863) and Gerrit Smith's *Stand by the Government* (1863). Brownson's support for Smith's view that the Rebellion must be put down and the Union preserved with or without slavery, but slavery will be abolished.

"Are Catholics Pro-slavery and Disloyal?" *Brownson's Quarterly Review* 25 (July, 1863):367-79. Review of Theodore Tilton's *The Negro* (1863). Brownson is hostile to slavery but opposed to "negro equality." American Catholics, especially in New York City, are generally pro-slavery, though that position is contrary to church teachings.

"Catholics and the Anti-Draft Riots." *Brownson's Quarterly Review* 25 (October, 1863):385-420; *Works* 17:412-47. Blames clergy for not educating rioters and for failing to resist Southern rebellion; most blame, however, belongs to pro-slavery Democrats in New York City.

"New England Brahminism." *Brownson's Quarterly Review* 25 (October, 1863):421-48. The history of Puritan theology out of which emerged the nineteenth century New England Brahminical class of writers whose cravings are ultimately for Catholicism.

"Return of the Rebellious States." *Brownson's Quarterly Review* 25 (October, 1863):481-511; *Works* 17:448-77. On the conditions of peace and on the reconstitution of the seceding states in the federal government."

"Note from O. A. Brownson." *New York Times* (October 15, 1863): 4.

1864

*"Atheism." *The New American Cyclopedia: A Popular Dictionary of General Knowledge.* ed. Charles Dana and George Ripley. 16 Vols. NY: D. Appleton, 1864. 1: 265-66.

"Introduction to the National Series." *Brownson's Quarterly Review* 26 (January, 1864):1-12. Brownson announces that *Review* will no longer be a theological review, but only national and secular.

"The Federal Constitution." *Brownson's Quarterly Review* 26 (January, 1864):12-44; *Works* 17:478-509. Brownson calls for constitutional means for re-admitting states that seceded from the Union; on Brownson's theory of the origins of constitutions.

"*Vincenzo; or, Sunken Rocks.*" *Brownson's Quarterly Review* 26 (January, 1864):45-70. Review of John Ruffini's *Vincenzo; or, Sunken Rocks* (1863). On religious and political affairs in Italy, and Ruffini's anti-clericalism.

"Popular Corruption and Venality." *Brownson's Quarterly Review* 26 (January, 1864):70-85. Review of Daniel Dougherty's *The Peril of the Republic the Fault of the People* (1863). On the loss of virtue in the American public.

"The President's Message and Proclamation." *Brownson's Quarterly Review* 26 (January, 1864):85-112; *Works* 17:510-36. Review of *Third Annual Message of President Lincoln to both Houses of Congress* (December 9, 1863). On Lincoln's "unconstitutional" plan for reorganizing the seceding states.

"General Halleck's Report." *Brownson's Quarterly Review* 26 (January, 1864):112-21. Review of *The Official Report of the General-*

in-chief to the Secretary of War (1863). On military matters in the Civil War and in defense of General Henry Wager Halleck's decisions.

"The Giobertian Philosophy." Part I of II. *Brownson's Quarterly Review* 26 (April, 1864):129-66; see July, 1864; "Vincenzo Gioberti," *Works* 2:211-70; *Gems*: 98-106. Review of Gioberti's *Teorica del Sovranaturale* (1850). How Gioberti is separated from rationalists, spiritualists, and Jesuits; Gioberti's intuition is not the intuition of theologians.

"Stevens on Reconstruction." *Brownson's Quarterly Review* 26 (April, 1864):166-86. Review of Thaddeus Stevens's *Reconstruction* (1864). The seceded States are no longer States in the Union and therefore have no constitutional rights. Against the blunders of the Lincoln administration, and especially the policies of William H. Seward, Secretary of State.

"Abolition and Negro Equality." *Brownson's Quarterly Review* 26 (April, 1864):186-209; *Works* 17:537-60. Review of *Speech of Wendell Phillips, Esq., at the Annual Meeting of the Anti-Slavery Society* (1864). Blacks inferior, but against deportation since blacks died to save union.

"The Next President." *Brownson's Quarterly Review* 26 (April, 1864):210-23. Review of Samuel Clarke Pomeroy's *The Next Presidential Election* (1864). Lincoln is totally deficient in administrative talent and not the man to be re-elected if a War Democratic candidate is proposed for election.

"Reade's *Very Hard Cash*." *Brownson's Quarterly Review* 26 (April, 1864):223-37. Review of Charles Reade's *Very Hard Cash* (1864). Brownson's defense of his recent focus upon political philosophy.

"Military Matters and Men." *Brownson's Quarterly Review* 26 (April, 1864):237-52. Review of Frank Moore's *Rebellion Record* (1864). On General George McClellan's candidacy for the presidency, which Brownson opposed, and criticisms of his military maneuvers.

"Fremont and Cochrane—Speeches by Dr. O. A. Brownson." *New York Times* (June 28, 1864):4-5.

"Dr. Brownson's Speech at the Fremont Meeting." *New York Times* (June 29, 1864):4.

"Civil and Religious Freedom." *Brownson's Quarterly Review* 26 (July, 1864):257-91; *Works* 20:308-42; RyanA: 349-56. Review of Charles R. F. de Montalembert's "L'Église libre dans l'État libre,"

Le Correspondant (August and September, 1863). The clerical dream of the Middle Ages, which the Jesuits still maintain, must be abandoned in favor of Montalembert's assertion of the freedom of the state in temporals and the freedom of the church realized in the freedom of the citizen.

"Giobertian Philosophy." Part II of II. *Brownson's Quarterly Review* 26 (July, 1864):292-315; see April, 1864; "Vincenzo Gioberti," *Works* 2:211-76.

"Literature, Love, and Marriage." *Brownson's Quarterly Review* 26 (July, 1864):315-39; *Works* 19:493-516; *Gems*: 107-32; *Modern*: 493-516. Review of Bayard Taylor's *Hannah Thurston* (1864). On nature of American literature; lack of virility in American culture.

"Lincoln or Fremont?" *Brownson's Quarterly Review* 26 (July, 1864):339-70. On the Baltimore Convention's nomination of Lincoln for re-election and Brownson's opposition to it and his support for the Cleveland Convention's nomination of John C. Fremont.

"General Fitz John Porter." *Brownson's Quarterly Review* 26 (July, 1864):371-77. On the removal of General Porter from the army and Brownson's support for Porter's loyalty and abilities.

"Note from Dr. Orestes A. Brownson." *New York Times* (July 2, 1864): 4.

"Are the United States a Nation?" *Brownson's Quarterly Review* 26 (October, 1864):385-420; *Works* 17:560-94. Review of *The Federalist* (1864). Brownson wants to find middle ground between state sovereignty and consolidation of all authority in federal government.

"Mr. Lincoln and Congress." *Brownson's Quarterly Review* 26 (October, 1864):420-50. Review of a series of documents on President Lincoln's *Proclamation of the Reconstruction Bill of Congress* (1864). A severe criticism of Lincoln's character and abilities, and a recounting of his administrative blunders and unconstitutional acts with respect to reconstruction of the governments of the Southern States.

"Liberalism and Progress." *Brownson's Quarterly Review* 26 (October, 1864):450-70; *Works* 20:342-61; *Kirk*: 161-90. Review of General Croaker's unpublished manuscript "Tendencies of Modern Society." Brownson asserts need for social aristocracy as in South; defines his position between liberalism and obscurantism.

"Explanations to Catholics." *Brownson's Quarterly Review* 26 (October, 1864):470-89; *Works* 20:361-81. Brownson defends his Catholicism, especially against those Catholics who have attacked his article on "Civil and Religious Liberty" (July,1864), and some of the changes in his theological perspective over the last ten years.

"Chicago, Baltimore, and Cleveland." *Brownson's Quarterly Review* 26 (October, 1864):490-506. Brownson favors John C. Fremont for President; under no circumstances would he support Lincoln. On the policies of the political parties and their candidates nominated at the Chicago, Baltimore and Cleveland conventions.

"Seward's Speech at Auburn." *Brownson's Quarterly Review* 26 (October, 1864):506-12. Review of *Speech of the Hon. Wm. H. Seward* (1864). On successful military affairs, the constitutional abolition of slavery after the cessation of the war, and Lincoln's re-election.

"Lincoln or McClellan—Note from Dr. Orestes A. Brownson." *New York Times* (October 28,1864):5.

1865

The American Republic: Its Constitution, Tendencies, and Destiny. New York: P. O'Shea, 1865; *La republique americaine, par O. A. Brownson.* trans. le Comte de Lubersac. Paris: Amyot, 1870; *Works* 18:1-222; RyanA: 68-102; Ellis: 383-85. Brownson's religious-constitutional theory of government; political authority is derived by the collective people or society from God through natural law.

Catholicity and Naturalism. Boston: Patrick Donahoe, 1865. *Works* 8:339-59. Naturalism denies supernatural revelation; there is development, but it unfolds only what was "originally in germ."

"Saint Worship." *Ave Maria* 1 (October 21, 1865):352-55; (November 4, 1865):389-91; (December 2, 1865):451-53; (December 30, 1865):513-14; 2 (February 3, 1866):70-71; (February 10, 1866): 82-83; (February 17, 1866):101-03; (February 24, 1866):116-117; (March 10, 1866):146-48; (March 24, 1866):182-84; (March 31, 1866):198-99; (April 7, 1866):214-15; (April 14, 1866):235-36; (May 12, 1866):294-95; "Miracles of the Saints" (May 26, 1866): 328-29; (June 2, 1866):341-42; "Worship of Relics, Crucifixes, etc." (September 22, 1866):593-95; (October 6, 1866):627-29; "Saint Worship" (October 20, 1866):657-58; *Works* 8:117-85; RyanT: 3-90. Nature of prayer; cult of the saints in Catholic piety based on doctrines of creation and redemption.

1866

"Moral and Social Influence of Devotion to Mary." *Ave Maria* 2 (June 16, 1866):377-80; (June 23, 1866):385-88; *Works* 8:86-104. Devotion to Mary promotes in the devotees the virtues (especially humility, maternity, and virginity or chastity) which they love, honor, and venerate in her, and has influenced Christian society as well as individuals.

"Herbert Spencer's Biology." *Catholic World* 3 (June, 1866):425-27. Review of Spencer's *The Principles of Biology* (1866), which is a manifestation of positivism and naturalism.

"Use and Abuse of Reading." *Catholic World* 3 (July, 1866): 463-73; *Works* 19:517-32; *Modern*: 517-32. On abuse of literature in depicting with delight the vices of nature; appeal to Catholic consciences to demand good books and journals.

"Independence of the Church." *Catholic World* 4 (October, 1866):51-64; *Works* 13:86-107. On the *Syllabus of Errors*; Catholicity and what it is not.

"Recent Events in Europe." *Catholic World* 4 (November, 1866):217-26; *Works* 18:466-81. On power plays in European politics.

"Dr. O. A. Brownson on the Suffrage Question and Reconstruction. Letter to the Editor." *New York Times* (November, 25, 1866):1.

"Reason and Religion." *Ave Maria* 2 (December 1, 1866):756-58; (December 15, 1866):788-90; 3 (January 5, 1867):4-6; (January 19, 1867):38-9; *Works* 8:324-39. On central Protestant principle of total depravity; Catholic Church on original sin.

1867

"Charity and Philanthropy." *Catholic World* 4 (January, 1867):434-46; *Works* 14:428-47. Sentimental culture has replaced moral; philanthropy separated from charity and love of God.

"Hopeful Tendencies." *New York Tablet* 10 (January 5, 1867):8. On religious movements toward Catholic unity, especially on the ritualistic movement in Anglican Church which is an "earnest desire for Catholic worship."

"The Future of Catholicity." *New York Tablet* 10 (January 5, 1867):8-9. On the loss of state support for Catholicism in Europe and the future benefits of separation. On the Second Plenary Council of Baltimore, one sign of growth in a free state.

"The Eastern Question." *New York Tablet* 10 (January 12, 1867):8. On the settlement of issues relating to the Christian population in Turkish empire and the roles of Western states in the settlement of the issues."

"The French Episcopate and the Roman Question." *New York Tablet* 10 (January 12, 1867):9. On conversion of French bishops to ultramontanism because of the spoilation of the Estates of the Church.

"Retraction." *New York Tablet* 10 (January 12, 1867):9. On a Mr. Riedel's reasons for retracting his conversion to Catholicism and his return to the Reformed tradition.

"Impeachment of the President." *New York Tablet* 10 (January 19, 1867):8. On insufficient grounds for impeachment of President Andrew Johnson.

"Church Union." *New York Tablet* 10 (January 19, 1867):9. On the newly established Evangelical journal *Church Union* (Brooklyn), its desire for reunion of the Churches, and Brownson's doctrine of life by communion.

"Theories of the Constitution." *New York Tablet* 10 (January 26, 1867):8. On five interpretations of American Constitution in the midst of Reconstruction problems.

"Church Union." *New York Tablet* 10 (January 26,1867):9. Defense of Brownson's views of ecclesiastical union based on Catholic principles.

"Bigotry and Superstition." *New York Tablet* 10 (January 26, 1867):9. A definition of the two terms.

"A Very Inconsistent *Observer.*" *New York Tablet* 10 (January 26, 1867):8. On the New York *Observer's* charges against the dogma of infallibility.

"The Church and Monarchy." *Catholic World* 4 (February, 1867):627-39; *Works* 13:107-27. On *Syllabus of Errors*; American republic founded by providence not men.

"The Altar and the Pulpit." *New York Tablet* (February 2, 1867):9. The *Liberal Christian* places pulpit above the altar; altar belongs to a past age.

"Baron Ricasoli and the Bishops." *New York Tablet* 10 (February 2, 1867):8. Absolute supremacy of the state under the guise of separation of Church and state in Italy; difference from American understanding of separation.

"Mary Mother of God." *Ave Maria* 3 (February 8, 1867):81-83.
Chalcedonian formula explained; Protestant view of Incarnation
is Nestorian.

"Congress and the President." *New York Tablet* 10 (February 9,
1867):8. Difference between president and congress on readmit-
ting Southern states into Union.

"Protection and Free Trade." *New York Tablet* 10 (February 9, 1867):9.
United States protective tariffs as unconstitutional.

"The Protective Policy." *New York Tablet* 10 (February 16, 1867):8.
Protective policies protect only the rich business corporations and
monopolies; Brownson neither free trader nor protectionist.

"A Fair-Sided View of 'Liberal Christianity.'" *New York Tablet* 10 (February 16, 1867):8-9. On the recent modifications in New England Unitarianism and the openness of "liberal searchers."

"Congress and Protestant Worship." *New York Tablet* 10 (February
23, 1867):8. Congress's concern with prohibition of Protestant
worship in Rome.

"Poland and Venice." *New York Tablet* (February 23, 1867):8-9. On
the fall from national status.

"The Tariff and Internal Taxes." *New York Tablet* 10 (February 23,
1867):9. Tariffs only enrich the few and make underconsumption
the basic problem in political economy.

"Proprieties and Improprieties of Indignation." *New York Tablet* 10 (February 23, 1867):9. On prohibition of Protestant worship in Rome.

"Sanctity Seeks Obscurity." *Ave Maria* 3 (March 2, 1867):132-34;
Carey: 267-71. On John 18:36. Sanctity frequently appears in the
unpretentious.

"Protestant Worship in Rome." *New York Tablet* 10 (March 2, 1867):8.
On religious liberty and protection of temporal sovereignty.

"'God Help the Pope.'" *New York Tablet* 10 (March 2, 1867):8-9.
On the pope's rights of temporal sovereignty and the imminence
of his loss of power.

"Protestant Alarm." *New York Tablet* 10 (March 2, 1867):9. On the
growth of Catholicism in the United States.

"Reconstruction—Note from Rev. O. A. Brownson." *New York Times*
(March 7, 1867):2.

"The Pope and Inductive Philosophy." *New York Tablet* 10 (March 9,
1867):8. On the difference between an inductive method and an

inductive philosophy; pope has not condemned an inductive method but only hypotheses that go beyond observable facts.

"The Pope and Civilization." *New York Tablet* 10 (March 16, 1867):8. Against those who charge the pope with condemning social programs of modern civilization; he condemns the materialism of so-called social programs, not true social programs.

"The Military Government Law." *New York Tablet* 10 (March 16, 1867):9. On bill providing for better government of the unreconstructed Southern States.

"Protestantism and Freedom of Worship." *New York Tablet* 10 (March 23, 1867):8. On suppression of religious liberty in Protestant countries.

"The New York 'Observer' and the Inquisition." *New York Tablet* 10 (March 30, 1867):8. Rome's prohibition of public worship for Protestants.

"The New York 'Herald' and the Pope." *New York Tablet* 10 (March 30, 1867):8. On James Gordon Bennett's assertion that Catholics everywhere are willing to abolish the temporal authority of the pope.

"Public Schools and the 'Nation.'" *New York Tablet* 10 (March 30, 1867):8-9. Public schools as dangerous to Catholic faith and morals; Catholic schools support intelligence, religion and country.

"The 'Church Union.'" *New York Tablet* 10 (March 30, 1867):9. Evangelical understanding of union of churches is devoid of doctrinal content.

"Union of Church and State." *Catholic World* 5 (April, 1867):1-14; *Works* 13:127-45. Separation of church and state brought about by conscience.

"Rev. Dr. Brann and St. Patrick's Day in Elizabeth, N. J." *New York Tablet* 10 (March 30, 1867):9. On Henry Brann's support for Irish patriots.

"Protestant Respect for the Rights of Catholics." *New York Tablet* 10 (April 6, 1867):8. On the rights of poor Catholic parents to provide religious education for their children.

"The 'Christian Intelligencer' Seeking Light." *New York Tablet* 10 (April 6, 1867):9. On Rome's right to protect a national religion; but state has no inherent rights over religion.

"Papal Infallibility." *New York Tablet* 10 (April 13, 1867):8. Papal infallibility not invoked in the Roman issue of religious liberty; pope not infallible as a temporal sovereign.

"The N. Y. Herald on Progress." *New York Tablet* 10 (April 13, 1867):8-9. Against the English custom of distributing property as a means of progress and reform because it violates the natural right to property.

"The N. Y. Observer—Under a Mistake." *New York Tablet* 10 (April 20, 1867):8-9. On Rev. G. H. Doane's pamphlet, *Exclusion of Protestant Worship from the City of Rome* (1867). Doane speaks of the rights of the Church in prohibiting worship; Brownson on the rights of Roman civil government.

"The Liberal Christian." *New York Tablet* 10 (April 20, 1867):9. Liberal Christian defined as one who accounts doctrine as nothing, but emphasizes common behavior and religious sentiment.

"Catholicity and Presbyterianism." *New York Tablet* 10 (April 27, 1867):8. Against the charge that Catholicism is a persecuting religion. Catholic Church is intolerant in theological order, but not in civil order.

"Roman Intolerance." *New York Tablet* 10 (April 27, 1867):8-9. Every state is sovereign under the law of God within its own dominions. State has no competence in spiritual matters—must protect liberty.

"An Old Quarrel." *Catholic World* 5 (May, 1867):145-59; *Works* 2:284-306. On nominalist-realist debates. Brownson tries to show that Anselm and Aquinas were not opposed to one another on knowledge of God; both accept the *a priori* foundation for our knowledge of perfect being.

"What is Protestantism?" *New York Tablet* 10 (May 4, 1867):8. Although Protestants hold many things in common with Catholic Church the distinctive essence of Protestantism is found in private interpretation.

"Papal Infallibility." *New York Tablet* 10 (May 4, 1867):8. Papal infallibility as a theological opinion, not an article of faith.

"The Christian Intelligencer." *New York Tablet* 10 (May 4, 1867):8-9. Religious liberty and prohibiting worship.

"Affairs Abroad." *New York Tablet* 10 (May 11, 1867):8. On changes in French foreign policy.

"Affairs at Home." *New York Tablet* 10 (May 11, 1867):8. On the Military Reconstruction Law and "negro suffrage."

"American Christian Review." *New York Tablet* 10 (May 18, 1867):8. Religious liberty.

"Christian Unity." *New York Tablet* 10 (May 18, 1867):8-9. Comments on Thomas S. Preston's *Lectures on Christian Unity* (1867). Christian unity is part of spiritual constitution of the Church and not the result of human engineering.

"Ritualism." *New York Tablet* 10 (May 18, 1867):9. A providential sign of a Protestant movement toward Catholicism in the reassertion of mediated grace.

"New York Observer on infallibility." *New York Tablet* 10 (May 25, 1867):9. Prohibition of Protestant worship in Rome.

"Victor Cousin and his Philosophy." *Catholic World* 5 (June, 1867):332-47; *Works* 2:307-29. On occasion of Cousin's death; for Cousin method over principle, reflection over intuition.

"Release of Jeff. Davis." *New York Tablet* 11 (June 1, 1867):8. On putting an end to punishing Southern leaders of "the rebellion."

"Private Judgment." *New York Tablet* 11 (June 1, 1867):8. Catholic as well as Protestant senses of private interpretation and interior illumination.

"Protestant Proselytism." *New York Tablet* 11 (June 1, 1867):8-9. On Protestant attempts to separate Catholic children from the Catholic faith.

"Affairs Abroad." *New York Tablet* 11 (June 15, 1867):8. On Victor Emmanuel and the pope; the Eastern Question, France, Prussia and Mexico.

"Social Despotism." *New York Tablet* 11 (June 15,1867):9. On individual freedom and the proper subjects of governmental action—against puritanical legislation.

"Extremes Meet." *New York Tablet* 11 (June 15, 1867):9. On suffrage as a trust, not an inalienable right.

"Universal Suffrage." *New York Tablet* 11 (June 22, 1867):8. On relationship between suffrage and the power of governing. Against suffrage as a natural right.

"The Church and the Bible." *New York Tablet* 11 (June 29, 1867):5. On the Protestant and Catholic understanding of the relationship of faith and authority.

"Catholic Congresses." *New York Tablet* 11 (June 29, 1867):8-9. On Belgian and German Catholic Congresses since 1848. Call for similar congresses in the United States.

"Guettée's Papacy Schismatic." Part I of II. *Catholic World* 5 (July, 1867):463-79; *Works* 8:474-500; see August, 1867. Review of Abbé

René François Wladimir Guettée's *The Papacy* (1867). Brownson objects to the ex-Catholic's attacks upon the papal claims to primacy and sovereignty, his conversion to Orthodoxy, and his view that the papacy was the cause of the East-West schism.

"Female Suffrage." *New York Tablet* 11 (July 6, 1867):8. Opposed on grounds that it is part of a movement to be freed from the restraints of all law.

"Hungering After the Truth." *New York Tablet* 11 (July 6, 1867):9. On Unitarian attempts to spread the truth by minimizing doctrine.

"Church Union." *New York Tablet* 11 (July 6, 1867):9. On separating the *Tablet* from the Evangelical movement toward Christian unity.

"Something More about Female Suffrage." *New York Tablet* 11 (July 13, 1867):8. On female suffrage which was opposed by the New York state constitutional convention.

"Hopeful Symptoms." *New York Tablet* 11 (July 20, 1867):8. Horace Greeley opposes female suffrage. Brownson's opposition to Negro suffrage.

"Homage to Catholicity." *New York Tablet* 11 (July 20, 1867):8-9. On theological developments among Universalists and the *Christian Intelligencer*'s Catholic arguments against Universalists' positions.

"The *Herald*'s Roman Correspondent." *New York Tablet* 11 (July 27, 1867):9. Announces a new council to be convoked to discuss whether pope personally infallible and to review the Council of Trent.

"Mazzini the Prophet." *New York Tablet* 11 (July 27, 1867):8. On Joseph Mazzini's new religion of progress. Opposes Mazzini's doctrine of progress by reasserting Brownson's doctrine of life by communion.

"The Methodist Speaks Truth." *New York Tablet* 11 (July 27, 1867):9. Sects are impediments in the way of truth.

"Guettée's Papacy Schismatic." Part II of II. *Catholic World*: 5 (August, 1867):576-93; see July, 1867; *Works* 8:474-500.

"'The Coming Crisis.'" *New York Tablet* 11 (August 3, 1867):8. On ritualism in the Protestant Episcopal Church and the tendency toward Catholic truth.

"The Age We Live In." *New York Tablet* 11 (August 10, 1867):8. Against the materialism of the age.

"An Important Need." *New York Tablet* 11 (August 10, 1867):8. The *Lutheran Observer* calls for a "living ministry and a living church."

"Catholic and Protestant Controversy." *New York Tablet* 11 (August 17, 1867):8. Differences between Catholics and Protestants is a difference between faith and opinion.

"The Churchman." *New York Tablet* 11 (August 24, 1867):8. On Anglican separation from the Catholic Church and the meaning of excommunication.

"The Western Record." *New York Tablet* 11 (August 24, 1867):9. On Catholic hostility to religious liberty.

"Marriage and Divorce." *New York Tablet* 11 (August 31, 1867):8. Protestant alarm at the increase and ease of divorce.

"France and the Italian Revolution." *New York Tablet* 11 (August 31, 1867):8. Protest French army in Rome.

"The Encyclical of 1864." *New York Tablet* 11 (August 31, 1867):9. An encyclical most needed by the circumstances of the age.

"The *Catholic World* and the New Englander." *New York Tablet* 11 (August 31, 1867):9. Against Congregationalist Leonard Bacon.

"Garibaldi and Rome." *New York Tablet* 11 (August 31, 1867):9. Garibaldi's preparation to descend upon Rome.

"Rome or Reason." *Catholic World* 5 (September, 1867):721-37; *Works* 3:298-314. Review of Francis Parkman's *The Jesuits in North America in the Seventeenth Century* (1867); Oliver Wendell Holmes's, *The Professor at the Breakfast Table* (1866); and "Rationalism and Catholicism," *Cincinnati Inquirer* (May 26, 1867). On essential Catholic synthesis; God's light is in both the church's authority and the self.

"Devotion to Mary." *Ave Maria* 3 (September 7, 1867):564-66. Premature to promote devotion to Mary among Protestants because they still hold Nestorian view of Incarnation.

"The Adroit Use of Words." *New York Tablet* 11 (September 7, 1867):8. On the charge of church's despotism.

"The Name Catholic." *New York Tablet* 11 (September 7, 1867):8-9. On Anglican use of the name "Catholic."

"Protestant Germany." *New York Tablet* 11 (September 14, 1867):9. Inability of Protestantism to battle the materialism of the age.

"The President, Sheridan, and Sickles." *New York Tablet* 11 (September 14, 1867):9. On false policies of Reconstruction.

"'Catholic and Protestant.'" *New York Tablet* 11 (September 14, 1867):9. On Anglican use of "Catholic."

"Dr. Bellows and Superstition." *New York Tablet* 11 (September 21, 1867):8. On Henry Bellows's assertion that Catholic Church is superstitious.

"The Church Journal." *New York Tablet* 11 (September 21, 1867):8-9. On Edmund S. Ffoulke's view of union of Greek, Roman and Anglican churches.

"The President's Proclamation." *New York Tablet* 11 (September 21, 1867):9. President Andrew Johnson's declaration of general amnesty to all engaged in the "rebellion."

"The Probable Alliance Between France and Austria." *New York Tablet* 11 (September 28, 1867):8. Such an alliance connected to Catholic spirit would prevent revolutionary upheavals.

"Who are the Enlightened?" *New York Tablet* 11 (September 28, 1867):8. On self-conceited enlightenment.

"Probable Alliance." *New York Tablet* 11 (September 28, 1967):8. Hopeful sign of union of Catholic powers.

"Public Grants to Catholic Institutions." *New York Tablet* 11 (September 28, 1867):9. Justice of public grants to Catholic social institutions.

"Rome and the World." *Catholic World* 6 (October, 1867):1-19. Antagonism between Rome and world, not Rome and reason; Catholicism as the atonement of reason and revelation, nature and grace.

"The Churchman's Reply." *New York Tablet* 11 (October 5, 1867):8. On the baptisms of Greeks and Anglicans, and excommunication.

"The Arrest of Garibaldi." *New York Tablet* 11 (October 5, 1867):9. Victor Emmanuel's assent.

"Protestant Rome." *New York Tablet* 11 (October 5, 1867):9. On Geneva and John Calvin.

"Protestant Churchmen." *New York Tablet* 11 (October 12, 1867):8. On "hopeless task" of ritualists Catholicizing Anglicanism.

"Heresies and Infidelity." *New York Tablet* 11 (October 12, 1867):9. Tendency of age is toward rationalism.

"Radical Reconstruction." *New York Tablet* 11 (October 19, 1867):8. Restoration of Southern states as counterpoise to Northern humanitarian or socialist democracy (i.e., radical reconstruction).

"'Decline of Popery.'" *New York Tablet* 11 (October 19, 1867):9. No evidence of decline despite loss of European governmental patronage of the Church.

"Rome and the Baptized." *New York Tablet* 11 (October 26, 1867):8. On baptisms of Anglicans and Greeks.

"The Cartesian Doubt." *Catholic World* 6 (November, 1867):234-51; *Works* 2:358-82. Review of "Science and God," *The Churchman* (August 31, 1867). On methods and principles; God as first principle in being and knowing, and the need for revelation and tradition.

"Heresy and the Incarnation." *Ave Maria* 3 (November 2, 1867):690-92; (November 23, 1867):742-44; (December 21, 1867):804-06; 4 (February 29, 1868):133-35; (March 14, 1868):197-99; (April 25, 1868):257-59; *Works* 8:186-219. On the living tradition; church as continuation of Incarnation.

"The Lambeth Conference." *New York Tablet* 11 (November 2, 1867):8. On Anglican episcopal attempts to affirm ritualism.

"Rome and Italy." *New York Tablet* 11 (November 2, 1867):9. Kingdom of Italy's desire to suppress temporal sovereignty of the pope.

"Romanism in America." *New York Tablet* 11 (November 2, 1867):9. Defense of "Rome and the World" (see *Catholic World* October, 1867) and attempts to convert United States to Catholicism.

"Reconstruction.—Negro Suffrage." *New York Tablet* 11 (November 9, 1867):8. Brownson's opposition to radical reconstruction and negro suffrage based on his sense of the common good, not on his sympathy for the South.

"Garibaldi and Protestantism." *New York Tablet* 11 (November 9, 1867):8. Protestant sympathy for Garibaldi.

"The Church and the World." *New York Tablet* 11 (November 9, 1867):8-9. On the necessary distinction between the two.

"Church Union." *New York Tablet* 11 (November 16, 1867):8. On corporate and federated church union among Protestants.

"The Peace Congress at Geneva." *New York Tablet* 11 (November 16, 1867):9. Peace without religious base is futile.

"The Late Elections." *New York Tablet* 11 (November 23, 1867):8. State elections revealed a distaste for radical reconstruction policies.

"Rome and the Revolution." *New York Tablet* 11 (November 23, 1867):9. On the *New York Tribune*'s opposition to papal sovereignty.

"Unitarianism." *New York Tablet* 11 (November 23, 1867):9. On Henry Bellows's Unitarian solution for peace—a form of rationalism.

"Decline of Protestantism." *New York Tablet* 11 (November 30, 1867):9. Need for a history of Protestantism and its decline.

"The White Man's Government." *New York Tablet* 11 (November 30, 1867):9. The sovereign people of the United States are "of the white race."

"Faith and the Sciences." *Catholic World* 6 (December, 1867):330-46; *Works* 9:268-91. Faith and science are independent and distinct orders yet not separated; error of science is in transcending the limits of the facts.

"The Church in Spain." *New York Tablet* 11 (December 7, 1867):8. On intolerance of Protestantism in Spain.

"The Temporal Power of the Papacy." *New York Tablet* 11 (December 7, 1867):9. Temporal power is only an "accident of history" and not essential to the survival of Catholicism.

"The Churchman." *New York Tablet* 11 (December 7, 1867):9. On the Cartesian doubt and Anglican principles.

"The President's Message." *New York Tablet* 11 (December 14, 1867):8. On the status of the Southern states.

"'The Temporal Power.'" *New York Tablet* 11 (December 14, 1867):8-9. *New York Tribune* argues that Rome belongs to the Italian people and not to the pope.

"To the Editor of the New York Tablet." *New York Tablet* 11 (December 14, 1867):9. *Tablet* not a partisan political paper.

"The Pope and Anti-Christ." *New York Tablet* 11 (December 21, 1867):8. Protestant charges of anti-Christ, although still present, are declining in vehemence.

"The Right of Revolution." *New York Tablet* 11 (December 21, 1867):8-9. The abuse of the term "right."

"Garibaldi King Yet." *New York Tablet* 11 (December 21, 1867):9. Protestant sympathy with European revolutionaries.

"The New York Observer on the Confessional." *New York Tablet* 11 (December 28, 1867):8. Protestant rejection of confession as spiritual despotism. Review of the novel *The Confession*.

"The Defeat of Garibaldi." *New York Tablet* 11 (December 28, 1867) 8-9. On the victory of Mentana when Roman and French army expelled Garibaldians from papal territory.

"Politics and the Religious Press." *New York Tablet* 11 (December 28, 1867):9. Abuse of the term "politics." Necessity of Catholic education in political theory and principles.

1868

"Nature and Grace." *Catholic World* 6 (January, 1868):509-27; *Works* 3:350-75; Carey: 283-306. There is no antagonism between nature and grace; they are distinct parts of one dialectical whole.

"Compulsory Education." *New York Tablet* 11 (January 4, 1868):8-9. On conditions that make compulsory education just.

"The Evangelicals and Ritualists." *New York Tablet* 11 (January 4, 1868):9. Internal Anglican quarrel.

"The European Conference." *New York Tablet* 11 (January 11, 1868):8. Napoleon, the European states, and the temporal sovereignty of the pope.

"Reconstruction." *New York Tablet* 11 (January 11, 1868):9. Restoring civil rights to all Southern states. Blunders of Federal Government.

"Political Ethics." *New York Tablet* 11 (January 11, 1868):9. Politicians losing sight of the promotion of common good as the end of government.

"Dr. Brownson in Boston." *New York Tablet* 11 (January 11, 1868):11. Reprint from *Boston Pilot* of Brownson's Boston lecture on the "Catholic method of reform."

"Are States that Secede Still States in the Union?" *New York Tablet* 11 (January 18, 1868):8. Difference between President and Congress on status of Southern states.

"The Church Union Association." *New York Tablet* 11 (January 18, 1868):9. Anglican High Churchmen form association to promote church principles.

"What does the Episcopal Church Teach in Regard to the Blessed Virgin Mary?" *New York Tablet* 11 (January 25, 1868):8. Some Anglicans hold that Mary was not a virgin, while others defend it.

"Argyll's Reign of Law." *Catholic World* 6 (February, 1868):595-606; *Works* 3:375-91. Review of Duke of Argyll's *Reign of Law* (1867). Law is not "will enforcing itself with power" (Argyll); but rather "will directed by reason."

"Liberty and Liberalism." *New York Tablet* 11 (February 1, 1868):8. Catholic Church as teacher and guardian of principles on which all true liberty (not liberalism) is based.

"The President and Disenfranchisement." *New York Tablet* 11 (February 1, 1868):9. President Johnson's wrong-headed policy.

"The Supreme Court." *New York Tablet* 11 (February 1, 1868):9. On the Court's decision regarding unconstitutional acts of Congress.

"'Expectations.'" *New York Tablet* 11 (February 8, 1868):8. Majority in the United States will become Catholic if Catholics are true to their principles.

"Holy Catholic, or Protestant Episcopal." *New York Tablet* 11 (February 8, 1868):9. The Struggle between sacramentalism and evangelicalism in the Protestant Episcopal Church.

"Unity of the Church." *New York Tablet* 11 (February 15, 1868):8. Catholic unity in opposition to liberalism and in support of true religious liberty.

"Sovereignty of the People." *New York Tablet* 11 (February 15, 1868):9. Catholic sense of sovereignty of the people.

"Liberalism and Protestantism." *New York Tablet* 11 (February 15, 1868):9. Protestant affinity with elements of infidelity and liberalism.

"The New York Herald on 'Toleration.'" *New York Tablet* 11 (February 15, 1868):9. Universal toleration supported, except for American Catholics.

"Worship of Angels and Spiritism." *New York Tablet* 11 (February 22, 1868):8. On Isaac Hecker's views of Catholicity and spiritism.

"'Perdition Literature.'" *New York Tablet* 11 (February 22, 1868):8-9. On relationship of literature to Christianity.

"Congress and the Roman Mission." *New York Tablet* 11 (February 29, 1868):8. Brownson never favored the Roman mission to the United States, but rejects its discontinuance on the grounds articulated by members of Congress because those grounds are insulting to Catholics.

"The Church and Her Attributes." *Catholic World* 6 (March, 1868):788-803; *Works* 8:552-73. On the meaning of the unity, sacramentality, holiness, visibility, indefectibility, authority, infallibility, catholicity, and apostolicity of the church.

"Impeachment of the President." *New York Tablet* 11 (March 7, 1868):8. Explains constitutional grounds for impeachment; was not in favor of impeachment voted on by Congress.

"'The Good City of Newark in Danger.'" *New York Tablet* 11 (March 7, 1868):8-9. Catholics of Newark seeking public funds for their school.

"The Church Review." *New York Tablet* 11 (March 7, 1868):9. On Brownson and Victor Cousin.

"Expectations Deceived." *New York Tablet* 11 (March 14, 1868):8. On division between Catholic and Protestant expectations of decline.

"Ignorance and Superstition." *New York Tablet* 11 (March 14, 1868):9. Charges against Catholicism.

"'What Can Rome Teach Us?'" *New York Tablet* 11 (March 21, 1868):8; see March 28, 1868. The Chicago Congregationalist *The Advance* outlines Catholic principles like the "unity and historic continuity of the Church" that Protestants need to reconsider.

"Education of Daughters." *New York Tablet* 11 (March 21, 1868):9. The French ministry of Public Instruction, opposed by Bishop Felix Dupanloup and the pope, has tried to secularize the education of young women.

"Calvin and Calvinism." *New York Tablet* 11 (March 21, 1868):9. Calvinism, in its evangelical and Methodist forms, though not as avid as in the days of Calvin, is very much alive.

"Catholicity and Rationalism." *New York Tablet* 11 (March 21, 1868):9. Objections to the assertion that both Catholicity and rationalism are basically consistent.

"The Progressive Age." *New York Tablet* 11 March 28, 1868):8-9. The meaning of progress.

"'What Can Rome Teach Us?'" *New York Tablet* 11 (March 28, 1868):9; see March 21, 1868. Catholic works and institutions of charity can teach Protestantism something.

"The Church Review and Victor Cousin." *Catholic World* 7 (April, 1868):95-113; *Works*, 2:330-57. Review of "O. A. Brownson as a Philosopher," *American Church Quarterly Review* (January, 1868). Refutation of charges leveled against Brownson's views on intuition and reflection.

"The Test of Democracy." *New York Tablet* 11 (April 4, 1868):8; see April 11, 1868. The real test of democracy is whether it can sustain the family and domestic virtues.

"Church Life." *New York Tablet* 11 (April 4, 1868):9. Liberal Christianity does not produce vital church life.

"The Union of Sects." *New York Tablet* 11 (April 4, 1868):9. Attempts to unite various Presbyterian sects.

"Democracy and the Church." *New York Tablet* 11 (April 11, 1868):8; see April 4, 18, 1868. Only the support of the Catholic Church can enable democracy to become a social success.

"How Protestantism Lives." *New York Tablet* 11 (April 11, 1868):8-9. On the historic evil and lies of Protestantism.

"The Christian Priesthood." *New York Tablet* 11 (April 11, 1868):9. Priesthood of all believers.

"How the Church Saves Society." *New York Tablet* 11 (April 18, 1868):8. Immigrant Catholics should Americanize, but they can contribute to the country only by resisting popular tendencies and supporting the virtues the church upholds.

"The Irish Church Establishment." *New York Tablet* 11 (April 18, 1868):8-9. On probable doom of Anglican Church establishment in Ireland.

"The Atlantic Monthly." *New York Tablet* 11 (April 18, 1868):9. Favorable reception of article on "Our Roman Catholic Brethren."

"The Irish Church Establishment." *New York Tablet* 11 (April 18, 1868):8. On English policy against the Irish.

"Is It Honest?" *New York Tablet* 11 (April 25, 1868):9. The honesty of charges against Catholicism questioned.

"Professor Draper's Books." *Catholic World* 7 (May, 1868):155-74; *Works* 9:292-318. Review of J. W. Draper's *Human Physiology* (1856); *History of the Intellectual Development of Europe* (1867); *History of the American Civil War* (1867). Philosophy not freed from ideal order; body not independent of soul.

"Is it Honest?" *Catholic World* 7 (May, 1868):239-55; Works 8:299-323. Review of the Rev. L. W. Bacon in *Brooklyn Times* (1868). On the honesty of Protestant attacks upon Catholics.

"'The Revolution.'" *New York Tablet* 11 (May 2,1868):8. On Susan B. Anthony's journal and the women's rights movement.

"'Le Correspondant.'" *New York Tablet* 11 (May 9, 1868):8. Describes French Catholic movement for a free church in a free society.

"The '*Catholic World*' May 1868." *New York Tablet* 11 (May 16, 1868):8. General praise for journal, with specific criticisms of its recent article on Tennyson.

"Sectarian Schools." *New York Tablet* 11 (May 23, 1868):8. On public grants of money to Catholic schools.

"The Pope and his Defenders," *New York Tablet* 11 (May 23, 1868):8-9. Criticisms of Italian revolutionaries.

"Alliance of Religion with Politics." *New York Tablet* 12 (May 30, 1868):8. On independence and self-sufficiency of the church.

"Protestant Mission and the Anniversaries." *New York Tablet* 12 (May 30, 1868):8. Comments on anniversary celebration of various Protestant missionary, Bible, and tract societies.

"The Church and Liberty." *New York Tablet* 12 (June 6, 1868):8. On Protestant charges of Catholic hostility to religious liberty.

"The Church and the Republic." *New York Tablet* 12 (June 13, 1868):8-9. On Isaac Hecker's Detroit lecture on the harmony of Catholicity with republican government.

"Ireland and Austria." *New York Tablet* 12 (June 20, 1868):8. On Count Montalembert and the separation of church and state.

"Materialism." *New York Tablet* 12 (June 20, 1868):8-9. Materialism in the medical profession.

"The Papacy." *Ave Maria* 4 (June 27, 1868):401-03. See "Guettée's Papacy Schismatic," *Catholic World* (July and August, 1867). Brownson responds to the charges in the *Catholic Mirror* (Baltimore) that he misrepresented Catholic teachings on the papacy and the procession of the Holy Spirit in the conflict with Greek Orthodoxy. The Greeks are not formally heretical on either position.

"The N. Y. Observer Outraged." *New York Tablet* 12 (June 27, 1868):8. Protestant protests of processions of New York German Catholics.

"Grasping at Power." *New York Tablet* 12 (July 4, 1868):8. On Protestant charge that Catholics want to control the country.

"Rome and Liberty." *New York Tablet* 12 (July 11, 1868):8. The civil administration of Rome has nothing to do with Catholic doctrine.

"Dr. McMullen and the Methodists." *New York Tablet* 12 (July 18, 1868):8. Chicago Methodists' labor against Catholic progress.

"Father Hecker's Lecture." *New York Tablet* 12 (July 18, 1868):8-9. On Hecker's lecture "Why am I a Catholic?"

"Problems of the Age." *New York Tablet* 12 (July 25, 1868):8; see August, 1868. Review of Augustine Hewit's *Problems of the Age* (1868).

"The Protestant Churchman on Papal Bulls, and Other Matters." *New York Tablet* 12 (August, 1, 1868):8. On the spiritual despotism of the papacy in reference to the new laws in Austria.

"'The Most Dangerous Enemy.'" *New York Tablet* 12 (August 1, 1868):9. Catholic Church dangerous to civil liberty.

"Church Property." *New York Tablet* 12 (August 1, 1868):9. Purposes of Church property and Anglican disestablishment in Ireland.

"Problems of the Age—Second Article." *New York Tablet* 12 (August 1, 1868):10; see July 25, 1868.

"Union and Disunion." *New York Tablet* 12 (August 8, 1868):8. On Anglican intercommunion with Eastern Orthodox Churches.

"The Methodists in a Fright." *New York Tablet* 12 (August 8, 1868):8-9. Methodists' charges against Catholic practices and political principles.

"Ecumenical Council." *New York Tablet* 12 (August 15, 1868):8. Suggests that Vatican Council may deal with issues of naturalism and rationalism in contemporary society, infallilibilty of the church, and union with Eastern churches.

"The Non-Catholic Press on Austria." *New York Tablet* 12 (August 15, 1868):8. The press's delight in the de-Catholicizing of Austria.

"The 'Churchman' on 'Romanism.'" *New York Tablet* 12 (August 15, 1868):9. On battles in Anglican Church.

"Infallibility." *New York Tablet* 12 (August 22, 1868):8. On the conflict between William G. Ward and Henry Ignatius Dudley Ryder on the infallibility of papal writings.

"The New York 'Observer' on Progress." *New York Tablet* 12 (August 22, 1868):9. On idolatrous worship of Mary among Catholics and their opposition to all progress.

"The Pope and Catholic Princes." *New York Tablet* 12 (August 29, 1868):8. Exclusion of ten princes from the Vatican Council.

"Romanism and Free Speech." *New York Tablet* 12 (August 29, 1868):8. On Catholics who were disciplined for differing with the church.

"The Methodists Have Made a Discovery." *New York Tablet* 12 (August 29, 1868):8-9. Methodists suggest love as a method for conquering and converting Catholics.

"The Rights of the Church." *New York Tablet* 12 (September 5, 1868):8; see "Political Conspiracy," September 12, 1868. Differences between Protestant and Catholic senses of religious liberty.

"The Church and Politics." *New York Tablet* 12 (September 12, 1868):8; see September 5, 1868. Self-sufficiency and independence of the Church.

"Political Conspiracy." *New York Tablet* 12 (September 12, 1868):8-9; see "Rights of the Church," September 5, 1868.

"The Churchman on Liberalism." *New York Tablet* 12 (September 19, 1868):8. On theological liberalism.

"Ritualists not Catholics." *New York Tablet* 12 (September 19, 1868):8. Protestant *Churchman* fears that ritualists are heading Rome-ward.

"'Religious Tyranny!'" *New York Tablet* 12 (October 3, 1868):8. On the pope's protest against religious intolerance in Austria.

"The 'Christian Intelligencer's' Reply to the 'Tablet.'" *New York Tablet* 12 (October 3, 1868):9. On *Tablet*'s misrepresentation of Protestant understanding of religious liberty.

"The Chicago 'Evening Post.'" *New York Tablet* 12 (October 10, 1868):8. *Post* defends itself against the charge that it is a Know-Nothing journal.

"Progress of Catholicity." *New York Tablet* 12 (October 10, 1868):9. Progress due primarily to immigration.

"Liberalizing Catholicity." *New York Tablet* 12 (October 10, 1868):9. Liberty, as understood by the age, cannot be harmonized with Catholicism.

"Uncompromising Catholicity." *New York Tablet* 12 (October 10, 1868):9. Against Catholic latitudinarianism.

"Revolution in Spain." *New York Tablet* 12 (October 17, 1868):8. History of forces leading to revolt against Queen Isabella.

"What Next?" *New York Tablet* 12 (October 17, 1868):8-9. Development of Anglican Benedictine monastic house for women.

"Education without Religion." *New York Tablet* 12 (October 24, 1868):8. Public education increasingly supports secularism or sectarianism.

"Infallibility of the Church." *New York Tablet* 12 (October 24, 1868):8-9. Necessity of infallibility for preservation of Christian truth.

"Protestantism a Failure." *New York Tablet* 12 (October 31, 1868):8. Report of lecture by Episcopalian F. C. Ewer.

"The Spanish Patriots and the Religious Orders." *New York Tablet* 12 (October 31, 1868):9. The Spanish Revolution's abolition of religious orders and confiscation of ecclesiastical properties.

"Popery at Work." *New York Tablet* 12 (November 7, 1868):8. Summary of charges against Catholics.

"More Religious Liberty." *New York Tablet* 12 (November 14, 1868):9. Revolution in Spain and liberalism.

"The Recent Elections." *New York Tablet* 12 (November 21, 1868):8-9. *Tablet* is not politically partisan, though it repeatedly supports sound political principles.

"The Bible and Catholics." *New York Tablet* 12 (November 28, 1868):9. Catholics respect Bible as Word of God, but not sole rule of faith.

"Godless Education " *New York Tablet* 12 (December 5, 1868):8. Support for denominational schools.

"Religious Liberty in Austria." *New York Tablet* 12 December 5, 1868):8. Liberalism the goal of rebellion in Austria.

"Protestantism in Spain." *New York Tablet* 12 (December 19, 1868):8. *Tablet's* opposition to Spanish revolution based on rejection of the secularism that is behind it and not based, as some charge, on fear of the reprisal of Protestantism.

"The Spanish Revolution." *New York Tablet* 12 (December 19, 1868):9. On French liberal Catholic support for the Revolution.

1869

"Protestantism a Failure." *Catholic World* 8 (January, 1869):503-21. Review of F. C. Ewer's "Failure of Protestantism, and Catholicism the Remedy," reprinted in *New York Times* (November 23, 1868):8, and New York *World* (November 16, 1868). Criticisms of Ewer's view that Catholicism is the unity of belief and practice of the Roman, Anglican, and Greek churches.

"The 'Churchman' and Father Weninger." *New York Tablet* 12 (January 2, 1869):8-9. The Episcopalian *Churchman's* refutation of F. X. Weninger's *The Apostolic and Infallible Authority of the Pope when Teaching the Faithful* (1868). Tradition must be the rule of interpretation when examining historical evidence on papal authority.

"Rossini, Havin, and Berreyer." *New York Tablet* 12 (January 2, 1869):9. On the deaths of three great Europeans.

"The Eastern Question." *New York Tablet* 12 (January 9, 1869):8. Scandal of European powers' failures to free Greek Christians from Turkish rule.

"Religious Liberty." *New York Tablet* 12 (January 9, 1869):8-9. United States the only country in the world where there is true and full religious liberty despite the limits in some states. That liberty comes from divine providence.

"Protestant Alarm." *New York Tablet* 12 (January 9, 1869):9. Conversions of Protestants in United States will not come about soon; Catholic efforts should be directed to conversion and religious education of the Catholic people.

"Who are Protestants?" *New York Tablet* 12 (January 9, 1869):12. Origin and meaning of "Protestant."

"Marriage and Divorce." *New York Tablet* 12 (January 23, 1869):8. Increase in divorce; marriage as a sacrament the only remedy.

"New York Observer." *New York Tablet* 12 (January 23, 1869):8. Religious liberty.

"The Sectarian Press." *New York Tablet* 12 (January 23, 1869):9. On Dr. F. C. Ewer's assertion of "the failure of Protestantism."

"Porter's *Human Intellect.*" Part I of II. *Catholic World* 8 (February, 1869):671-86; see March, 1869; *Works* 2:383-427. Review of Noah Porter's *The Human Intellect* (1868). Ideal intuition made clear; against Coleridge and Transcendentalists' views of reason and understanding.

"The Churchman." *New York Tablet* 12 (February 6, 1869):8. Relation of infallibility and reason.

"Republicanism in Spain." *New York Tablet* 12 (February 6, 1869):8. Revolutionary republicanism in Spain as in other European countries aims at suppression of the church.

"Dr. Ewer and his Opponents." *New York Tablet* 12 (February 6, 1869):9. On church as an organism.

"The Church not a Foreigner." *New York Tablet* 12 (February 13, 1869):8. On American spirit and Catholicism.

"The Future Religion of America." *New York Tablet* 12 (February 13, 1869):9. Response to Isaac Hecker's Chicago lecture on Catholic Church as future of religion in United States.

"Positivism." *New York Tablet* 12 (February 20, 1869):8. On the explicitly anti-Christian First Positivist Society of New York.

"Via Media." *New York Tablet* 12 (February 20, 1869):9. Anglicanism, Puritanism and Catholicism.

"Gen. Grant and the Politicians." *New York Tablet* 12 (February 27, 1869):8. Grant's presidential aims for the economy and the expected resistance from the politicians.

"State Religion." *New York Tablet* 12 (February 27, 1869):12. Isaac Hecker's true aim not a state religion of Catholicism, but a conversion of the United States to Catholicism.

"Porter's *Human Intellect.*" Part II of II. *Catholic World* 8 (March, 1869):767-84; see February, 1869; *Works* 2:383-427.

"The Relation of Capital and Labor." *New York Tablet* 12 (March 13, 1869):8. Labor does not get a just share of profits.

"The Fortieth Congress." *New York Tablet* 12 (March 13, 1869):9. Negative review of its work. *Tablet's* opposition to a religion of the state in opposition to the *Syllabus of Errors* (1864).

"'The *New York Tablet* Anathema!.'" *New York Tablet* 12 (March 20, 1869):9. *Hartford Churchman* declares anathema on *Tablet* because it asserts against the *Syllabus of Errors* that the Church neither expects nor wishes to be the religion of the State.

"The New Administration." *New York Tablet* 12 (March 27, 1869):8. On President U. S. Grant's inaugural address.

"The Christian Intelligencer Ruffled." *New York Tablet* 12 (March 27, 1869):9. Ruffled by *Tablet's* assertions that Protestant principles, which tend toward rationalism, could not do battle with the rising naturalism and positivism.

Conversations on Liberalism and the Church. New York: D. & J. Sadlier, 1869; *Works* 13:1-86. Against objections of liberalism; church is unmoved mover, the source of progress while never changing herself.

"The Bishops of Rome." *Catholic World* 9 (April, 1869):86-97; *Works* 13:146-61. Review of "The Bishops of Rome," *Harper's Magazine* (January, 1869). On relation of religion and civilization. Protestants have many false views of the history of popes.

"Denominationalism." *New York Tablet* 12 (April 3, 1869):8-9. Various Protestant solutions to the problem of sectarianism.

"The Age of Light." *New York Tablet* 12 (April 3, 1869):9. Many new questions, like women's suffrage, have old solutions.

"'Pious Paganism.'" *New York Tablet* 12 (April 10, 1869):9. On the Catholic doctrine of grace and works.

"The 'Christian Intelligencer' Not Ruffled." *New York Tablet* 12 (April 24, 1869):8. Catholicism and American republicanism.

"Can a State Secede?" *New York Tablet* 12 (April 24, 1869):9. Chief Justice Salmon Portland Chase and the status of Southern states.

"The Woman Question." Part I of II. *Catholic World* 9 (May, 1869):145-57; see *Brownson's Quarterly Review* (October, 1873); *Works* 18:381-98. On Brownson's grounds for opposing female suffrage and eligibility.

"Pope or People." *Catholic World* 9 (May, 1869):212-21. Review of *The Congregationalist and Boston Recorder* (March 4, 1869). On the Catholic understanding of the relationship between reason, the interior illumination of the Holy Spirit, and an external infallible authority.

"The Tablet Replies." *New York Tablet* 12 (May 1, 1869):8. No conflict between faith and reason in the doctrine of Transubstantiation.

"The Relation of Capital and Labor—No. II." *New York Tablet* 12 (May 1, 1869):9; see March 13, 1869. On political economists.

"The General Council." *New York Tablet* 12 (May 8, 1869):8. Prediction about agenda of Vatican I.

"The Watchman and Reflector." *New York Tablet* 12 (May 8, 1869):9. On Isaac Hecker's Boston lecture on the present religious tendencies of the sectarian world.

"Mr. Ffoulkes and Anglicans." *New York Tablet* 12 (May 8, 1869):9. Edmund Salusbury Ffoulkes's views on reunion of Rome, Constantinople and Canterbury.

"Religious Liberty." *New York Tablet* 12 (May 15, 1869):9. The *Christian Intelligencer*'s views.

"'Romanism in the United States.'" *New York Tablet* 12 (May 22, 1869):8. Sectarian press's fear of growth of Catholicism.

"'The Churchman' Studies the 'Tablet.'" *New York Tablet* 12 (May 29, 1869):8. On the *Syllabus* and its interpretation.

"Transubstantiation." *New York Tablet* 12 (May 29, 1869):9. The *Christian Intelligencer* on faith and reason.

"Spiritism and Spiritists." *Catholic World* 9 (June, 1869):289-302; *Works* 9:332-51; *Gems*: 23-42. Review of Epes Sargent's *Plancette, or the Despair of Science* (1869), Joseph Bizouard's *Des Rapports de l'Homme avec le Demon* (1863-1864), and Miles Grant's *Spiritualism Unveiled* (1866). Brownson's traditionalism and intuitionism against inductive method's *a priori* refusal to admit spirit-manifestations.

"'Rome's Aggressive Policy.'" *New York Tablet* 13 (June 19, 1869):8. Against the view that Rome seeks to destroy all free institutions.

"Secularizing Education." *New York Tablet* 13 (June 26, 1869):8. *Tablet's* opposition to such secularization.

"Common Schools." *New York Tablet* 13 (June 26, 1869):8. On public aid to private schools and anti-Catholicism of common schools.

"The Physical Basis of Life." *Catholic World* 9 (July, 1869):467-76; *Works* 9:365-79. Review of "New Theory of Life. A Lecture by T. H. Huxley," *New York World* (February 18, 1869). Against Huxley's reduction of life to its physical basis; must go beyond physical laws in order to find principles.

"Lecky on Morals." *Catholic World* 9 (July, 1869):529-40. Published with "The Conversion of Rome," September, 1869, in "Lecky on Morals," *Works* 14:379-95. Review of William E. H. Lecky's *History of European Morals* (1869). Creation as ground of obligation—moral law takes its obligation from God as final cause.

"The Protestant Protest." *New York Tablet* 13 (July 10, 1869):8. German Protestant rejection of papal invitation to Vatican I.

"The Spanish Regency." *New York Tablet* 13 (July 10, 1869):8. On the Constitution of the new Spanish revolutionaries.

"The Apostolic Times." *New York Tablet* 13 (July 17, 1869):8. Catholic methods of gaining influence in the United States.

"New Austria." *New York Tablet* 13 (July 17, 1869):8. A new haven for liberalism.

"Protestants and the Council." *New York Tablet* 13 (July 24, 1869):8. Papal invitation to Protestants was attempt to bring them back to church.

"Common Schools." *New York Tablet* 13 (July 24, 1869):8-9. On proposed legislation to give public aid to private schools; and on the purpose of education.

"Secularism." *New York Tablet* 13 (July 24, 1869):9. Increasing triumph of secularism in world governments.

"A New Protest." *New York Tablet* 13 (July 24, 1869):9. Protestant protest against the name "Catholic."

"The Council Again." *New York Tablet* 13 (July 31, 1869):8. Protestant anxiety over the calling of Vatican I.

"French Affairs." *New York Tablet* 13 (July 31, 1869):8. French now swinging to real republicanism.

"The Church and Liberty." *New York Tablet* 13 (July 31, 1869):8-9. On Catholic meaning of religious liberty.

"Our Established Church."' *New York Tablet* 13 (July 31, 1869):9. Protestants against public funds for Catholic uses in New York.

"Our Established Church." *Catholic World* 9 (August, 1869):577-87. Review of *Putnam's Monthly Magazine* (July, 1869). New York State and City subsidies to Catholic charitable institutions do not constitute church establishment.

"Spiritualism and Materialism." *Catholic World* 9 (August, 1869):619-34; *Works* 9:379-400. No antagonism between spiritual and material; "fundamental error of the age is the denial of creation."

"Mental Slavery." *New York Tablet* 13 (August 7, 1869):8. Charge against Catholicism. Freedom and faith in Catholic Church.

"The Church as Civilizer." *New York Tablet* 13 (August 7, 1869):9. Danger of the arguments for or against the influence of religion upon civilization.

"Neither Sectarian Nor Partisan." *New York Tablet* 13 (August 14, 1869):8-9. Imperialism would be as anti-Catholic in United States as it is already in Europe.

"Giving Money for Sectarian Uses." *New York Tablet* 13 (August 14, 1869):9. Common schools might be considered sectarian institutions.

"Rev. Mr. Bacon's Pamphlet." *New York Tablet* 13 (August 21, 1869):8. Leonard Bacon on refutations of Protestant and Catholic charges against each other.

"Senator Casserly's Speech." *New York Tablet* 13 (August 28, 1869) 8-9. Brownson's political theory of government and his agreement with Eugene Casserly's opposition to the thirteenth, fourteenth, and fifteenth amendments.

"The Independent on the Council." *New York Tablet* 13 (August 28, 1869):9. Sarcastic report on *Independent*'s ridicule of the Vatican Council.

"Primeval Man." *Catholic World* 9 (September, 1869): 746-56; *Works* 9:318-32. Review of Duke of Argyll's *Primeval Man* (1869). Brownson's arguments for a doctrine of creation against Sir John Lubbock's theory of biological evolution, and Brownson's belief that the savage state is not the primitive state of humans.

"The Conversion of Rome." *Catholic World* 9 (September, 1869):790-803. Published with "Lecky on Morals" (July, 1869) in "Lecky on Morals," *Works* 14:395-414.

"Correction of a Mistake." *Catholic World* 9 (September, 1869):855. On reason's ability to demonstrate the spirituality not the immateriality of the soul.

"Partisan and Sectarian Schools." *New York Tablet* 13 (September 4, 1869):8-9. On the American system of education, the use of the Bible in the schools, and the incompetence of the State in spiritual matters.

"Woman's Rights." *New York Tablet* 13 (September 18, 1869):8. Opposition to Catholics who support women's rights movement.

"Papal Infallibility." *New York Tablet* 13 (September 18, 1869):9. The divine origin of infallibility.

"An Imaginary Contradiction." *Catholic World* 10 (October, 1869):1-12; *Works* 3:407-23. Review of the "Spirit of Romanism," *The Christian Quarterly* Cincinnati (July, 1869), which criticized Hecker's *Aspirations of Nature*. Brownson's view of the dialectical synthesis between reason and revelation, creation and redemption.

"James Sadlier." *New York Tablet* 13 (October 2, 1869):8. Obituary signed "O. A. B."

"The Western Catholic." *New York Tablet* 13 (October 2, 1869):9. Against the view that ten million Catholics have been lost to the faith.

"The Bible." *New York Tablet* 13 (October 2, 1869):9. On English versions of the Bible.

"Pere Hyacinthe." *New York Tablet* 13 (October 9, 1869):8. On the reported defection of the Carmelite monk and renowned preacher Hyacinthe [Charles Jean Marie] Loyson.

"The Difference Between Us." *New York Tablet* 13 (October 9, 1869):8-9. Catholic-Protestant differences; Church against sects.

"Cuba and Spain." *New York Tablet* 13 (October 9, 1869):9. On reports of revolutionary disturbances in Cuba and the U. S. Government's entanglement.

"The Ecumenical Council." *New York Tablet* 13 (October 9, 1869):9. Sectarian predictions of council splitting the Catholic Church.

"Pere Hyacinthe Again." *New York Tablet* 13 (October 16, 1869):8. He has left his religious order, protesting the divorce between Catholic Church and nineteenth century society.

"Papal Infallibility." *New York Tablet* 13 (October 16, 1869):8. On divine origin of infallibility, and difference between impeccability and infallibility.

"Liberal Christianity." *New York Tablet* 13 (October 16, 1869):9. Unitarians linked with other sectarians and Republican Party to oppose the Catholic Church.

"Death of Mr. James Sadlier." *Ave Maria* 5 (October 23, 1869):693-94. Reprint of *New York Tablet* (October 2, 1869).

Pere Hyacinthe Once More." *New York Tablet* 13 (October 30, 1869):8. The internal Catholic battle over church's relation to the age.

"Political Atheism." *New York Tablet* 13 (October 30, 1869):9. Defines statolatry and political atheism.

"Free Religion." *Catholic World* 10 (November, 1869):195-206; *Works* 3:407-23; *Gems*: 43-60. Review of *Proceedings of 2nd Annual Meeting of the Free Religion Association* (1869). Principle of Catholicism is not authority (as Francis Ellingwood Abbott believes) but the Incarnation.

"The Dark Ages." *New York Tablet* 13 (November 6, 1869):8-9. On the validity of the designation "Dark Ages."

"The Intelligencer and Infallibility." *New York Tablet* 13 (November 6, 1869):9. The issue with the Protestants is the infallibility of the church, not papal infallibility.

"The Church Union." *New York Tablet* 13 (November 6, 1869):9. The journal seeks Christian unity on the basis of dogmatic and ecclesiastical indifference.

"The Enemy at the Polls." *New York Tablet* 13 (November 13, 1869):8-9. No Catholic unanimity at the polls.

"'The Christian Union.'" *New York Tablet* 13 (November 13, 1869):9. The journal, formerly the *Church Union*, reflects Henry Ward Beecher's evangelicalism and naturalism.

"The American and Foreign Christian Union." *New York Tablet* 13 (November 20, 1869):8. On anti-Catholicism of the *Union* and exclusive salvation.

"The Bible in the Schools." *New York Tablet* 13 (November 20, 1869):8-9. Cincinnati's school board votes Bible out of schools, and thereby promotes godless education.

"The Future of the Public Schools." *New York Tablet* 13 (November 20, 1869):9. Suggests a system of denominational public schools, as in Europe.

"Religion in the Schools." *New York Tablet* 13 (November 27, 1869):8-9. A large number of Protestants do not want godless education.

"'Liberal Catholicism.'" *New York Tablet* 13 (November 27, 1869):8-9. On the internal Catholic battles between liberals and ultramontanes.

"Beecher's Norwood." *Catholic World* 10 (December, 1869):393-401; *Works* 19:533-44; *Modern*: 533-44. Review of Henry Ward Beecher's *Norwood* (1868). Brownson characterizes traits of various New England states and argues that Beecher's book aims to undercut New England theological and moral doctrines.

"Dr. Bellows on the School Question." *New York Tablet* 13 (December 4, 1869):8-9. Henry W. Bellows asserts that Catholics are only tolerated in this country, and thus the country cannot put education into Catholic hands.

"Christian Courtesy." *New York Tablet* 13 (December 4 1869):9. *Tablet* has violated courtesy by insulting Henry Ward Beecher.

"Anglicans Politely Snubbed." *New York Tablet* 13 (December 11, 1869):8. Relations between Canterbury and Constantinople.

"The Late Albert D. Richardson." *New York Tablet* 13 (December 11, 1869):8-9. On the murder of Richardson and his violation of the marriage bond before his murder.

"The Presbyterians and Politics." *New York Tablet* 13 (December 11, 1869):9. On the right of Christian pastors to promote the exercise of Christian conscience at the polls.

"Opening of the French Chambers." *New York Tablet* 13 (December 11, 1869):9. The European reaction to revolution seems to be gaining some ground.

"Health Officer." *New York Tablet* 13 (December 18, 1869):9. Support for H. S. Hewit's application as Health Officer for the Port of New York.

"The President's Message." *New York Tablet* 13 (December 18, 1869):8. U. S. Grant's first message to Congress sensible, but not entirely satisfactory.

"The Richardson Tragedy." *New York Tablet* 13 (December 18, 1869):9; see December 11, 1869. On the public disapproval of Richardson's immorality.

"The President's Message." *New York Tablet* 13 (December 25, 1869):8. On Grant's financial policies and the government coming under the mob of businessmen.

"The 'Tribune' on Common Schools." *New York Tablet* 13 (December 25, 1869):9; see November 10, 1869. *N.Y. Tribune's* opposition to the *Tablet's* proposals on education.

1870

"The Coming Fight." *New York Tablet* 13 (January 1, 1879):8-9. Use of public funds for Catholic schools.

"Father Hyacinthe's Discourses." *New York Tablet* 13 (January 8, 1870):8. Leonard Bacon published Hyacinthe's *Discourses on Various Occasions* (1869) and used the ex-Carmelite's views against Catholic Church. Attack upon French-style liberal Catholicism.

"The Governor's Message." *New York Tablet* 13 (January 16, 1870):8-9. Favorable view of New York's governor John Thompson Hoffman's annual message to New York State legislature.

"Marriage and Free Love." *New York Tablet* 13 (January 16, 1870):9; see December 11, 1869. Secular and sectarian press's rejection of free love in the Richardson affair.

"Common Schools." *New York Tablet* 13 (January 22, 1870):8-9. The majority against the *Tablet's* position on the school question.

"Error LXXX of the Age." *New York Tablet* 13 (January 22, 1870):9. The *Syllabus* and the prohibition of the Catholic Church's reconciliation with liberalism, as that term is understood in Rome.

"How History is Written." *New York Tablet* 13 (January 29, 1870):8. Defense of Isaac Hecker and attack on Hyacinthe's misrepresentations of Hecker's positions.

"The Truth About Romanism." *New York Tablet* 13 (January 29, 1870):9. Need for real conversion of Catholics.

"Future of Protestantism and Catholicity." Part I of IV. *Catholic World* 10 (January, 1870):433-48; see February, March, and April, 1870; *Works* 13:162-84. Review of l'Abbé Martin, *De l'Avenir du Protestantisme et du Catholicisme* (1869). On Puritanism and the state; against the romantic notion that the church is necessary for salvation of civilization.

"Putnam's Defense." *Catholic World* 10 (January, 1870):542-47. See also *Catholic World*, August, 1869. Response to *Putnam's Magazine's* "The Unestablished Church"(December, 1869), which defended its attack upon New York State's subsidies to Catholic institutions.

"Future of Protestantism and Catholicity." Part II of IV. *Catholic World* 10 (February, 1870):577-89; see January, March, and April, 1870; *Works* 13:184-201.

"The 'Catholic World' and the Puritans." *New York Tablet* 13 (February 5, 1870):8. On virtues of Puritans in comparison to liberal Protestants like Henry Ward Beecher.

"Sir Walter Scott and Catholicity." *New York Tablet* 13 (February 5, 1870):8-9. Catholic characters in Scott's novels.

"The Papal Infallibility." *New York Tablet* 13 (February 12, 1870):8-9. Arguments in favor of defining papal infallibility.

"The 'Post' on Education." *New York Tablet* 13 (February 12, 1870):9. Religion should be the prevailing principle of all education.

"Religion in Schools." *New York Tablet* 13 (February 19, 1870):8. Use of Bible in the schools.

"The 'Catholic World.'" *New York Tablet* 13 (February 19, 1870):8-9. On *Catholic World*'s liberalism.

"The Ecumenical Council." *New York Tablet* 13 (February 19, 1870):9. Press reports on Vatican Council.

"The Council and Papal Infallibility." *New York Tablet* 13 (February 26, 1870):8-9. In favor of decree on papal infallibility.

"Grants to Sectarian Schools." *New York Tablet* 13 (February 26, 1870):9. Public funds for Catholic schools.

"Civil and Political Liberty." Part III of IV. *Catholic World* 10 (March, 1870):721-35; see January, February, and April, 1870; "The Future of Protestantism and Catholicity," *Works* 13:201-22.

"The Romish School Question." *New York Tablet* 13 (March 5, 1870):8-9. Public aid.

"Congress." *New York Tablet* 13 (March 5, 1870):9. Lack of statesmen in Congress.

"Religion and Politics." *New York Tablet* 13 (March 12, 1870):8. On separation of religion from politics.

"The Bible and the School Fund." *New York Tablet* 13 (March 19, 1870):8. Catholic right to establish schools and teach religion equal to Protestant right to use the Bible in common schools.

"The State Not Infidel." *New York Tablet* 13 (March 19, 1870):9. Cincinnati, Ohio, decision on Bible in schools. Catholics should not favor godless education by voting for the exclusion of Bible from common schools.

"Count Charles De Montalembert." *New York Tablet* 13 (March 26, 1870):8. Obituary.

"Civil and Political Liberty." Part IV of IV. *Catholic World* 11 (April, 1870):1-14; see January, February, and March, 1870; "The Future of Protestantism and Catholicity," *Works* 13:222-41.

"The School Question." *Catholic World* 11 (April, 1870):91-106; *Works* 13:241-62. On history of development of common schools and the organized union of religion and education in the United States; the present exclusion of Catholicism from these schools.

"The New York Times on the Public Schools." *New York Tablet* 13 (April 2, 1870):8. *Times* charges that Catholic demands for equal rights in education are exorbitant; it misrepresents Catholic arguments.

"The Syracuse Methodist Convention." *New York Tablet* 13 (April 2, 1870):9. The political agenda for the Convention.

"The Christian Intelligencer." *New York Tablet* 13 (April 2, 1870):9. School question.

"Rev. G. H. Hepworth and Catholicism." *New York Tablet* 13 (April 9, 1870):8. On church and state relations. Signed O. A. Brownson.

"Church of the Messiah." *New York Tablet* 13 (April 9, 1870):8-9. The school question and Americanization.

"Infallibility." *New York Tablet* 13 (April 9, 1870):9. On rumors of Vatican I discussion of papal infallibility.

"The Truth About The School Question." *New York Tablet* 13 (April 16, 1870):8. *New York Times*'s denials that it is unfair to Catholics on the school question.

"The State in Danger!—Inroads of Catholicism in Our Country!" *New York Tablet* 13 (April 16, 1870):8. The real danger comes not from true Catholics but from political Catholics who see no connection between religion and politics.

"The School Question." *New York Tablet* 13 (April 16, 1870):9. Response to William Seton on the state's duty to teach.

"Hepworth on Allegiance to The Pope." *New York Tablet* 13 (April 23, 1870):5. G. H. Hepworth's assault on Catholicism motivated by desire to increase his church's membership.

"The Times on the School Question." *New York Tablet* 13 (April 23, 1870):8. Use or misuse of Bible in the schools is not the true issue for Catholics.

"The Late Count Montalembert." *New York Tablet* 13 (April 23, 1870):8-9. His liberalism in the years prior to his death.

"Harshness and Imprudence." *New York Tablet* 13 (April 23, 1870):9. Catholic charges against *Tablet* with regard to school question and papal infallibility.

"Frightened, Are We?" *New York Tablet* 13 (April 23, 1870):9. School question and the *New York Times*.

"An American Catholic." *New York Tablet* 13 (April 30, 1870):5. The Bible is not just a "potent weapon of the Protestant power."

"State Religion." *New York Tablet* 13 (April 30, 1870):8. On a Protestant proposed amendment to the Constitution that would acknowledge the Christian religion.

"The 'Advance' on the School Question." *New York Tablet* 13 (April 30, 1870):9. No such thing as Christianity in general, which can be the basis of a common religion in the schools.

"Church and State." *Catholic World* 11 (May, 1870):145-60; *Works* 13:263-84; RyanA: 357-70. State subject to law of God, but only as people understand it.

"Emerson's Prose Works." *Catholic World* 11 (May, 1870):202-11; *Works* 3:424-38; RyanA: 174-84. Review of *The Prose Works of Ralph Waldo Emerson* (1870). Examination of Emerson's idealism and pantheism, and Brownson's doctrine of creation.

"Mr. Ffoulkes and the 'Catholic World'." *New York Tablet* 13 (May 7, 1870):8. On various historical charges Edmund Salusbury Ffoulkes makes against the Catholic Church.

"Shall We Be Frightened?" *New York Tablet* 13 (May 7, 1870):9. On frightening the N. Y. legislature to prohibit aid to Catholics.

"The Doctrine of The Late Archbishop Francis Patrick Kenrick— An Error of The 'N.Y. Herald' Corrected." *New York Tablet* 13 (May 21, 1870):8. On Peter Richard Kenrick's letter to Martin John Spalding on his brother's doctrine of infallibility.

"The Vatican Council." *New York Tablet* 13 (May 28, 1870):8. On Arthur Cleveland Coxe's *A Letter to Pius the Ninth, Bishop of Rome* (1870).

"Catholic Education." *New York Tablet* 13 (May 28, 1870):8-9. On Brownson's former (1860s) opposition to separate Catholic schools and their poor quality.

"Papal Infallibility." *New York Tablet* 14 (June 4, 1870):8-9. Archbishops P. R. Kenrick and John Purcell against Archbishop M. J. Spalding at Vatican I.

"Mr. Coxe to Pius the Ninth." *New York Tablet* 14 (June 11, 1870):8; see May 28, 1870. On Anglicans and Catholics.

"Church and State." *New York Tablet* 14 (June 11, 1870):9. Obedience to God prior to and above obedience to state.

"Cardinal Antonelli's Reply to the Note of Count Daru."*New York Tablet* 14 (June 11, 1870):9. On papal infallibility and subjection of state to the absolute authority of the church.

"The 'Weekly Register,' Brooklyn." *New York Tablet* 14 (June 11, 1870):9. A new Catholic journal.

"Dr. Marcy's Life Duties." *New York Tablet* 14 (June 18, 1870):8-9. Review of Erastus Edgerton Marcy's *Life Duties* (1869). On Catholic doctrine, which carried the name but not the substance of the Catholic tradition (especially in relation to its Eucharistic doctrine).

"The Dead Novelist." *New York Tablet* 14 (June 18, 1870):9. On Charles Dickens.

"Have We Gained or Lost?" *New York Tablet* 14 (June 25, 1870):8. School question. The loss of state support for Catholic schools, but the gain in strengthening relations of religion and education.

"President Grant and Sectarianism." *New York Tablet* 14 (June 25, 1870):9. On Grant's support for the sectarian Evangelical World Alliance which is anti-Catholic.

"Papal Infallibility." *New York Tablet* 14 (June 25, 1870):9. On Protestant and Catholic forms of infallibility.

"Red Cloud and the Administration." *New York Tablet* 14 (June 25, 1870):9. On government's swindling of the Indians.

"'The Bible Does No Good.'" *New York Tablet* 14 (July 2, 1870):8. On the Bible and Tract societies.

"'The Churchman.'" *New York Tablet* 14 (July 2, 1870):9. Anglican bishops.

"The Protestant Conspiracy." *New York Tablet* 14 (July 9, 1870):8. Conspiracy to prevent Catholic appointments to public offices.

"Correction." *New York Tablet* 14 (July 16, 1870):8. Isaac Hecker's *Aspirations of Nature* incorrectly cited.

"Dr. Brownson on Gallicanism." *New York Tablet* 14 (July 16, 1870):8. Signed O. A. Brownson.

"The Late Riot at Elm Park—Orangeism in New York." *New York Tablet* 14 (July 23, 1870):8. Both Catholic and Protestant Irish to blame for the riot, but Catholics were provoked.

"Blackstone and Papal Infallibility." *New York Tablet* 14 (July 23, 1870):9. What William Blackstone said of the authority of the King of England "surpasses what Catholics claim for the pope in spirituals."

"The Future of Protestantism and Catholicity." *New York Tablet* 14 (July 23, 1870):8-9. On the future council of the Evangelical World Alliance compared to the Vatican Council.

"The Franco-Prussian War." *New York Tablet* 14 (July 30, 1870):8. Support for France in the reported war between France and Prussia.

"'The Claim of Rome.'" *New York Tablet* 14 (July 30, 1870):8-9. Catholics in all areas of life, even in politics, should act upon Catholic principles dictated by the Word of God.

"France and Prussia." *New York Tablet* 14 (August 6, 1870):8. Sympathies with France in current war.

"The Syllabus and Democracy." *New York Tablet* 14 (August 6, 1870):8. Religion superior to politics.

"The Future of England." *New York Tablet* 14 (August 6, 1870):9. Latitudinarian and revolutionary principles will undermine England's peace and order in the future.

"Infallibility." *New York Tablet* 14 (August 6, 1870):9. Papal infallibility is not absurd; acknowledged as possible.

"The 'N.Y. World' on Papal Infallibility." *New York Tablet* 14 (August 13, 1870):8. Papal infallibility does not mean that the Pope is the final court of appeal, as the Supreme Court is.

"'The Blunder Proclaimed.'" *New York Tablet* 14 (August 13, 1870):9. Papal infallibility no blunder nor inexpedient.

"The French and the Prussians." *New York Tablet* 14 (August 20, 1870):8. Signed "O.A.B." Our hopes for the French have been disappointed. Napoleon has proved himself an incompetent general.

"'The Capstone Put On.'" *New York Tablet* 14 (August 20, 1870):9. On the meaning of papal infallibility.

"Is the Negro Dying Out." *New York Tablet* 14 (August 20, 1870):9. If country remains predominantly Protestant the Negro will die out. The Negro race is inferior.

"The War in Europe." *New York Tablet* 14 (August 27, 1870):8. France is losing the war.

"The Pope and his Friends." *New York Tablet* 14 (August 27, 1870):8-9. On the succession of Peter.

"What Makes Paupers?" *New York Tablet* 14 (August 27, 1870):9. Poverty a concomitant of "the modern mercantile and industry system."

"Hereditary Genius." *Catholic World* 11 (September, 1870):721-32; *Works* 9:401-17. Review of Francis Galton's *Hereditary Genius* (1870). Brownson rejects Galton's thesis; abilities belong to soul not body, and soul is created not generated.

"The Protestant Press and the Protestant Pulpit on the War." *New York Tablet* 14 (September 3, 1870):8. Protestant and secular press side with Prussia.

"Papal Infallibility Since Haguenau." *New York Tablet* 14 (September 3 1870):9. No connection between papal infallibility and France's losses during the war.

"The War." *New York Tablet* 14 (September 10, 1870):8. France is prostrated.

"A Good Nomination." *New York Tablet* 14 (September 10, 1870):9. Support for General Martin T. McMahon for Congress.

"France and the Revolution." *New York Tablet* 14 (September 17, 1870):8. Signed O.A. Brownson. On the collapse of the Second French Republic, Napoleon's failures, and the future of Catholicism.

"The Pope and Italian Unity." *New York Tablet* 14 (September 17, 1870):8-9. Pope's future in face of fall of Rome.

"Thoughts for Catholics." *New York Tablet* 14 (September 24, 1870):8. On the "evil times."

"The Apostolate." *New York Tablet* 14 (September 24, 1870) 8. On Peter's successors in the apostolate.

"Union with the Church." *Catholic World* 12 (October, 1870):1-16; *Works* 3:438-59. Reviews of "Union with the Church," *Mercersburg Review*, (July, 1870), Henry Harbaugh's *Union with the Church* (1867), and Israel Knight's [Ellen Tryphosa Harrington Putnam] *Where is the City?* (1868). Brownson's views on the necessity and meaning of church unity.

"The War." *New York Tablet* 14 (October 1, 1870):8. Signed O. A. Brownson. On Brownson's debt to French literature and love of France.

"Not Peace, But A Sword." *New York Tablet* 14 (October 1, 1870):8-9. Papal infallibility not the only concern of Vatican I. On the grounds of the definition.

"'Downfall of the Pope.'" *New York Tablet* 14 (October 8, 1870):8-9. Downfall supposed because of lack of temporal sovereignty, a mere accident of history.

"France and the Church." *New York Tablet* 14 (October 8, 1870):9. Support for Gallicanism the fault of France.

"The Apostolic Office." *New York Tablet* 14 (October 15 1870):8-9. Apostolic succession.

"Plebiscitum." *New York Tablet* 14 (October 15, 1870):9. Italian people have no right to depose the pope of his temporal sovereignty.

"A Mistake." *New York Tablet* 14 (October 15, 1870):9. Faults in Catholic countries.

"The Anglican Position." *New York Tablet* 14 (October 22, 1870):8. On the Catholic nature of Anglicanism.

"Rome and Italy." *New York Tablet* 14 (October 22, 1870):9. On the survival of papacy despite the loss of temporal support.

"Supervision of Politics." *New York Tablet* 14 (October 22, 1870):9. On the authority to prescribe Christian morals in politics.

"The 'Churchman.'" *New York Tablet* 14 (October 29, 1870):8. Authority in Christianity.

"The Great Commission." *Catholic World* 12 (November, 1870):187-200; *Works* 8:359-78. Review of John Harris's *The Great Commission* (1870). Charges against Protestants' authentic commission to preach, teach and save—they have neither communion nor doctrine.

"Signs of the Times." *New York Tablet* 14 (November 5, 1870):8. Signs of true piety in the midst of revolutionary Europe.

"The *Catholic World.*" *New York Tablet* 14 (November 5, 1870):8. The valuable contributions of this journal.

"The 'American Churchman.'" *New York Tablet* 14 (November 5, 1870):9. The Anglican claims to Catholic communion.

"The Apostolic Office." *New York Tablet* 14 (November 5, 1870):9. Apostolic succession.

"Church and State—No. I." *New York Tablet* 14 (November 12, 1870):8; see November 19, 1870; December 10, 1870; December 31, 1870; January 21, 1871; February 4, 1871. On the various theories of the relation between church and state.

"Can't Make a Creed." *New York Tablet* 14 (November 12, 1870):9. Unitarians and doctrinal statements.

"Church and State—No. II." *New York Tablet* 14 (November 19, 1870):8; see November 12, 1870.

"The Napoleonic Error." *New York Tablet* 14 (November 19, 1870):9. Denial of the religious foundation of government.

"The Psychology of Perversion." *New York Tablet* 14 (November 26, 1870, 9. On Anglican claims.

"St. Paul and the Popes." *New York Tablet* 14 (November 26, 1870):8-9. The qualifications of an apostle, and apostolic succession.

"Steps of Belief." *Catholic World* 12 (December, 1870):289-304; *Works* 8:379-99. Review of James Freeman Clarke's *Steps of Belief* (1870). Against Leibniz; Brownson's view that belief precedes unbelief.

"Answers to Difficulties." *Catholic World* 12 (December, 1870):328-40; *Works* 9:566-83. On the progress and the necessity of Catholicism for true progress and civilization.

"European Politics." *New York Tablet* 14 (December 3, 1870):8-9. On the relative political strength of various European governments.

"Resemblance between the Buddhist and the Roman Catholic Religion.'" *New York Tablet* 14 (December 10, 1870):8. Review of article in *Atlantic Monthly* (December, 1870) by Maria L. Child.

"Church and State —No. III." *New York Tablet* 14 (December 10, 1870):9; see November 12, 1870.

"The 'Napoleonic Error' and the 'Christian Intelligencer'—Causes of the Decadence of the Catholic Nations." *New York Tablet* 14 (December 17, 1870):8-9. Cause of decadence not because of the Catholic Church, but in spite of it.

"The Temporal Power of the Pope." *New York Tablet* 14 (December 17, 1870):9. The distinction between the right and the necessity of the pope's temporal sovereignty.

"Changing Its Tune." *New York Tablet* 14 (December 24, 1870):8-9. The *New York Observer*'s hostility toward the temporal sovereignty of the pope.

"Church and State—No.IV." *New York Tablet* 14 (December 31, 1870):8-9; see November 12, 1870.

1871

"Beecherism and its Tendencies." *Catholic World* 12 (January, 1871):433-50; *Works* 3:460-84. Review of Henry Ward Beecher's *Sciences* (1869-70). Protestants make very little use of intelligence in order to make room for sentiment and emotions.

"*Mrs. Gerald's Niece.*" *Catholic World* 12 (January, 1871):546-57; *Works* 19:544-59; *Modern*: 544-59. Review Lady George Fullerton's novel (1870). Brownson on the weakness of novels, especially those by women; but his praise for Fullerton's work.

"Religious Orders." *Ave Maria* 7 (January 28, 1871):65-67; (February 4, 1871):81-83; (February 18, 1871):113-15; (April 8, 1871):233-34; (July 1, 1871):425-26; (July 22, 1871):473-75; (August 5, 1871):505-07; (August 12, 1871):521-23; (August 26, 1871):553-55; (September 9, 1871):585-87; *Works* 8:219-63. On poverty, chastity and obedience; Brownson's realization of God's freedom was central point of his conversion.

"Treatment of Catholics." *New York Tablet* 14 (January 7, 1871):8. On Leonard Bacon's "condescension" to Catholics.

"The Pope as a Subject." *New York Tablet* 14 (January 14, 1871):8. Pope not subject to any temporal power.

"The Reckless 'Christian Intelligencer.'" *New York Tablet* 14 (January 14, 1871):8-9. The conditions of Catholic countries.

"The Arrogance of Rome." *New York Tablet* 14 (January 14, 1871):9. On arrogance of Protestants without the claim of infallibility.

"Church and State—No. V." *New York Tablet* 14 (January 21, 1871):8-9; see November 12, 1870.

"Church and State—No. VI." *New York Tablet* 14 (January 28, 1871):8; see November 12, 1870.

"Church and State—No. VII." *New York Tablet* 14 (February 4, 1871):8-9; see November 12, 1870.

"'St. Peter.'" *New York Tablet* 14 (February 11, 1871):8. On a tasteless Catholic journal established to defend the pope.

"Unity and Infallibility." *New York Tablet* 14 (February 11, 1871):8-9. On the Evangelical Alliance's sense of these terms.

"'The Pope Not a Subject.'" *New York Tablet* 14 (February 11, 1871):9. Relation of church and civil law.

"Cabinet Changes." *New York Tablet* 14 (February 18, 1871):8-9. On President Grant's contemplated reconstruction of his cabinet.

"Manning's Vatican Council." *New York Tablet* 14 (February 18, 1871):9. Review of Henry Edward Manning's *The Vatican Council and its Definitions* (1871).

"What Dollinger Thinks of the Pope's Temporal Power and Italian Unity." *New York Tablet* 14 (February 18, 1871):9. On Johann Joseph Ignaz von Dollinger's 1861 support for the temporal power.

"Proscription." *New York Tablet* 14 (February 25, 1871):9. On prohibiting appointments to civil offices because of a person's Catholicism.

"Baring-Gould on Christianity." *Catholic World* 12 (March, 1871):764-81; *Works* 3:484-508. A critical review of Sabine Baring-Gould's *The Origin and Development of Religious Belief* (1870) because he bases the truth of Christianity upon the facts or wants of human nature. Baring-Gould lacks a sense of the communion of the objective and the subjective dimensions of life and thought, and thus distorts the fundamental doctrines of Christianity.

"A Lenten Meditation for the 'Christian Intelligencer' on its Spiritual Ancestors." *New York Tablet* 14 (March 5, 1871):8-9. On the execution of medieval heretics.

"From the 'Christian Union.'" *New York Tablet* 14 (March 5, 1871):9. Protests against movements to establish a state religion.

"The Witless 'Christian Intelligencer.'" *New York Tablet* 14 (March 11, 1871):8-9. Religious intolerance.

"Incipient Innovators." *New York Tablet* 14 (March 11, 1871):9. On liberal Catholics.

"The Higher Education." *New York Tablet* 14 (March 18, 1871):8. Deficiencies in Catholic education.

"Liberalism and the War." *New York Tablet* 14 (March 18, 1871):9. Liberalism responsible for the Franco-Prussian War and the prostration of France.

"Dr. Bellows on Church and State." *New York Tablet* 14 (March 25, 1871):8. The liberal Christian view of separation of church and state.

"Popish Views of the Bible." *New York Tablet* 14 (March 25, 1871):8-9. Defense of Catholic approach to Scripture.

"Unification and Education." *Catholic World* 13 (April, 1871):1-14; *Works* 13:284-302. Review of Henry Wilson's "New Departure of the Republican Party," *Atlantic Monthly* (January, 1871). Against Wilson's desire for national unification and national education and his support for will of majority. Brownson asserts the few should lead and the many follow.

"The Insurrection in Paris." *New York Tablet* 14 (April 1, 1871):8. Revolutionary liberalism.

"The Reds Successful in Paris." *New York Tablet* 14 (April 1, 1871):9. Red Republicanism in France and future prospects for the Catholic Church.

"The 'Churchman' Delighted." *New York Tablet* 14 (April 8,1871):8-9. Anglicans on church and state.

"Which Shall Triumph?" *New York Tablet* 14 (April 8, 1871):9. Catholicity or Protestantism.

"Rev. Henry Ward Beecher." *New York Tablet* 14 (April 15, 1871):8. Review of Beecher's writings and positions.

"Is It Ignorance or Malice?" *New York Tablet* 14 (April 15, 1871):9. On the *New York Observer's* views of Catholicism.

"The 'Methodist' and Liberalism." *New York Tablet* 14 (April 15, 1871):9. European liberalism and Methodist sympathy for it.

"Reign of Terror in Paris." *New York Tablet* 14 (April 22, 1871):8-9. Hostilities to Catholic Church.

"Answer to a 'Subscriber.'" *New York Tablet* 14 (April 22, 1871):9. On the elections of senators and representatives in Congress.

"France and 'the Kingdom of Italy.'" *New York Tablet* 14 (April 29, 1871):8. The Garibaldians and the revolutionary troubles in France.

"Sectarian Education." *New York Tablet* 14 (April 29, 1871):8-9. Reactions to Brownson's "Unification and Education" in the *Catholic World*, April 1871.

"The Church Accredits Herself." *Catholic World* 13 (May, 1871):145-58; *Works* 3:399-417. Review of Henry Edward Manning's *The Vatican Council and its Definitions* (1871). Church is witness to herself; she is today totally identical with apostolic age, witnessing to revelation in same sense.

"The Progress of 'Liberty' in Paris." *New York Tablet* 14 (May 6, 1871):8-9. Imprisonments of Archbishop of Paris and a number of clergy.

"Dr. Dollinger." *New York Tablet* 14 (May 13, 1871):8. Intellectual pride his fault.

"'The True Woman.'" *New York Tablet* 14 (May 20, 1871):8-9. Recommends the new journal, edited by Charlotte E. McKay, because it opposes woman's rights movement.

"Sardinia and the Holy Father." *Catholic World* 13 (June, 1871):289-304; *Works* 18:445-66. Italian unification brought about by lawlessness which violates principles of religion; atheism is real threat of modern world; papacy is symbolic of predominance of spiritual.

"Dollinger and the German Catholics." *New York Tablet* 15 (June 10, 1871):8-9. Press has made Dollinger's defection from the Catholic Church an event of world-wide importance, which it is not.

"The Revolution Checked." *New York Tablet* 15 (June 10, 1871):9. Defeat of Communists in Paris.

"Dr. Dollinger's Case." *New York Tablet* 15 (June 17, 1871):5. Dollinger's defection and European revolutionaries.

"Rome and the Civil Power." *New York Tablet* 15 (June 17, 1871):8. Independence of church from civil power.

"About Papal Europe." *New York Tablet* 15 (June 17, 1871):8-9. On the general Catholic acceptance of the doctrine of papal infallibility against the minority view of Dollinger and Hyacinthe.

"The Pope's Encyclical on the Papal Guarantees." *New York Tablet* 15 (June 17, 1871):9. Pope declares that he will not compromise with the Italian government.

"Origin of Civilization." *Catholic World* 13 (July, 1871):492-504; *Works* 9:418-34; *Gems*: 144-64. Review of John Lubbock's *The Origin of Civilization and the Primitive Condition of Man* (1871). Move from barbarism to civilization possible only by external and supernatural influence, not by self-generation.

"France and Germany." *New York Tablet* 15 (July 1, 1871):8. Political affairs in both countries.

"Counsellors For The Pope." *New York Tablet* 15 (July 1, 1871):8. Protestant advice on temporal and spiritual powers of pope.

"Wanted, A Live Anti-Popery Society." *New York Tablet* 15 (July 1, 1871):9. Leonard Bacon's new anti-popery plan.

"A Mystery Cleared Up." *New York Tablet* 15 (July 8, 1871):5. On opposition to papal infallibility by bishops Peter R. Kenrick, John Purcell and Félix Dupanloup because of its inopportuneness; their subsequent acceptance of the doctrine.

"Sectarian Associations and Conspiracies." *New York Tablet* 15 (July 8, 1871):8. On a new catholic, but not Roman, church.

"Catholicity and Republicanism." *New York Tablet* 15 (July 15, 1871):8. All governing power comes from God, and all governments hold their power as a trust.

"Catholics and the Common Schools." *New York Tablet* 15 (July 15, 1871):9. Protestant fears of Catholic positions.

"Independence of the Clergy." *New York Tablet* 15 (July 22, 1871):4. Clergy not above the law, but exempt from jurisdiction of the civil courts.

"The Problem of The Age." *New York Tablet* 15 (July 22, 1871):6. The education question.

"The Right Arm of The Revolution." *New York Tablet* 15 (July 22, 1871):9. The International Society of Workingmen.

"If The 'Infallible' Pontiff Please!" *New York Tablet* 15 (July 29, 1871):8. Origin of the state's power not from pope.

"The Bigots of New York." *New York Tablet* 15 (July 29, 1871):8. On Harper and Brothers's publishing firm, and *Harper's Weekly.*

"Jesuit Schools." *New York Tablet* 15 (July 29, 1871):9. Arthur Coxe on the "Jesuit morality," which is now recognized by infallible authority.

"The Real 'Dangerous Classes.'" *New York Tablet* 15 (July 29, 1871):9. Not the Irish lower classes, but *Harper's Weekly* represents the dangerous classes.

"The Secular Not Supreme." *Catholic World* 13 (August, 1871):685-701; *Works* 13:303-26. Review of Henry W. Bellows's *Church and State in America* (1871), and E. P. Hurlbut's *A Secular View of Religion and State, and of the Bible in the Public Schools* (1870). Against the "political atheism" of these two proposals for a complete divorce of church and state in order to defeat Evangelicals who want to declare the country Christian, and Catholics who want a share of public funds for education. The church and religion are necessary to sustain the republic.

"The Revolution Crowned in Rome." *New York Tablet* 15 (August 5, 1871):8. The American press's joy over a United Italy motivated by sympathy with revolutionaries and hatred of the pope.

"The Riot of the Twelfth, Again." *New York Tablet* 15 (August 5, 1871):8. The Orange riot, mob rule, and New York's Governor John Thompson Hoffman.

"The Evangelical Conspiracy." *New York Tablet* 15 (August 5, 1871):8-9. The movement to amend preamble of Constitution to declare this country Christian.

"The 'Accomplished Fact.'" *New York Tablet* 15 (August 12, 1871):8. The final usurpation of pope's temporal authority.

"Italian Unity in New York." *New York Tablet* 15 (August 12, 1871):8. New York Italians who favor "Italy United."

"Lessons of the Riot." *New York Tablet* 15 (August 12, 1871):8-9. Catholic Church did not support Orange Riot of July 12, 1871.

"By Their Fruits." *New York Tablet* 15 (August 19, 1871):8. Catholic immorality exists in spite of the church.

"The 'American Churchman' and the Ritualists." *New York Tablet* 15 (August 19, 1871):9. Anglican fears of Romanizing tendencies of ritualists.

"Catholics of Germany." *New York Tablet* 15 (August 26, 1871):8. Only religion can save government.

"Obligation of the Probable." *New York Tablet* 15 (August 26, 1871):9. On John Henry Newman, probability, and papal authority.

"Petty Spite." *New York Tablet* 15 (August 26, 1871):9. On papal question becoming a "farce."

"The Reformation not Conservative." *Catholic World* 13 (September, 1871):721-37; *Works* 14:447-69; *Gems*: 203-21. Review of Charles P. Krauth's *The Conservative Reformation and its Theology* (1871). Brownson's views that the Lutheran Reformation and conservatism "belong to different categories"; the Reformation in principle and effect is "decidedly revolutionary."

"Romanism and Government." *New York Tablet* 15 (September 2, 1871):8. Church and State, as understood by the *Tablet*.

"Meaning of Freedom of Speech." *New York Tablet* 15 (September 2, 1871):8-9. On Catholics violating the free speech of an apostate priest in Ogdensburg, New York.

"Romanism and Politics." *New York Tablet* 15 (September 9, 1871):8. On religious liberty and Catholic appeals for equality of civil rights.

"True Proportions of Dollinger." *New York Tablet* 15 (September 9, 1871):8-9. *New York Times*'s assertion that Dollinger is Catholic Church's most formidable enemy.

"The Triple Alliance." *New York Tablet* 15 (September 9, 1871):9. Germany, Austria, and Italy against Russia and France.

"Dissensions in the Catholic Church." *New York Tablet* 15 (September 16, 1871):8. Between liberals and conservatives.

"Why Dollinger Will Not Be Luther." *New York Tablet* 15 (September 16, 1871):8-9. Dollinger declares himself, despite excommunication, to be in the Church.

"The Reform Movement in Germany." *New York Tablet* 15 (September 16, 1871):9. On the formation a German Catholic Church.

"Bishop Strossmeyer's [*sic*] Speech." *New York Tablet* 15 (September 16, 1871):9. A fraudulent construction of Bishop Joseph Georg Strossmayer's speech during the Vatican Council.

"The Dead 'Leader of The International.'" *New York Tablet* 15 (September 23, 1871):8. On the death of Karl Marx.

"Responsibility of Freedom." *New York Tablet* 15 (September 23, 1871):8-9. Henry Ward Beecher and the excessive burden of his sense of freedom and his subjection to the tyranny of public opinion.

"Political Parties." *New York Tablet* 15 (September 30, 1871):5. Association of the Republican Party with anti-Catholic prejudices.

"Roman Education Under The Pope." *New York Tablet* 15 (September 30, 1871):5. The misinformation on education in Rome.

"The City Government." *New York Tablet* 15 (September 30, 1871):8-9. On fraud and corruption in New York City politics and necessity of reform.

"The 'Herald' and The Jesuits." *New York Tablet* 15 (September 30, 1871):9. Rumors that Jesuits expelled from Rome.

"Christianity and Positivism." *Catholic World* 14 (October, 1871):1-15; *Works* 2:428-47. Review of James McCosh's *Christianity and Positivism* (1871). Relationship between ontologism and traditionalism (which complements and corroborates the ontological argument); how one can demonstrate God's existence.

"The Riot of the Twelfth." *Catholic World* 14 (October, 1871):117-26. On the injustices of the Irish Catholic rioters and the Orange parade that provoked them.

"Mr. Seton's Letter." *New York Tablet* 15 (October 7, 1871):8-9. On compatibility of true republicanism and Catholicism.

"An Illogical Reference." *New York Tablet* 15 (October 7, 1871):9. Catholic clergy, who fail to instruct their people, are responsible for revolutionary victories in Europe.

"Romanism Politically." *New York Tablet* 15 (October 14, 1871):8-9. School question.

"A House That Needs A Lesson." *New York Tablet* 15 (October 14, 1871):9. *Harper's Weekly* and Thomas Nest. Suggests boycotting the publishing firm.

"The 'Christian Union' and The Public Schools." *New York Tablet* 15 (October 21, 1871):8-9. On the role of religion in education.

"Protestant Episcopal Convention." *New York Tablet* 15 (October 28, 1871):8. Declaration on the meaning of baptismal regeneration.

"Dollinger and Thiers." *New York Tablet* 15 (October 28, 1871):9. France and restoration of religion.

"The 'Old Catholics' of Munich." *New York Tablet* 15 (October 28, 1871):9. On a recent convention of Old Catholics.

"Authority in Matters of Faith." Part I of II. *Catholic World* 14 (November, 1871):145-57; see *Brownson's Quarterly Review*, (October, 1874); *Works* 8:574-92. Catholic tradition contains whole revelation whether written or unwritten, and this tradition is able to interpret Sacred Scripture infallibly.

"The 'Churchman' on Dr. Dollinger." *New York Tablet* 15 (November 4, 1871):8-9. Dollinger not a Luther because of his consistent opposition to Protestantism.

"The Riot of The Twelfth." *New York Tablet* 15 (November 11, 1871):8. Catholic Church not cause of riots and not involved in politics.

"The Pope and The Nations." *New York Tablet* 15 (November 11, 1871):9. No Catholic nations remain.

"The 'Tribune' on 'Irish Immigrant Guiees [*sic*].'" *New York Tablet* 15 (November 18, 1871):8. On John O'Hanlon's *Irish Emigrant's Guide* (1851) and moral advice to immigrants.

"Beecher on the Rights of Conscience." *New York Tablet* 15 (November 25, 1871):8-9. School question and State's obligation to respect Catholic consciences.

"Recent Events in France." *Catholic World* 14(December, 1871):289-304. *Works* 18:481-502. On the absolutism of monarchies against the absolutism of people as the real war in nineteenth-century Europe.

"Municipal Affairs." *New York Tablet* 15 (December 2, 1871):8. City elections, defeat of Tammany Hall, and triumph of reform.

"Our Imperial Guest." *New York Tablet* 15 (December 2, 1871):8-9. Grand Duke Alexis of Russia should be welcomed by Catholics.

"Sectarian Aid." *New York Tablet* 15 (December 2, 1871):9. Public aid to Catholic Institutions in New York.

"Rise and Decline of the Romish Church." *New York Tablet* 15 (December 9, 1871):8. Assertions of Henry Bellows.

"The Woman Movement." *New York Tablet* 15 (December 16, 1871):8. The purposes of the movement are free love, abolition of Christian marriage, and the destruction of the family.

"President's Message." *New York Tablet* 15 (December 16, 1871):8-9. Review of Grant's proposals and call for political changes.

"M.F. Walworth and Dollinger." *New York Tablet* 15 (December 30, 1871):8-9. Walworth's rejection of papal infallibility.

1872

"The Protestant Rule of Faith." *Catholic World* 14 (January, 1872):488-513; *Works* 8:418-39. Review of Charles Hodge's *Systematic Theology*, Vol. 1 (1872). Catholics have infallible teacher in the pope who preserves and applies tradition; Sacred Scripture is the foundation, but not the rule of faith.

"The Bible In Schools." *New York Tablet* 15 (January 6, 1872):8. Against the use of the Protestant Bible in the schools and recent history of that use.

"The Proposed City Charter." *New York Tablet* 15 (January 6, 1872):9. On proposed changes in New York City government.

"The Irrepressible Conflict." *New York Tablet* 15 (January 13, 1872):8. Between ecclesiastical and civil courts.

"The 'New York Witness.'" *New York Tablet* 15 (January 20, 1872):8. Protestant bigotry under the guise of openness to Catholicism.

"The Governor's Message Again." *New York Tablet* 15 (January 20, 1872):8. On reform of New York City government to avoid centralized democracy.

"Romanism In America." *New York Tablet* 15 (January 27, 1872):8. Methodists, not Catholics, are antagonistic to American freedom.

"Hepworth and the Unitarians." *New York Tablet* 15 (January 27, 1872):9. His apparent renunciation of Unitarianism, but his continued heterodox ideas on Trinity.

"The Cosmic Philosophy." *Catholic World* 14 (February, 1872):633-45; *Works* 9:439-56. Review of Herbert Spencer's *First Principles of a New System of Philosophy* (1871). Spencer misapprehends relation of religion and science because he does not understand the doctrine of creation which is the nexus between the two.

"The International Association." *Catholic World* 14 (February, 1872):694-707. Review of *The Dublin Review* (October 1871) and Wendell Phillip's "The Labor Movement," *New York Tribune* (December 7, 1871). On the unequal and relentless battles between capital and labor manifested most clearly by the International Association of Workingmen, and the necessity of religion to heal the wounds of class strife.

"The City Government." *New York Tablet* 15 (February 3, 1872):8. On proposed new charter of city government— judiciary department; against the election of judges.

"Civil Service Reform." *New York Tablet* 15 (February 10, 1872):9. Importance of public opinion in reforming civil service appointments.

"Mr. Sumner's Supplementary Civil Rights Bill." *New York Tablet* 15 (February 17, 1872):9. Against legislating the social equality of Negroes.

"Christianizing the Constitution." *New York Tablet* 15 (February 24, 1872):8. Against the Methodist movement to make Protestantism the national religion.

"Owen on Spiritism." *Catholic World* 14 (March, 1872):803-12; *Works* 9:352-65. Review of R. D. Owen's *The Debatable Lord* (1872) and *Footfalls on the Boundary of Another World* (1860). Against Owen's views of spirit-manifestations, which he identifies with biblical miracles, Christian inspiration and revelation.

"The Church and Republicanism." *New York Tablet* 15 (March 2, 1872):8. No incompatibility between the two.

"Is Suffrage A Natural Right Or A Trust?" *New York Tablet* 15 (March 9, 1872):8. A trust.

"Old Catholics." *New York Tablet* 15 (March 16, 1872):8. No New or Old Catholics because Catholicism is the Kingdom of God.

"Anglican Catholics." *New York Tablet* 15 (March 16, 1872):9. Misapplication of the term "Catholic."

"The New York 'Evangelist' on Sectarian Subsidies." *New York Tablet* 15 (March 23, 1872):8. Public aid to Catholic institutions not unconstitutional.

"The 'New York Herald' on Joseph Mazzini." *New York Tablet* 15 (March 23, 1872):8. On Mazzini's death.

"Elevation of the Working Classes." *New York Tablet* 15 (March 23, 1872):9. On social equality of working class.

"Is Suffrage a Natural Right or a Political Trust?" *New York Tablet* 15 (March 30, 1872):8-9. A trust.

"The Crisis in the Catholic Church." *New York Tablet* 15 (March 30, 1872):9. Crises are nothing new in the historic church's relationship with secular society.

"The Alabama Claims." *New York Tablet* 15 (April 6, 1872):8. United States claims for damages against Great Britain for its part in the Civil War will not be resolved.

"The Vicar of Christ." *New York Tablet* 15 (April 13, 1872):8-9. Central question between Protestants and Catholics is authority.

"Exclusive Salvation." *New York Tablet* 15 (April 20, 1872):8. "No salvation outside the Church."

"The Insurrection in Spain." *New York Tablet* 15 (May 4, 1872):8. Uprising of Don Carlos and the religious party in Spain against revolutionary regime.

"The Outlook For The Church." *New York Tablet* 15 (May 4, 1872):9. Public opinion against the church, but hope for church based upon her supernatural origins.

"The Greeley-Brown Ticket." *New York Tablet* 15 (May 18, 1872):8. Horace Greeley's nomination for President.

"Mary, Mother of God." *New York Tablet* 15 (May 18, 1872):9. Catholic theology of Mary.

"France–Thiers–Gambetta." *New York Tablet* 15 (May 25, 1872):8-9. Political divisions in France.

"The Washington Treaty." *New York Tablet* 16 (June 1, 1872):8-9. Conflicting claims between United States and Great Britain. See April 6, 1872.

"State Education Is State Religion." *New York Tablet* 16 (June 8, 1872):8-9. Public education is a form of union between church and state.

"Secularizing Education." *New York Tablet* 16 (June 8, 1872):9. Secular schools present no danger to Protestantism because American culture itself is Protestant.

"Satan Worshippers." *New York Tablet* 16 (June 15, 1872):8. England and Prussia have bowed to the prince of this world.

"The Disturbing Element." *New York Tablet* 16 (June 15, 1872):9. Catholic Church is the element that disturbs Methodists and society.

"The Methodist Conference." *New York Tablet* 16 (June 22, 1872):8-9. On the conference's various proceedings.

"Union of the Sects." *New York Tablet* 16 (June 29, 1872):8. Meaning of Christian union.

"The New Reformation." *New York Tablet* 16 (June 29, 1872):9. Old Catholics in Germany and general religious indifference.

"The Papacy the Only Safeguard to Liberty, Civil and Religious."
New York Tablet 16 (July 6, 1872):8. The independence of the
spiritual order.

"Bismarck Against The Jesuits." *New York Tablet* 16 (July 13, 1872):8-
9. Reichstag's bill excluding Jesuits from the German Empire.

"Greeley and the Democracy." *New York Tablet* 16 (July 20, 1872):8.
Prefers Grant to Greeley for President.

"Germany and The Jesuits." *New York Tablet* 16 (July 20, 1872):8.
Catholics enjoy full religious liberty in no Protestant country.

"The 'Times' Measure of Bismarck." *New York Tablet* 16 (July 27,
1872):9. Support for German Jesuits expelled from German Empire.

"The Rev. Beecher on Religious Warfare." *New York Tablet* 16 (July
27, 1872):9. H. W. Beecher advises Protestants to cease assaults
on Catholics.

"The Pope's Letter." *New York Tablet* 16 (August 3, 1872):8. European Catholics under governments of Protestants or infidels.

"The Protestant Idea of the Jesuits." *New York Tablet* 16 (August 10,
1872):8. Fear of Jesuits' historic political manipulations.

"Pope and Emperor." *New York Tablet* 16 (August 24, 1872):8. German persecution of Catholic Church pleases American sects.

"Catholic Reform in Germany." *New York Tablet* 16 (August 31,
1872):8. Old Catholics as national church.

"The Presidential Election." *New York Tablet* 16 (August 31, 1872):8-
9. Support for Grant over Greeley.

"A Free Church in a Free State." *New York Tablet* 16 (August 31,
1872):9. The meaning of the phrase according to Camillo Benso
Cavour and Charles Montalembert.

"Bigotry." *New York Tablet* 16 (September 7, 1872):8. Catholics can
never reason with Protestants.

"St. Louis." *New York Tablet* 16 (September 7, 1872):8-9. Catholic
children in Protestant Sunday schools.

"Die Alt-Katholiken." *New York Tablet* 16 (September 14, 1872):8.
Old Catholics as a religious movement in Germany.

"Grant or Greeley?" *New York Tablet* 16 (September 21, 1872):8.
Grant, but support for Greeley's party.

"The Jesuits." *New York Tablet* 16 (September 21, 1872):8. Protestants and liberal Catholics oppose Jesuits as a first blow against
the papacy and the church.

"The Louisville Convention and Its Candidates." *New York Tablet* 16 (September 28, 1872):8. Democrats ruined themselves by nominating Greeley.

"Mr. Hyacinthe Loyson on His Marriage." *New York Tablet* 16 (September 28, 1872):9. His marriage not valid in Catholic Church. Celibacy and a married clergy.

"Low Churchmen Demanded of the Church." *New York Tablet* 16 (October 5, 1872):8-9. Meaning of union with the church, and Old Catholics.

"Letter From Dr. Brownson." *New York Tablet* 16 (October 5, 1872):9. Brownson announces reasons for resumption of his *Quarterly.*

"Heathenism and Christianity." *New York Tablet* 16 (October 5, 1872):9. On Hindu religion.

"We Want An Honest Legislature." *New York Tablet* 16 (October 12, 1872):8. An honest legislature demands an honest electorate.

"St. Bartholomew's Massacre." *New York Tablet* 16 (October 19, 1872):4. On past and present Catholic evaluations of the massacre.

"The Church of The Future." *New York Tablet* 16 (October 19, 1872):4. Church is organic body, not just an organized society.

"The Meeting of the Emperors." *New York Tablet* 16 (October 19, 1872):8. Prussia, Austria, and Russia.

"The Old Catholics Again." *New York Tablet* 16 (October 19, 1872):9. Divisions among Old Catholics.

"Evangelization in Italy." *New York Tablet* 16 (October 26, 1872):8. Failure of Protestant proselytizing in Catholic countries.

"Fairly Acknowledged." *New York Tablet* 16 (October 26, 1872):8-9. Gallicanism and Ultramontanism.

"Brownson's Review." *Ave Maria* 8 (November 2, 1872):708-09. Reprint of "Letter to the Editor," *New York Tablet* September 24, 1872.

"Infallibility." *New York Tablet* 16 (November 2, 1872):8. Infallibility does not belong to the person of the pope.

"Satan's Last Move." *New York Tablet* 16 (November 2, 1872):8-9. The demand for secularized education.

"Dr. Hodge On A Romish Question." *New York Tablet* 16 (November 9, 1872):5. Charles Hodge's views of railroad companies giving land to Catholics for building churches.

"History Vs. Infallibility." *New York Tablet* 16 (November 9, 1872):8. On the massacre of St. Bartholomew's Day.

"The Jews and the Roumanians [*sic*]." *New York Tablet* 16 (November 9, 1872):9. Anti-Jewish sentiments; on the persecution of Jews.

"Forewarned, Forearmed." *New York Tablet* 16 (November 16, 1872):8. School question.

"Catholicity and Patriotism." *New York Tablet* 16 (November 16, 1872):9. Loyalty to Catholicism not incompatible with patriotism, but is above patriotism.

"The Conflict of the Two Powers." *New York Tablet* 16 (November 23, 1872):8. The *New York Herald* on church and state.

"The Office, Not The Man." *New York Tablet* 16 (November 23, 1872):8-9. Papal infallibility belongs to the office.

"The Elections." *New York Tablet* 16 (November 23, 1872):9. Grant and Republicans win. Democrats abandoned principle.

"Jews and Roumanians [*sic*]." *New York Tablet* 16 (November 23, 1872):9. Jews are sworn enemies of Christianity.

"The Christian (Methodist) Advocate." *New York Tablet* 16 (November 30, 1872):8-9. In conflicts between the Catholic Church and the state, Protestant journalists generally take the side of the state's opposition to the church.

"Drift of Opinion on Education." *New York Tablet* 16 (December 7, 1872):4. Toward secularization.

"Protestants Drop The Old Catholics." *New York Tablet* 16 (December 7, 1872):8-9. Old Catholics are not becoming Protestant reformers.

"Death of Horace Greeley." *New York Tablet* 16 (December 7, 1872):9. Eulogy on Greeley.

"The President's Message." *New York Tablet* 16 (December 14, 1872):8. Nothing new, but Grant articulates a dangerous principle: no policy against the will of the people.

"Political Crisis in France." *New York Tablet* 16 (December 14, 1872):9. Apparent conflict between National Assembly and Marie Joseph Louis Adolphe Thiers.

"Non-Catholic Zeal For Education." *New York Tablet* 16 (December 21, 1872):8. Zeal motivated by hostility to Catholic Church.

"The Combat Deepens." *New York Tablet* 16 (December 28, 1872):8-9. Protestant-Catholic battles.

1873

"Introduction" to Sarah M. Brownson, *Life of Demetrius Augustine Gallitzin*. New York; Cincinnati: Pustet, 1873. On the current political condition of Russia and the Russian Orthodox church, and the need and possibility of reunion with Rome. Such a reunion would free the Russian church from its political dependency.

"Introduction to the Last Series." *Brownson's Quarterly Review* 27 (January, 1873):1-8; *Works 20:*381-88. On Brownson's reasons for resuming the *Review* and on his uncompromising Catholicism in the spirit of the *Syllabus of Errors.*

"The Papacy and the Republic." *Brownson's Quarterly Review* 27 (January, 1873):9-33; *Works 13:*326-51. Church is kingdom of God on earth; church has nothing to do with politics.

"The Dollingerites, Nationalists and the Papacy." *Brownson's Quarterly Review* 27 (January, 1873):34-53; *Works 13:*351-69. Dogma is above history as church gives true sense of facts of history; pope is "central all" of organism and Gallicanism is "inchoate Manicheeism."

"Religious Novels, and Woman versus Woman." *Brownson's Quarterly Review* 27 (January, 1873):53-69; *Works 19:*560-75; *Modern*: 560-75. Review of Sister Mary Francis Clare's *Hornehurst Rectory* (1873); Lady Georgiana Fullerton's *Mrs. Gerald's Niece* (1870); and Mary Agnes Tincker's *The House of Yorke* (1872). Brownson's comments on novels that deal with Puseyism, and Catholicism, and his criticisms of novels that are half theology and half romance.

"Archbishop Manning's Lectures." *Brownson's Quarterly Review* 27 (January, 1873):69-84; *Works 13:*370-84. Review of Henry Edward Manning's *Lectures on the Four Great Evils of the Day* (1872). Brownson's views on the modern denials of divine sovereignty over intellect, will, and society, as well as the need for papal infallibility.

"What is the Need of Revelation?" *Brownson's Quarterly Review* 27 (January, 1873):85-95; *Works 3:*509-18. On the initial and teleological orders of existence; nature is the initial and supernature is the teleological order.

"The Political State of the Country." *Brownson's Quarterly Review* 27 (January, 1873):95-111; *Works 18:*520-35. Grant is bad but Greeley would have been worse; in favor of the nation's "natural aristocracy."

"European Politics." *Brownson's Quarterly Review* 27 (January, 1873):111-29; *Works 18*:502-19. On the power changes in Europe; Catholics should not place trust in political alliances, but work for the reconversion of Europe to the church.

"Synthetic Theology." *Brownson's Quarterly Review* 27 (April, 1873):145-74; *Works 3*:536-64. Review of Peter Rossi's *I Principii di Filosofia Sopranaturale* 3 vols. (1868-1872). On the Giobertian-like attempts to articulate the dialectical synthesis between the natural (initial) and the supernatural (teleological) orders through the doctrines of creation (generation) and Incarnation (regeneration), and on the necessity and priority of the synthetic over the analytical method in theology.

"Photographic Views." *Brownson's Quarterly Review* 27 (April, 1873):174-84. Review of F. X. Weninger, *Photographic Views* (1873). A book of spiritual reading which asserts that nature is symbolic of a meaning beyond its visible appearance, and Brownson's views on symbolism and Platonism.

"Catholic Popular Literature." *Brownson's Quarterly Review* 27 (April, 1873):185-205; *Works 19*:575-94; *Modern*: 575-94. Review of *All-Hallows-Eve* (New York Catholic Publication Society, 1872) and Emily C. Agnew's *Geraldine* (1872). Brownson's reflection on a literature produced by Catholics, for Catholics, and informed by Catholic spirit.

"The Primeval Man not a Savage." *Brownson's Quarterly Review* 27 (April, 1873):205-35; *Works 9*:457-85. Review of Nicholas Wiseman's *Lectures on Connections between Science and Revealed Religion* (1872). While Christian tradition is test of truth there is no conflict between real science and divine revelation.

"The Democratic Principle." *Brownson's Quarterly Review* 27 (April, 1873):235-59; *Works 18*:223-45; *Kirk*: 191-226. Reminiscences of an old man. Brownson believed in democracy until the "hard cider" campaign of the 1840s.

"Bismarck and the Church." *Brownson's Quarterly Review* 27 (April, 1873):259-75; *Works 13*:384-400. Review of lecture on "The Old Catholic Movement in Europe" by A. N. Littlejohn, Episcopal Bishop of Long Island. Brownson appeals to history of papacy and church to prove that church is ultimately victorious over secular powers.

"Whose is the Child?" *Brownson's Quarterly Review* 27 (July, 1873):289-301; *Works* 13:400-12. On the church's, parents' and state's right and authority to educate children.

"Science, Philosophy, and Religion." *Brownson's Quarterly Review* 27 (July, 1873):301-22; "Professor Bascom's Lectures," *Works* 2:448-61. Review of John Bascom's *Science, Philosophy, and Religion* (1871). Although Bascom believes in suprasensible ideas, he tries to prove objective reality via inductive method, which is unjustifiable; Brownson places understanding beyond the criticisms of skepticism.

"Papal Infallibility." *Brownson's Quarterly Review* 27 (July, 1873):322-40; *Works* 13:412-29. Response to sermon preached by Michael Domenec, bishop of Pittsburgh, on papal infallibility; an extreme application.

"Darwin's *Descent of Man.*" *Brownson's Quarterly Review* 27 (July, 1873):340-52; *Works* 9:485-96. Darwin's theory is untenable; any theory of progress demands a creator God.

"The Church above the State." *Brownson's Quarterly Review* 27 (July, 1873):352-67; *Works* 13:430-44. Review of Richard Gilmour's *Lenten Pastoral on Christian Education and other Catholic Duties* (1873). Natural and revealed law are part of one dialectical whole, distinct but not separate.

"True and False Science." *Brownson's Quarterly Review* 27 (July, 1873):367-98; *Works* 9:497-528. Inadequacy of inductive method when used to demonstrate existence of God, spirituality of soul, liberty and free will.

"Sisters of Mercy." *Brownson's Quarterly Review* 27 (July, 1873):399-409. Review of Mary Teresa Austin Carroll's *Life of Catherine McAuley* (1871). On McAuley, the Sisters of Mercy, and the work of women who combine the contemplative with the active in the world.

"Essay in Refutation of Atheism." Part I of III. *Brownson's Quarterly Review* 27 (October, 1873):433-65; see January and April, 1874; see also *Essays in Refutation of Atheism*, ed. by Henry F. Brownson. Detroit: T. Nourse, 1882; *Works* 2:1-32. Brownson originally wrote this work in 1871 and early 1872, and intended that it be published as a separate work. Brownson considers this essay to be preamble to faith; the problem to be resolved is whether there is a God who has created the world from nothing and is both our first and last cause.

"Protestantism Antichristian." *Brownson's Quarterly Review* 27 (October, 1873):465-88; *Works* 8:439-61. Review of Thomas William M. Marshall's *My Clerical Friends* (1873) and *Church Defense* (1873). Brownson's assertion that contemporary Protestantism as a system is anti-Christian because of its indifference to truth and its loss of faith in objective truth.

"Father Thebaud's *Irish Race.*" *Brownson's Quarterly Review* 27 (October, 1873):488-508; *Works* 13:547-66. Review of Augustine Thébaud's *The Irish Race* (1873). Irish have preserved primitive Christianity and have mission of converting English speaking world.

"The Woman Question." Part II of II. *Brownson's Quarterly Review* 27 (October, 1873):508-29; see *Catholic World,* May, 1869; *Works* 18:398-418.

"At Home and Abroad." *Brownson's Quarterly Review* 27 (October, 1873):534-45; *Works* 18:535-45. Caesarism in republican as well as in monarchial governments.

"Colonel H. S. Hewit, M. D." *Brownson's Quarterly Review* 27 (October, 1873):545-53. Obituary for Dr. Henry Stewart Hewit who was Brownson's physician for seventeen years.

1874

"Essay in Refutation of Atheism." Part II of III. *Brownson's Quarterly Review* 28 (January, 1874):1-37; see October, 1873, April, 1874; *Works* 2:32-67.

"Education and the Republic." *Brownson's Quarterly Review* 28 (January, 1874):37-54; *Works* 13:445-61. On education, the "perfectibility of man," and the insufficiency of natural means for perfection in education.

"Holy Communion-Transubstantiation." *Brownson's Quarterly Review* 28 (January, 1874):55-77; *Works* 8:264-79. Prefers Aristotle over Plato as philosopher, and Augustine's explanation of real presence over Aquinas's.

"The Most Rev. John Hughes, D. D." *Brownson's Quarterly Review* 28 (January, 1874):78-93; *Works* 14:485-500. Review of Lawrence Kehoe's edition of the *Complete Works of the Most Rev. John Hughes* (1873). Character sketch of Hughes and evolution of his works and relations to the American public.

"Evangelical Alliance." *Brownson's Quarterly Review* 28 (January, 1874):93-106; *Works* 8:461-73. Diatribe against Protestantism as private judgement separated from Incarnation.

"Archbishop Spalding." *Brownson's Quarterly Review* 28 (January, 1874):107-21; *Works* 14:500-14. Review of John Lancaster Spalding's *The Life of the Most Rev. M. J. Spalding* (1873). On infallibility of pope; Satan was first Protestant.

"Home and Foreign Politics." *Brownson's Quarterly Review* 28 (January, 1874):121-38; "The Political Outlook," *Works* 18:546-61. On the recent election losses for the Republican party and the evils of the credit system.

"Essay in Refutation of Atheism." Part III of III. *Brownson's Quarterly Review* 28 (April, 1874):145-79; see October 1873, January 1874; *Works* 2:67-100.

"Religion and Science." *Brownson's Quarterly Review* 28 (April, 1874):179-97; *Works* 3:519-36. Review of Joseph Le Conte's *Religion and Science* (1874). Diatribe against Le Conte—good scientist, ignorant theologian; science and religion, reason and faith, nature and grace are all parts of uniform whole.

"Constitutional Guaranties [sic]." *Brownson's Quarterly Review* 28 (April, 1874):197-220; *Works* 18:246-68. Legislators have responsibility to the Constitution not to the fickled will of the people; Brownson against absolute sovereignty of the people, i.e., centralized democracy.

"Extra Ecclesiam nulla Salus." *Brownson's Quarterly Review* 28 (April, 1874):220-245; *Works* 5:572-79. Brownson against liberal interpretations of this doctrine and his assertion that invincible ignorance excuses from sin, but it confers no virtue and is purely negative, having no power to save.

"Count de Montalembert." *Brownson's Quarterly Review* 28 (July, 1874):289-313; *Works* 14:515-38. Review of C.F. Audley's *Count de Montalembert's Letters to a Schoolfellow, 1827-1832* (1874). On French Revolution and reactions to it.

"Gallicanism and Ultramontanism." *Brownson's Quarterly Review* 28 (July, 1874):313-38; *Works* 13:462-83. Nature of papal and temporal powers; apostolic authority belongs to Pope.

"Ontologism and Psychologism." *Brownson's Quarterly Review* 28 (July, 1874):357-76; *Works* 2:468-86. Review of Petro Fournier's *Institutiones Philosophicae* (1854), Franc Rothenflue's *Institutiones*

Philosophicae Theoreticae (1846), Salvatoris Tongiorgi's *Institutiones Philosophicae* (1867), and William Hill's *Elements of Philosophy* (1873). Brownson defends himself against Augustine Hewit's and the *Catholic World*'s charges that his views on the knowledge of God are heterodox. Brownson tries to establish the *a priori* conditions of thought.

"Constitutional Law—The Executive Power." *Brownson's Quarterly Review* 28 (July, 1874):376-92; "The Executive Power," *Works* 18:269-81. Evaluation of Adolphe de Chambrun's *The Executive Power of the United States* (1874) and Brownson's views of the advantages and limits of the president's executive power.

"Early and Recent Apostates." *Brownson's Quarterly Review* 28 (July, 1874):393-408. Review of John Joseph Franco's *Tigranes* (1874). An historical novel on Julian the Apostate which unrealistically encourages the evangelical counsels for laity. On the new (Bismarck) as well as the old (Julian) promoters of the absolute supremacy of the state under the guise of liberalism.

"Letter from Dr. Brownson." *Boston Pilot* (July 11, 1874): 4.

"Answer to Objections." *Brownson's Quarterly Review* 28 (October, 1874):433-65; *Works* 20:389-419. Response to article in the *Boston Pilot* criticizing Brownson's view of exclusive salvation, and to a correspondent's objections to his views on hell.

"Controversy with Protestants." *Brownson's Quarterly Review* 28 (October, 1874):465-82. The burden of proof in all controversies between Catholics and Protestants should fall upon Protestants, not Catholics who can claim prior possession of truth. On the controversy over the incompatibility of Catholicism and American ideas.

"The Problem of Causality." *Brownson's Quarterly Review* 28 (October, 1874):482-510; see "Hume's Philosophical Works," October, 1855; *Works* 1:381-407. Review of *The Philosophical Works of David Hume* (1854).

"Authority in Matters of Faith." Part II of II. *Brownson's Quarterly Review* 28 (October, 1874):510-31; see *Catholic World*, November, 1871; *Works* 8:592-98. Review of Dwight H. Olmstead's *De l'Autorité ou de la Philosophie du personalisme. Lettre adressée au Rev. Père I. T. Hecker, suivie d'un appendice sur la Souveraineté du Peuple* (1874).

"Letter to the Editor." *Brownson's Quarterly Review* 28 (October, 1874):532-48; *Works* 20:420-35. Response to a Jesuit criticism that Brownson is too harsh on contemporary Jesuits' philosophical positions, their inability to understand Aquinas, and their indiscreet zeal in promoting devotion to the Sacred Heart.

"The Outlook at Home and Abroad." *Brownson's Quarterly Review* 28 (October, 1874):548-60; *Works* 18:562-73. Review of Robert Montagu's *On Some Popular Errors Concerning Politics and Religion* (1874). Brownson's views on religion and politics.

"The Review for 1875." *Brownson's Quarterly Review* 28 (October, 1874):571-72. Brownson states that he has tried to write all the articles for the *Review* since he revived it, but now that task has become impossible and, given the need to train young reviewers for the future, undesirable.

1875

"Professor Tyndall's Address." *Brownson's Quarterly Review* 29 (January, 1875):1-20; *Works* 9:528-47. Negative assessment of John Tyndall's *Inaugural Address before the British Association* (1874). On Tyndall's "false charges" that the theologians are opponents of the progress of science and the study of nature.

"The Last of the Napoleons." *Brownson's Quarterly Review* 29 (January, 1875):20-42. Review of *Le Dernier des Napoléons* (1874) and Brownson's outline of the downfall of Napoleon III who betrayed the divine authority and thus the leadership of the modern European world.

"Maria Monk's Daughter." Brownson's Quarterly Review 29 (January, 1875):43-75. Review of Mrs. L. St. John Eckel's *Maria Monk's Daughter: An Autobiography* (1874). On Eckel's conversion to Catholicism and Brownson's views on corelation of interior illumination and communion with the apostolic and Catholic church.

"Mary Queen of Scots." *Brownson's Quarterly Review* 29 (January, 1875):75-105. Review of John Morris's edition of *The Letter Books of Sir Amias Poulet, Keeper of Mary Queen of Scots* (1874). On the conspiracy to have Mary Queen of Scots executed.

"Papal Infallibility and Civil Allegiance." *Brownson's Quarterly Review* 29 (January, 1875):105-22; *Works* 13:483-99. On the theory of development; nature and the supernatural "two parts of dialectical whole."

"The Conflict of Science and Religion." *Brownson's Quarterly Review* 29 (April, 1875):153-73; *Works* 9:547-66. Review of John William Draper's *History of the Conflict between Religion and Science* (1874). Science and religion are two parts of one dialectical whole and, therefore, there can never be a conflict between the two if they are both authentic and true to their purposes.

"Reforms and Reformers." *Brownson's Quarterly Review* 29 (April, 1875):174-86. Review of *Next Phase of Civil Progress* (1874). Brownson's views on progress, reform in city and federal governments, the power of wealth in government, the virtues of the laboring classes, and the need to reform corrupt public opinion.

"The Prisoners of St. Lazare." *Brownson's Quarterly Review* 29 (April, 1875):186-202. Review of Pauline de Grandpre's *The Prisoners of St. Lazare* (1872). On necessity of establishing houses of correction, reform, and rehabilitation for prostitutes—houses like the French house of St. Lazare.

"Newman's Reply to Gladstone." *Brownson's Quarterly Review* 29 (April, 1875):231-46; *Works* 13:499-514. On obedience to pope; papal powers from the beginning of Christianity.

"Our Colleges." *Brownson's Quarterly Review* 29 (April, 1875):246-60. On the intellectual deficiencies in Catholic colleges and the need for a Catholic university.

"Father Hill's Philosophy." Part I of II. *Brownson's Quarterly Review* 29 (April, 1875):260-80; see October, 1875; *Works* 2:487-506. Criticisms of Hill's scholastic philosophy from the view point of Brownson's modified ontologism.

"The Constitution of the Church." *Brownson's Quarterly Review* 29 (July, 1875):297-314; see January, 1856; *Works* 8:527-51. Introduces his January 1856 article of the same title by referring to the fundamental change in ecclesiology that accompanied Vatican I, namely that the primacy of Peter would thereafter become the first part of treatises on the church, and the body of the church the second part.

"The Church and Civil Power." *Brownson's Quarterly Review* 29 (July, 1875):334-70. Review of a series of pamphlets by Joseph Fessler, William E. Gladstone, Henry Edward Manning, John E. E. D. Acton, John Henry Newman, and William Bernard Ullathorne on Vatican I and civil allegiance. The article is primarily a republication of "The Two Orders, Spiritual and Temporal," *Brownson's Quarterly Review* (January, 1853).

"Women's Novels." *Brownson's Quarterly Review* 29 (July, 1875):370-81; *Works* 19:595-605; *Gems*: 182-202; *Modern*: 595-605. Review of Mary Agnes Tincker's *Grapes and Thorns* (1874); J. W. Lawson's *Brockley Moore* (1874); and Christian Reid's *Hearts and Hands* (1875). Brownson's criticisms of women novelists as sentimental.

"Our Lady of Lourdes." *Brownson's Quarterly Review* 29 (July, 1875):381-401; *Works* 8:104-17; Carey: 272-82. Review of Louis Gaston de Segur's *The Wonders of Lourdes* (1875). On the Incarnation as the basis of the cult of the saints, and of Christian devotion to Mary.

"Protestant Journalism." *Brownson's Quarterly Review* 29 (October, 1875):441-69; *Works* 13:567-94. Review of Thomas William Marshall's *Protestant Journalism* (1874). Against Catholic and secular as well as Protestant journalism; diatribe against all kinds of nationalism.

"The Family, Christian and Pagan." *Brownson's Quarterly Review* 29 (October, 1875):469-89; *Works* 13:526-46. Review of Auguste Riche's *The Family* (1875). Assertions on the sanctity, unity and indissolubility of marriage.

"Hill's *Elements of Philosophy*." Part II of II. *Brownson's Quarterly Review* 29 (October, 1875):490-515; see April, 1875; *Works* 2:506-31.

"The Public School System." *Brownson's Quarterly Review* 29 (October, 1875):516-38; *Works* 13:515-25. Review of Edmund F. Dunne's *Our Public Schools: Are they free for all, or are they not?* (1875). Brownson calls for a united Catholic effort on the school question to obtain justice from the state.

"Home Politics." *Brownson's Quarterly Review* 29 (October, 1875):539-64; *Works* 18:574-98. Against the absolute will of the people as the ruling principle in contemporary politics and against the evils of the credit system of economics.

"Valedictory." *Brownson's Quarterly Review* 29 (October, 1875):578-80; *Works* 20:436-38. Brownson's reasons for ceasing to publish his *Review*.

1876

"Philosophy of the Supernatural." *American Catholic Quarterly Review* 1 (January, 1876):22-33; *Works* 2:271-83. Review of Peter Rossi's *I Principii di Filosofia Sopranaturale* (1868-74). Written three months before his death; against the scholastics and the analytical method in theology.

Index

"Luther and the Reformation," 85
Lutheran Observer, 116
Lynch, Patrick, 70

M
MacCabe, William B., 88
"Madness of Antichristians," 66
Maine, Liquor law in, 85, 90
Maitland, Samuel Roffey, 73
Malan, C., 96
Manahan, Ambrose, 96
"Manahan's Triumph of the Church," 96
Manicheeism, 159
Manning, Henry Edward, 145, 147, 159,166
Manning, Robert, 65
Mansel, Henry L., 97
"Manual Labour Schools," 40
Manual of Political Ethics (Lieber), 49
Marcy, Erastus Edgerton, 140
Maret, H. L. C., 91, 94
"Maret on Reason and Revelation," 91
"Maria Monk's Daughter" (Eckel), 165
Marriage, 107, 116, 128, 135-36, 152, 157, 167
"Marriage and Divorce," 116, 128
Marshall, Thomas William M., 162, 167
Martin, Abbé, 136
Martineau, Harriet, 40
Martinet, Abbé Antoine. *See* Gyphendole, Evariste
Marx, Karl, 8, 151
Mary, Mother of God
and Anglicans, 120

devotion to, 80, 109, 116, 125, 167
and saints, 24, 108
theology of, 111, 155
worship of, 108, 125
"Mary Mother of God," 155
Mary Lee (Peppergrass), 96-97
"Mary Queen of Scots," 165
Maryland, colonial, 89
Masonic Temple, 45
Mass, 51-52
Massachusetts Anti-Slavery Society, 45
Massachusetts, Legislature, 86
Materialism, 112, 124,
and culture, 116
and spiritualism, 132
Mazzini, Joseph, 115, 154
McAuley, Catherine, 161
McCosh, James, 151
McClellan, George, 106, 108
McColloh, J. H., 82-83
McKay, Charlotte E., 147
McMahon, Martin T., 142
McMullen, Dr., 124
McSherry, James, 78
"Mediation of the Church," 57
Mediatorial Life of Jesus (Brownson), 56
"Meditations of St. Ignatius," (Siniscalchi) 102
M'Elheran, John, 96
"Memoir of Saint-Simon," 38
Menschenseele und Physiologie (Froschammer), 104
Mentana, Victory of, 119
Mercersburg,
hypothesis, 83
Mercersburg Review, 74-75, 83,